James Fawcus

The Letters of the Late James Fawcus, M.D.

For Private cCirculation

James Fawcus

The Letters of the Late James Fawcus, M.D.
For Private cCirculation

ISBN/EAN: 9783337016531

Printed in Europe, USA, Canada, Australia, Japan

Cover: Foto ©ninafisch / pixelio.de

More available books at **www.hansebooks.com**

THE LETTERS

OF THE LATE

JAMES FAWCUS, M.D.

FOR PRIVATE CIRCULATION.

EDINBURGH: THOMAS AND ARCHIBALD CONSTABLE

PRINTERS TO THE QUEEN, AND TO THE UNIVERSITY.

1877.

CONTENTS.

CHAPTER I.
EARLY YEARS, ... 1

CHAPTER II.
JOURNAL OF THE VOYAGE TO THE EAST, AND LETTERS FROM THE HELLESPONT, ... 20

CHAPTER III.
LETTERS FROM PARIS, STRASBURG, VIENNA, Etc., . 63

CHAPTER IV.
LETTERS FROM INDIA AND CHINA, . . . 80

CHAPTER V.
LETTERS FROM NEW ZEALAND AND INDIA, . 126

CHAPTER VI.
LETTERS FROM CALCUTTA, ... 147

CHAPTER VII.
THE LAST LETTERS FROM INDIA, . . 180

CHAPTER VIII.
LAST LETTERS, ... 187

ACCOUNT OF THE LAST WEEKS, . . . 195

APPENDIX I., ... 203

APPENDIX II., . . 204

LETTERS OF JAMES FAWCUS.

CHAPTER I.

EARLY YEARS.

"The child is father of the man."

I DID not think to look upon my young brother's grave, or to tell the story of his life when it was ended.

I shall try to convey to his children some idea of their gentle good father, although I know well that I can never picture him to others as he lives in my memory.

It was a sunny spring afternoon—April 19, 1833—when my brother, James Fawcus,[1] was born in Dockwray Square, North Shields. He was the seventh son of our parents, the youngest of their eleven children. He was a lovely child, very fair, with deep blue eyes, and hair of a silvery brightness. A most angelic and sweet expression rested on his fine softly-moulded features. We used to watch, as he lay in his cot, for the smile which always came as soon as he wakened and recognised us. In babyhood, as in after years, he was noted for sweetness of temper. His loving nature was expressed in his outward form and in all his ways. He used to give his little hand so trustingly, and in all his behaviour was charming. I have often asked him for toy or sweetmeat, that I might see the gladness with which he would present them.

Obedience, the virtue of childhood, seemed to belong to his nature. He never quarrelled with his brother or playmates, because he was free from selfishness, and ready to oblige and yield. He was always fond of animals, especially of dogs; often in his letters from far countries he inquires for his dumb

---

[1] We learn from the parish records of births, marriages, and deaths, kept in Warkworth Church (Northumberland), and from the inscriptions on the family tombstones in the adjoining churchyard (the dates of which go back to 1698), that previous to my grandfather's time our name was not spelt "Fawcus," but "Fawkes," and sometimes "Foulkes."

favourites. He early showed his brave nature and fearlessness of danger for himself. Once, when he was five and I nineteen, he placed himself between me and some cattle, bidding me not to be afraid, saying, "I will defend you, Allie." Often since, thinking of my faithful, true-hearted champion, the words of the bereaved father in the old Border ballad have come home to me—

> "I durst hae ridden the world round
> Had Christy Graeme been at my back."

My father died at the age of forty-six, when James was only four years old. He was a kind and good father,—a brave, sincere, God-fearing man.

Though James was thus early bereft of a father's care,

> "Yet pleasantly his childhood sped
> Upon his mother's sheltering bosom,
> His life was like a garden spread,
> Each day was like an opening blossom.
>
> And soon his merry boyhood came,
> Each day he grew in strength and stature,
> But kept his childhood's heart the same,
> His winning ways and gentle nature." [1]

Three months after we lost our father, death came again to our home, and gathered a sweet flower,—a sister, six years of age. All day we had watched the dying child, and often our little Jamie's joyous voice and laughter had been heard in the distance during these sad hours. In the evening he was brought into the sick-room in his night-dress to be kissed as usual. I held him up to give a last kiss to Margaret's cheek. "Dood night, Maggie," said he, smiling; and then, as she made no answer, nor regarded, a look of wonder and gravity came over his bright features. The contrast between the two was most touching: Jamie, radiant with health and beauty, bending like a bright cherub over his dying sister; and she, unconscious, pale, and wan, passing into her last sleep.

I have another vivid recollection of James on a happier occasion,—his seventh birthday. He was a frequent guest with us, the bright morning star of our home as well as of his mother's. A short time before, we had given a magic-lantern party, which he had greatly enjoyed, and he therefore made a proposal to "bring his birthday" to his sister's house. We gladly assented. I think I see him now in his blue dress coming to our door, a maid-servant along with him bearing a

---

[1] Lines to James, written by his brother-in-law.

basket of cakes,—the birthday in a visible shape,—a troop of little friends following with rosy, smiling faces. It was the happiest of parties.

The good old custom of perpetuating family names was followed by our parents. James was named after one of my mother's grandfathers, James Hunter, a saint-like character, who retired from the world after the death of his wife, and led a sort of hermit life for more than forty years afterwards in the house of his daughter on the banks of the Tyne. His grave is in the beautiful churchyard of Ryton. My mother's ancestors were mostly Puritans. By nature and training she was strongly imbued with religious sentiments. "The peace which passeth understanding" disclosed itself in all her looks and movements. She had a sweet, serene temper, and was full of the milk of human kindness. She was orderly and clever in the management of her large family. In all relations of life she was faithful, much loved by her father, husband, children, and friends. James, as he shows in his letters, had a deep and tender affection for his mother. She was his ideal of what a woman ought to be. It was his highest praise to say of any one, "She is like my mother." When first left a widow, her youngest, with his sweet gracious ways, was an especial comfort to her. As he lay on her bosom in early mornings, she used to teach him hymns and Bible stories. He was nurtured in an atmosphere of love. The love of God and of his fellow-men was implanted in his childhood, and these religious lessons and precepts, learnt from his mother, bore fruit in riper years, even though he might then imagine he had "reached a purer air," and no longer had faith in "her early heaven, her happy views."[1]

James's first lessons were taught by his sisters. His home was by the sea, and in his early childhood he used to play on the rocks and sands of Tynemouth Haven.

Isabella, our eldest sister, who since has been laid in the tomb by the side of her young brother James, was his kindest and best teacher.

Isabella's delight was to make the younger children happy. She had a most felicitous way of managing them, understanding their feelings, sympathising in their pleasures. She resorted to no punishment, nor desired unnecessarily to impose *her* will. Her banner over them was love. She spent hours on the shore

---

[1] My dear mother is living yet (1877), in her eighty-sixth year. But her life of active usefulness, of "unhasting, unresting" diligence, is ended. She is helpless from paralysis, but patient, sweet, and uncomplaining, having only loving thoughts. Her mind is kept in perfect peace. Nothing grieves her, nothing troubles her now. She seems already to belong to that world where sorrow is unknown.

directing their play. She herself loved the open air and the fresh sea-breezes. In summer days James and the others would run barefoot on the sands, sporting at the edge of the waves. Isabella was never angry with the unfortunate,—those who, too venturesome, were overtaken by a wave, or who slipped and fell as they retreated from its advance: she was the consoler on these occasions.

Often I have seen her returning with a joyous band, assisting the flagging steps of the wearied ones, not hurrying nor dragging them on, laden herself with spades or pails or sea-treasures, sparing every one but herself. My brave, true-hearted, unselfish sister,—she also has left a blessed memory.

When James was nearly ten years old he was sent to Mill Hill School, where he remained for two years, winning optimes and commendations. In 1844 he spent his summer holidays with us in a farm-house near Kenilworth, where we then lodged. During that time he wrote daily letters to his mother. The docile child of eleven did the appointed task well. The simple record of those days is before me, carefully and clearly written. I give one letter as a specimen; it is characteristic of his gentle nature.

TO HIS MOTHER.

VILLIERS HILL, *July 3d*, 1844.

IT is a fine rainy day for me to write you a long letter, which I intend to do. L., Henry, and I were fishing yesterday in a pond. In the first pond that we went to, L. caught an asp, or what you call in the north "ask." We then went away from that pond to another, and I caught a perch. After that we went to a very nice pond. I put my line in beside a bush, and went to sit next to L., and watch my line. I saw a bird go into the bush two or three times, so I went to see what was there, and I found a nest with a dead bird in it. I pulled it out, and I went to sit beside L. again. The bird that the nest belonged to began to chirp very loud. I went again to the place, and saw a young bird, which I caught hold of, and the mother fluttered about, and made a great noise. When I found what distress the mother was in I put the nest in its place, and the young one in it. By and by when I came to look at it, the mother had taken it away to take care of it.

In January 1846 James entered Leamington College as a day-pupil, having his home with us. Very pleased he and I were with the change. The following year, when we left Leamington, my mother came to live there in our house, that her two youngest boys might continue to have the advantage at once of a home and a good public school. She had comfort and pleasure in watching the progress of her youngest children. James was alike a favourite with boys and masters. One of the latter, an exiled Pole, used to call him an "exemplarry boy."

At Christmas 1848 James left Leamington College, and came to us in Cumberland, pursuing his studies under my husband's direction. He decided to enter the medical profession, and diligently worked in preparation for that object. My husband and he used to take long mountain excursions, and James thus became well acquainted with the country round Derwentwater, learning mineralogy and other lore from the book of Nature. He was a steady and docile pupil, needing no pressing, but ever fulfilling the tasks appointed him. It is a time of pleasant memories, of rambles by river and lake and mountain-sides, of kind farewells, of welcome returns after brief absences. How often I have watched from the How Hill, in the winter afternoons or evenings, when the ground was crisp with frost, in the twilight, or by the light of moon or stars, until I saw Fanny (the white pony) crossing the bridge over the river Derwent; and then as I listened, the hooting of the owls alone breaking the stillness, I would hear the tramp of Fanny's feet, and a clear young voice would send shouts to me along the lane (knowing that I was there), and presently the forms of both would be at the gate, and I would feel the fresh cheek pressed to mine, and breath of "caller air," as he stooped from the pony to embrace me.

Lately, as my husband and I were passing a spot near Bassenthwaite Lake, we recalled a sunny afternoon in the summer of 1847. Isabella, my good sister, and James had gone with us in the pony-phaeton to enjoy a picnic. I seemed to see the fair gentle boy of fourteen, with the usual sweet look of content on his beautiful face. I have many visions of him of that summer; riding bare-backed on the pony to the brook, laughing joyously; or with can in hand going to catch minnows in the river Derwent; or rowing in the boat on the lake,—always innocent and gay. There were many small jokes at that time, at which we used to laugh until the tears ran down our cheeks. And now, those jokes, those days that are no more, are remembered with the sad tears of sorrowful recollection.

James used to join heartily in sports, but I never knew him say or do anything rude or unkind. His tolerance of shortcomings or infirmities of temper in others was remarkable, even in his boyhood. Like a good Newfoundland dog, he would bear with cheerfulness the quips and sallies which might have vexed another.

I have letters of every year of his life, beginning when he was eleven. We used to say of his boyish letters that they only contained bare facts. He was always sincere and modest, made no pretence nor display on any occasion. To me in their unbroken sequence all these ever kind amiable letters, with simple details of his daily life, are full of interest.

These few extracts from letters to his mother will suffice to indicate his progress until he was eighteen.

TO HIS MOTHER.

THE HOW, KESWICK, *Feb.* 26*th*, 1849.

I HAVE begun Rollin's Ancient History, and when I have finished the introduction I have to make an abstract of it from recollection. I have also begun Turner's Chemistry, and now I am busy making an extract of it. I am reading Eutropius in Latin. L. also questions me when we are out walking together. I have ordered a book on Vegetable Physiology. When you come will you bring Mrs. Marcet's Conversations on Chemistry?

TO THE SAME.

March 5th, 1849.

L. and I went up to the black-lead mines in Borrowdale. On our way we saw the salt spring, which is at the other end of the lake. L. thinks it might be made more useful if it were known. After we had explored and planned how the place could be beautified we proceeded on our way to Borrowdale. We went by the Bowder Stone, which, I think, I have already told you of, but when you come you shall see all these wonders. The black-lead mines you would not like to see for various reasons. You have to carry a tallow-candle in your hand; dirty water drops down from the top of the mine, and in some places the red water mixed with clay is two or three inches deep—unpleasant to walk through. There was also a strong sulphurous smell, which I know you are not fond of. The vein runs horizontally into the mountain. The black-lead lies beside a dark rock which is very hard, and has also a little black-lead in it. After we had gone 450 yards, the mine goes straight down. L. descended, but he would not let me go with him, because it looked so dangerous. The country people in Borrowdale formerly used the black-lead for marking their sheep. The ore was discovered by an ash-tree being blown down, and pulling some black-lead up with its roots.

TO THE SAME.

THE HOW, *April* 13*th*, 1849.

L. and I rode to Lorton yesterday. There is a mineral spring not far from the village; it tastes much like Leamington waters. We took a walk along the Cocker, and went into Lorton churchyard, where we saw a musical gravestone, which rung like a gong when we hit it with our hands, even though we were sitting upon it. We saw lambs for the first time this year on the mountains. Our dog Wag went with us, and he is very tired this morning. I finished the introduction to Rollin the other night, and have begun Vegetable Physiology. I would feel very much obliged if William could get me an air-gun, because the summer is coming on, and I want to get some small birds, which will soon be leaving us.

TO THE SAME.

DERWENT BANK, *March* 31*st*, 1850.

I WRITE to wish you many happy returns of your birthday, and to tell you how much we would like to be with you on that day, but as that cannot be accomplished, we must be content with meeting about the 14th of April, and spending my birthday together. I intended to send you a bunch of violets as a birthday present, knowing that that would be as acceptable as anything I could send you, but I could only find a few sweet-scented ones. I am glad you like the little spruce-fir that Isabella brought you; it is a very healthy one, but I am afraid it will not live more than two or three years in the smoky atmosphere of Shields. The larch-tree which you admired in our front field—one the poet Southey helped to plant in commemoration of Waterloo—is coming out in leaf and flower. The light green of the early spring contrasts beautifully with the little red flowers. I send you two or three of the flowers, because perhaps you do not remember them, or may never have seen them. I think you would enjoy coming here for a fortnight; the country is beginning to look very beautiful.

In the summer of 1851 James passed his entrance-examination at University College. It was the time of the Great Exhibition, and my mother and I went up to London with him to see him comfortably settled. In a brief memoir of him which appeared in the *British Medical Journal*, Nov. 1871, it is said, " By his love for his profession, the sweetness of his temper, and utter unselfishness of his nature, he won the love of his teachers and fellow-students." He used to confide all that interested or occupied his mind to us, sure of our sympathy. He was as a son as well as a brother to us. Of medical and scientific subjects he wrote to my husband, on more trifling matters to me. Often he would send me extracts from books which had pleased his fancy or which he thought would please me. I quote one extract from *Guesses at Truth* (p. 248), which seems to me now to express the yearning and reverence of my own heart for him.

TO ALLIE.

"During the last few pages I seem to have been walking through a churchyard, strewn with the graves of those whom it was my delight to love and revere, of those from whom I learnt with what excellent gifts and powers the spirit of man is sometimes endowed. The death of India's excellent bishop, Reginald Heber, in whom whatsoever things are lovely are found, has already been spoken of. Coleridge, who is mentioned along with him, has since followed him. The light of his eye is also quencht, none shall listen any more to the sweet music of his voice, none shall feel their souls teem and burst as beneath the breath of spring, while the life-giving words of the poet-philosopher flow over them. Niebuhr too has past from the earth, carrying away a richer treasure of knowledge than was ever lockt up in the breast of a single man. And the illustrious friend, to whom I alluded just now,—he who was always so kind, always so generous, always so indulgent to the weaknesses of others, while he was always endeavouring to make them better than they were,—he who was unwearied in acts of benevolence, ever aiming at the greatest, but never thinking the least below his notice, who could descend, without feeling that he sank, from the command of armies and the government of an empire, to become a peacemaker in village quarrels,—he in whom dignity was so gentle, and wisdom so playful, and whose laurelled head was girt with a chaplet of all the domestic affections,—the soldier, statesman, patriot, Sir John Malcolm, he too is gathered to his fathers. It is a sorry amends that death allows us to give utterance to that admiration which, so long as its object was living, delicacy commands us to suppress. A better consolation lies in the thought that, blessed as it is to have friends on earth, it is still more blessed to have friends in heaven.

"But in truth, through the whole of this work, I have been holding converse with him, who was once the partner in it, as he was in all my thoughts and feelings, from the earliest dawn of both. He too is gone. But is he lost to me? Oh no! He whose heart was ever pouring forth a stream of love, the purity and inexhaustibleness of which betokened its heavenly origin, as he was ever striving to lift me above myself, is still at my side, pointing my gaze upwards. Only the love which was then hidden within him has now overflown, and transfigured his whole being; and his earthly form is turned into that of an angel of light.

> "Thou takest not away, O Death,
> Thou strikest; Absence perisheth;
> Indifference is no more.
> The future brightens on the sight,
> For on the past has fallen a light,
> That tempts us to adore."

Dear Allie, I send you this extract in order that you may know what sort of a man Julius Hare is. Although he is one of the most learned men in Europe, he makes not the least display of his learning, and seems scarcely to be aware of it.

I have not been careful in choosing this extract, but I think it is characteristic, and one in which his modesty and love is truly shown. I think the allusions to his brother Augustus are especially beautiful, but you shall judge of the whole book for yourself in a short time.

TO HIS MOTHER.

LONDON, *July* 14*th*, 1851.

You will be glad to hear that I have passed my examinations. It is a great relief to me, for this last has been a very anxious week. I am going up for honours in Chemistry, but it is no consequence if I fail in that, which I am almost sure to do, as the other students that are going up have been taught by the examiner himself, and he will be sure to ask such questions as he laid most stress upon during his lectures.

In the spring of 1852 James spent some holidays with his mother in Derbyshire. They had invited me to join them there, but I was prevented doing so.

They had a pleasant time together. James was an accurate observer of Nature, and my mother delighted to listen to his explanations of all they saw. He had already acquired much scientific knowledge, and he had a most happy mode of conveying information, making things simple and clear in his own quiet modest way.

In his early manhood he retained much of the simplicity of his childhood, and the same ingenuous expression of countenance. As his brother-in-law used to say, he carried a letter of introduction in his face.

Before he got his appointment in Renkioi Hospital he had to have an interview with Sir James Clark. There had been some objection made to his youth; he was only twenty-two. He said to Sir James that he had been told by a lady that he looked like thirty. Sir James smiled, and remarked, " I think she must have been a very young lady."

The thoughtful and intelligent expression of his countenance was beyond his years; but his fair ruddy complexion, slender figure, and a certain look of candour and trust, made him seem youthful enough.

TO HIS SISTER.

MATLOCK, *April 23d*, 1852.

WE received your letter, and were sorry to find that we could not have the pleasure of seeing you just now. The weather has been fine, but exceedingly dusty. Mother says that the roads remind her of Cheltenham, and I suppose all roads on the limestone rock are dusty in dry weather. The rocks here are very perpendicular and picturesque, and are full of caverns and rents like those at Caldbeck.

There are a great number of old mines in them, supposed to have been worked by the Romans. A small quantity of lead is still got out of some of them, but there is so little of it that it was passed by the old workers as not worth the labour of working.

We have seen Chatsworth, Haddon Hall, and Bakewell since I wrote to you. You will see from the small picture which I send you that Chatsworth has quite the look of a modern house, although part of it is very old. The gardens are laid out in the most expensive manner, and I should think are among the finest in the world, with large conservatories and hot-houses, running streams and fountains. We saw one *jet-d'eau* playing which was ninety feet high, but sometimes one is playing which rises as high as two hundred feet on high days, visits from the Queen, etc. I will send you two or three pictures which will give you a good idea of the scenery round Matlock.

TO L.

BUXTON, *April 25th*, 1852.

BEFORE I received Allie's letter in which she said you wished me to see Buxton, mother and I had agreed to spend two or three days there, in order that we might see the caves of Castleton and other places near more conveniently. We left Matlock at ten this morning, I on the top and mother inside the coach.

The day was as fine as we could wish it to be, the sky clear, with a few fleecy clouds, and scarcely any wind. The distance from Matlock to Buxton is twenty miles, and the scenery between these two places, I should think, is as fine as any in Derbyshire. You can imagine how much I would enjoy the drive after coming from London. There were many things which reminded me of Cumberland, and I was thinking of you and your country all the way. The pass over the Peak is like some part of Whinlater, but the rocks on each side being limestone fissured, covered with ivy, and having yews here and there growing amongst them, are more picturesque and beautiful. On a stormy day I should think the pass of the Peak would look very wild, for the hills are bare and the stone walls and crags look very grey and cold; but it will never look anything like so grim as we in our journeys together have seen many of the passes in Cumberland.

The dark yews to-day in the bright sunlight contrasted beautifully with the light grey limestone crags.

On our road we passed Haddon Hall, one of the oldest baronial houses in England. Part of it was built by the first of the Peverils. The next time I read *Peveril of the Peak* I shall enjoy it more. There are many descriptions of scenery in it of which I have but a dim recollection, and which I was rather apt to skip, from the greater interest which I took in the story.

We arrived here at two o'clock, and after walking about until six, we had a bath. The temperature of the water is 80°. It has very little taste. The solid contents are small, and consist chiefly of chloride of magnesium, and sodium and carbonate of lime. The wonderful effects which it is said to produce are supposed to be due to the nitrogen which it holds in solution. It contains about one cubic inch of carbonic acid and four cubic inches of nitrogen in the gallon. The Duke of Devonshire is doing a great deal for Buxton. A large piece of ground to the west of the town is just now being laid out by Paxton as pleasure-grounds to be open to the public. The town is very clean, built of sandstone. Half of the houses, I should think, are lodging-houses. It is rather too much exposed, and will be too cold for invalids in the months of spring, but in summer I think it will be very pleasant. There is a theatre and public billiard-rooms to enliven the persons drinking the water. We intend going to Castleton to-morrow, and parting on Thursday or Friday. Mother cannot go round by Keswick this time. She hopes to see Allie in July.

P.S.—I shall write to you when I am in London, and tell you all the rest I have seen, and I hope it will be a better letter than this.

TO HIS MOTHER.

Nov. 14th, 1852.

ALTHOUGH it is a long time since you heard from me, I have not the less been thinking of you—indeed, I fancy rather more of late. . . I go to the College every day, and return home again, each day being a repetition of the day before. On Saturday, however, I made a little variety, and went down to Chelsea with the intention of seeing the Duke lying in state, but I was obliged to rest satisfied with seeing the crowd. I should think there never was a more dense crowd. Six persons died from the pressure, and numbers fainted. From the outside the perspiration upon the people appeared to rise like smoke from a chimney. They looked as if they were on fire, and some who had retreated appeared to be melting. Several of our students who had attempted to get in were glad to escape, thankful that their ribs were not crushed. I penetrated for a short distance into the crowd, but when I felt my ribs pressed so that I breathed with difficulty, I thought the good to be obtained was not in proportion to the suffering to be gone through, and therefore made my retreat.

TO HIS SISTER.

Oct. 14th, 1853.

I AM quite ashamed of having been so long in writing to you, and can scarcely forgive myself for my neglect, but still hope for your forgiveness. I am much more occupied this year than I was last, although the work which I have had to do is easier. Most of my time is spent at the hospital, where I am officiating as clinical clerk to one of the physicians. My chief duty is to write what are called "histories" of the patients previous to their admission into the hospital. It would be better to call them biographies, or memoirs, for none are sufficiently long to merit the dignified name of history. I like my present course of study much better than that of last year. I am thankful to have got out of the dissecting-room. I have got a ward full of women to look after. Most of them behave very well, some the contrary. There are three nice little girls in at present. It is painful to see one sinking gradually, but the pleasure of seeing the other two recovering makes up for it.

TO HIS MOTHER.

Nov. 4th, 1853.

I HAVE been so busy this week that I have scarcely had a moment to spare. Just now I am what is called "active dresser," that is, I am busy at the hospital the greater part of the day dressing ulcers, stumps, drawing teeth, etc., and I am generally very tired before my day's work is accomplished. Last night the students did me the honour of electing me secretary to the Medical Society, a post which will entail on me a good deal of work in the way of letter and report writing, but which, although troublesome at present, will be of benefit to me.

TO THE SAME.

December 5, 1853.

I HAVE just finished a long report of a Medical Society meeting, and I cannot finish off my evening's work better than by writing to you. It is a long time since I have heard from you, but I shall see you in less than three weeks, and that is far better than receiving letters.

I have been dining out the last two days. My friend Adams is in London, and invited me to dine at his father's house. I called to see Mr. William Smith[1] (whom you met in Cumberland), and he dissected a brain with me at my lodgings, and I showed him some curiosities with my microscope. I dined with him yesterday at his sister's, Mrs. Weigall.

There were two daughters and a son at home. All were nice people. I was particularly pleased with the eldest daughter. Eustace Smith was also of the party. In the evening we went to church together, and heard the son of your old friend Mr. Bickersteth.

TO HIS SISTER.

February 27, 1854.

YOUR letters are always very acceptable, and eagerly looked for in the Post-Office window every morning. I am now busier than ever, for in addition to my other duties I have accepted the post of clerk to Dr. Jenner at the Children's Hospital. The time for visiting the little patients is 8.30 A.M., and the hospital is distant from my lodgings about a mile and a half, so you see I have to commence work pretty early in the day. . . . Time passes very quickly with me. It seems a very short time since I left you at Christmas; I hope the six weeks which separate us will pass equally quickly.

I heard David Masson, our Professor of English Language, deliver a splendid lecture on Education at the opening of the

---

[1] The author of *Thorndale*.

Arts end of the College to-day. I think him the most eloquent man I have ever heard. "Ardent, vivid, vivacious, yet sober and quiet withal," so Carlyle describes him.

TO HIS MOTHER.

March 9, 1854.

... The Children's Hospital was formerly one of the residences of the nobility, so that its external appearance is less formal than that of most other hospitals, and when in the interior the difference is still more striking. The floor is strewn with toys, with which many of the children are joyously playing; few are so bad as to lose all relish for amusement. I am very glad that I have been appointed clerk, because this will enable me to become well acquainted with the diseases of children.

TO THE SAME.

September 2, 1854.

THE cholera gives us a great deal to do, that I had forgotten to answer your letter. ... You must not expect to see me at Shields. I should like to remain here until the cholera is gone.

TO HIS SISTER.

September 7, 1854.

... If you knew how much I have had to do during the last fortnight, you would not be surprised that I forgot to answer mother's letter. The cholera has been dreadful. Five of my patients died last night. The mortality is above 50 per cent. I have had more than my share of work to do. My colleague was knocked up, and has left London. I have been up four nights this week, but it is all over now. I shall not have much more to do, for we have got additional help. It is a most melancholy sight to see the poor patients dying, no remedy producing the least effect in the latter stage of the disease. But it is a still more melancholy sight to see the friends of the patients, and to tell them of the death of their relatives. We have admitted three of one family at different times, and they have died one after another. Two of the same family have died in other hospitals. I have had to tell a father first of the death of his wife, and then of two of his children. I myself am as well as ever I was in my life, notwithstanding the work which I have to go through. Don't show this letter to mother. It will make her anxious.

P.S.—I shall not think of leaving London until the epidemic is over.

His conduct during this epidemic was greatly admired. He took double duty, and "was up" four nights in succession. He feared nothing for himself, and his brave spirit probably preserved him. He came to Derwent Bank as soon as his duties were over, to have the change of air and repose he so much needed.

Many sad details he gave us. I remember he mentioned how a mother who had left her daughter ill the previous night, and had been admitted in the morning unwittingly by one of the nurses, looked for a moment rejoicingly at the bed on which another young woman about the same age, and with hair of similar colour, was lying convalescent. At first the poor mother thought it was her own child, but in an instant she saw her mistake, and utered a shriek of despair as the truth was revealed to her mind. Her child had died in the night, and another had taken her place on the same pallet.

James had made *post-mortem* examinations, and been incessantly occupied.

TO L.

June 26th, 1854.

I WAS at King's College Hospital on Saturday, and saw Fergusson do some minor operations. There were no cases of cleft palate in the hospital, but a student told me that about a month ago Fergusson operated very successfully on two cases. When they left the hospital little peculiarity could be detected in their voice; before being operated on they spoke scarcely intelligibly. Fergusson, in the last edition of his Surgery, says that he has operated on twenty-six cases, and has been successful in all but three. The failure in these three cases he attributed to "want of skill in dealing with the stitches." In one case also the patient was too young.

With respect to the voice he says: "In some instances there has scarcely been an appreciable difference, but in others, and I am glad to say the majority, the effect has been most gratifying. In some the change of tone has been perceptible at once, while in others many months have elapsed ere much could be noticed; in all instances where there has ultimately been great improvement, correct modulation of tone has been acquired only after the lapse of some considerable time."

I was rather amused at Fergusson's magnificence. He drove up to the hospital door in a very large carriage with two horses, and footmen before and behind. Every one seemed to treat him with great respect, and there was such a bustle when he appeared. He walked along the hospital passage in a stately manner, graciously smiling and nodding to a few of the students.

It was like a triumphal procession; the sound of the trumpet alone was wanting. The few small operations that he did were performed in a most elegant manner. He used the knife as if he were playing with it, just as you see some people cutting up apples after dinner. The expression of his face was peculiar, indicating coolness and indifference. It was evidently partially assumed. He now and then stopped, made some remark, and smiled whilst performing the operation. He has a habit of elevating his eyebrows, pouting his lips, and approximating the right angle of his mouth to the eye of the same side, by which he appears to mean to say—"See how cool I am!"

TO L.

... It is rather difficult to answer your question about the amount of water in the human body, but I should think a rough calculation would be sufficient for your purpose. In 100 parts of blood there are 79 of water; in 100 of muscle, tendons and cartilage, etc., 70; in 100 of the animal matter of bone, 70; in 100 of bone there are 33 parts of water. Thus from this we get—in 100 of blood and bones together, 70; in 100 of the other constituents of the body, 70. It will not be very far wrong to say that the body contains 70 per cent. of water. But mummies also contain a great deal of water, I cannot say how much—very likely as much as a piece of dry fir-wood. I will talk with any scientific friends that I have on the subject of burning the dead, and will communicate results to you.

P.S.—Seven weeks more of hard work for the M. B., and then I shall see you.

TO HIS SISTER.

FEVER HOSPITAL, *Feb.* 19*th*, 1855.

I THINK I must devote this letter to giving you a description of the Fever Hospital, and my life in it. I shall not say anything about the external appearance of the hospital, for you must know it as well as I do. It is the first large red brick building which we used to pass every day when we lodged in Theberton Street, on the way to the "Hangel." I hold no office here, but am just staying with my friend Dr. Buchanan to help him to look after the patients. The central portion of this building is the dwelling-house of the resident medical officer. ... The male wards are on one side of us, and the female on the other, and both are separate from the house by a passage which is exposed to the purifying winds of heaven. We get up rather late during the cold weather, but for all that much time is not spent in bed. Hospital officers never go to bed early. You know sick people are always worst for the first few hours of the night. We spend a considerable part of the time between breakfast and dinner in the wards or in the *post-mortem* house. We both find that the Fever House agrees well with our health, and think that we might do worse than recommend it to people wanting a change of air. The evening we spend in the drawing-room, where we have tea, and amuse ourselves with reading entertaining and instructive books, medical and others, trying to play on the flute, talking, etc., until bed-time and after it. You see this is a very delightful sort of life, but unfortunately it must not last long. I must retire shortly into lodgings to read, for I have read but little for the last year, my time has been so much taken up with the practical study of medicine. I have proposed March 1st as our parting day, which neither of us likes, although we both see the necessity of it. I have lately become acquainted with Morley, the editor of the *Examiner*. He is one of the cleverest and best-natured men I know, remarkably gentle and amiable for a literary man. His style of writing is very charming to me, it is so simple and melodious. I think you would do well to order some of the books for your club, such as the *Life of Palissy the Potter*, or *Jerome Cardan*. The weather here is frightfully cold. Last night the thermometer was 23° below freezing. On Friday night I was down at Blackfriars Bridge from eleven until two, looking at a tremendous fire, which illuminated London and the country for ten miles around. The windows of the houses two miles off were quite brilliant with the reflection of the flames. The fire was close by the waterside. The Thames looked extremely beautiful. Large blocks of ice covered with white crisp snow were floating up it; the fire made them appear pink, and the intervening water was of a brilliant red. The bridge was crowded with people, and cabs having spectators on the tops, shafts, steps, and wheels. Every now and then, when a roof fell in, or the flames blazed up unusually high, such a curious murmur arose from the crowd— not loud at all, but so diffused and universal, produced by each individual making a slight exclamation. Have you read Thackeray's *Rose and the Ring*? It is so clever and pretty, and so beautifully illustrated. One little picture of Betsinda dancing before the king and queen is exquisite. I should like to be at Keswick now for the sake of the skating. I should think the lake is frozen a foot thick, and if this weather continues will soon get frozen to the bottom. In London there is nothing attractive in cold weather.

B

TO L.

March 18*th*, 1855.

It is very unlikely that I caught small-pox at the hospital, as I at first supposed, for I find that the incubation period of small-pox is fourteen and not seven days, and I did see a slight case of varioloid a week before going with you to the Small-pox Hospital. Please tell Allie that I am much obliged to her for her offer to nurse me, but I cannot think of accepting it; I should be in continual fear of her catching the disease. The old hospital nurse is very attentive. I have not begun to get better yet, but I am little worse than when I first wrote to you. I think the disease has now reached a crisis. I shall not regret having had small-pox; it will teach me to sympathise with my patients. The last week has appeared to me like a year. I have been restless and full of pain. I shall be able to go about small-pox patients now without fear. I am afraid my letter is not very clear. It just reflects the condition of my head.

P.S.—Mother might know now, perhaps.

TO HIS MOTHER.

Fever Hospital, *March* 19*th*, 1855.

Since I last wrote to you, as you already know, I have had small-pox, which I can now tell you from personal experience is anything but an agreeable disease. For one week I was very ill. My nights appeared interminably long. I scarcely closed my eyes for three nights. L. came up to see me, but I had just awoke from sleep, and was recovering when he came into the room. I am happy to say that my misery is now all over, and the blessings of convalescence are in store for me. I have agreed with L. to be in Keswick in a few days, and should be delighted to see you there. I have been remarkably fortunate in having a nice sick-room. Directly I discovered the eruption I came here, and I have been treated with extreme kindness by Dr. Buchanan. Dr. Jenner also has seen me every day.

TO HIS SISTER.

27 Euston Place, *June* 1855.

John has just been here, and brought with him what Carlyle would call an Eidōlon of you. I am sorry to say it is nothing more than the Eidōlon or ghost of what a likeness of you ought to be. For some time I hesitated whether it should share the fate of your other likeness, but at last I came to the conclusion that it is better than nothing, and have therefore resolved to keep it. I enclose you two extracts from a book of poems by Gerald Massey.

June 14th.—Mother and I expect that you will come to London, and shall be much disappointed if you do not arrive to-morrow. London is very delightful just now. The country around is looking very beautiful, and the Opera and Royal Academy are open. Dr. Carlyle is in London, and he expressed a great desire to see you. Do not be later than Monday, for fear that I may be gone before you arrive, and so not have time to see anything with me.

I went gladly and helped to prepare his outfit for the East.[1] He delighted to show mother and me the sights of London, and he took me to the Opera, of which he was passionately fond. My mother had to leave us a few days before James sailed, and I was left alone with him until the day of his departure. How often I have bade him farewell, and always the parting was sad, the last "casting its shadow before."

[1] He was appointed assistant physician to the hospital of Renkioi on the Dardanelles, which was established, under the superintendence of Dr. Parkes, in the rear of the hospitals in the Crimea and at Scutari. He also volunteered for the Crimea, and was for some time attached to the hospital of the Light Division at the front. For his services there he received the thanks of the officers, and afterwards Sir William Codrington procured him the Crimean medal. It was characteristic of him that he left immediately after the duties were over, that he might not in any way share the merit of his military medical friends. After returning to Renkioi, where he served till the end of the war, he was also appointed assistant-surgeon to the Land Transport Corps, which had at that time over six thousand mules at the Dardanelles and a large number of men. Here, at Abydos, he remained some time. "He discharged," says Dr. Parkes, "both sets of duties with great zeal and very ably. He was at that time only twenty-two years old, full of vigour, very strikingly handsome, and with a sweet, never-ruffled temper which made him a favourite with all. His service in the East was very pleasant to him, and he enjoyed greatly the active, energetic life he led there."

CHAPTER II.

JOURNAL OF THE VOYAGE TO THE EAST, AND LETTERS FROM THE HELLESPONT.

PART I.—EXTRACTS FROM THE JOURNAL.

> "And all we met was fair and good,
> And all was good that Time could bring."
> *In Memoriam.*

July 9th, 1855.

July 4th.—Came on board the "Bacchante" this afternoon about eight o'clock with anything but a pleasurable sensation, although I had been so long looking forward to that event joyfully. The captain had not received orders to take us on board, so we had to wait until orders came from London.

July 5th.—Sailed this morning about three o'clock. Got up about seven, and saw the banks of the Thames on either side. Passed Ramsgate, Deal, Dover, Hastings. Saw the masts of a steamboat like our own, which had come in contact with another ship, and sunk opposite Deal. Made the acquaintance of my fellow-passengers,—Mrs. Hall, Miss Parkes. Talked a good deal with Bader about the state of the peasants in Switzerland, etc. He expresses himself very strongly against the Austrians and Prussians, especially against the latter.

July 6th.—To-day we have been sailing along the south coast of England, but at a great distance from shore. Paid farewell to England: Start Point was the last piece of land we saw.

July 10th.—Last night a wave or two came in upon Playne and me in the midst of our sleep. I would like sailing if I could only get properly washed. This evening passed the Busting Rocks and Cape Penitchi. The coast appears very beautiful. We can see windmills, houses, churches, but we are not sufficiently close to see the people. The weather is still colder than when we left London.

July 11th.—This is the first day at sea that I have really enjoyed. We sailed with a favourable wind all day at the rate of eight miles an hour all day. Turned the point of Cape St. Vincent in the middle of the day and began to sail eastward. The rocks at Cape St. Vincent are very bold and high; they remind me much of Marsden in Durham. At the extreme point there is a lighthouse, and behind it a convent, the windows of which we could distinctly see, but up to this time we have not seen a single human being. The people appear to be fond of keeping indoors; they don't properly appreciate their beautiful country. It must be taken from them, and given to some who can make use of it. It is now in a fit state to be overrun again by Goths or people from the north. The English if they are turned out by the Russians had better settle here; the country would have a very different appearance if inhabited by them. The stars appeared beautiful this evening; Venus was directly over the stern of the ship and reflected a silver path on the sea. I learnt several constellations from a young doctor.

July 12th.—The wind this morning was strong against us as we passed Cape Trafalgar and through the Straits of Gibraltar. The African coast is very fine and bold. There are several steep overhanging barren rocky mountains, and some valleys which appear fertile. One very steep bare rock is placed exactly opposite Gibraltar. The mists were disposed about them very beautifully. As we sailed into the harbour of Gibraltar (about four P.M.) the water became perfectly smooth, and we began to feel the power of the sun, but it was not too hot to be pleasant to me. We sailed near the shore for a short distance and saw cactuses, aloes, and palms growing among the rocks. When we arrived at the landing-pier there were several naked Spanish boys, quite brown, diving and turning head-over-heels into the water, at the same time gesticulating vehemently and calling to each other in Spanish. The German and I did not wait for the ladder, but jumped on shore from the ship. We were immediately accosted by a wideawake-looking inhabitant, whom we afterwards found to be half African and half English. He scarcely left us all the time we were on shore, and took care that we should see all the wonders of the place. We first walked up the main street of the town; saw some Highlanders getting drilled in the sun on an open place by the roadside. The groups of people that we met in the street appeared very singular to me. We met Moors, Jews, Spanish, English soldiers and officers in successive groups. The Spanish women go about without bonnets, many of them carrying merely a fan to keep off the sun, and to keep themselves cool. Some of them are extremely beautiful. We bought oranges and plums in the marketplace very cheap. They smelt nice, but that part of the town had an intolerable smell of onions. I have been told the Spanish are very abstemious, eating nothing almost but an onion with water for dinner and supper every day. We saw one very fine Moor, with a beautiful smooth brown skin, well supported by adipose tissue. He excited our admiration, for he looked so good-natured, contented, and happy, but at the same time alive and intelligent. The groups of children, too, were delightful to behold. The fair Scotch and English girls contrasted prettily with the Spanish, with their dark brilliant black eyes and well-defined eyebrows and olive-coloured skins. I don't know which I preferred. The slight superiority of the Spanish in sprightliness of expression was fully compensated for by the charming innocence of the north-country children. I was pleased to see the way in which several of the Spanish little girls received plums which I gave them. Some of the young Spanish women appeared amused at my behaviour to the children. I felt highly gratified at seeing so many pretty women after my long sea-voyage with the nurses. After we had taken a good survey of the town we made our way up the hill in a broiling sun towards the galleries of fortifications, but notwithstanding the heat, in consequence of our pleasure in being on shore in a beautiful country, we toiled joyfully and vigorously up-hill. We were amply repaid for all our labour. The views were magnificent. I never enjoyed scenery so much in my life. Water, a wide expanse in three directions, bounded by hills and mountains; the water smooth and blue, with many ships sailing about; beneath us the town; soldiers drilling, and a very bad band playing, which nevertheless sounded well at our distance. In climbing, sometimes we were almost fried, and at other times the wind was almost strong enough to blow us away. I was wet through with perspiration, but I toiled away, perfectly happy and joyful. The German and I were the only two who got to the top of the fortifications. In the evening we bathed in the harbour. The water was very refreshing, neither too hot nor too cold. It was full of little phosphorescent animalcules, which emitted light wherever the water was disturbed. We durst not swim out far for fear of sharks, which it was too dark to see; neither of us liked the idea of having even a toe carried off. After my bath I had a splitting headache, felt completely paralysed, and then was sick, but after that I felt as well and happy as possible. Went into the town again, and drank iced ginger-beer. Then I came on deck again and smoked and talked with Bader for an hour, and so my day at Gibraltar ended,—about as happy a one as I ever passed. I feel as if I shall never be able to live in England again without longing for the south.

July 13*th*.—This morning we sailed again at five; I wished to have another bathe, but we sailed an hour earlier than I expected.

Tuesday, July 17*th*.—For the last few days we have been sailing monotonously across the sea. The first day, land on the south of Spain was just in sight, but we could only see the outlines of a few mountains, which appeared to be very high. We have occasionally seen porpoises and turtles swimming about. On the 14th we passed two boats picturesquely rigged with long pointed sails reaching higher than their masts. These the captain considered to be pirates on the look-out for a becalmed sailing vessel. There was a heavy swell on the sea all that day without a breath of wind. The waves, as the prow of our ship struck against them, very much impeded our progress, so that we scarcely sailed more than four miles an hour. The weather has been warm, but not too hot. I am looking forward to another swim at Malta, which I am sure will do me good. To-day we are between Sardinia and Africa, opposite the island and rocks of Galita, where Captain Marryat was drowned in the "Avenger." The rocks are steep, high, and barren, running directly into the sea without any extension of base.

July 22*d*.—We arrived at Malta about seven o'clock on the morning of Thursday (July 19th), and left it about one P.M. of the same day. Upon the whole I was not so much pleased with Malta as with Gibraltar, although I was very glad to get on shore again, and enjoyed myself very much; I bathed twice— before landing and before coming on board again. The second time I stayed in the water about twenty minutes; I was so warm that I could have remained in much longer. The Maltese boys got a great many pennies from our ship's company by diving; they are very clever divers; I don't think they missed catching a single copper.

The town of Malta (Valetta) has a much more foreign appearance than Gibraltar. Several of the streets are composed of stairs. The windows of nearly all the houses project somewhat in the Elizabethan style. The town has a general aspect of cleanliness, and all the houses are built of light yellow stone, of a texture nearly identical with that of the new Houses of Parliament. We went into the church where all the knights are buried. The general effect of it was grand, but we had not time to enter into minutiæ or to criticise. A great number of people of all classes were kneeling, saying prayers and counting beads. Several priests with three-cornered black hats were walking about the church. Malta seems to swarm with these men. One of them, who had a better countenance than the rest, appeared to be dying of phthisis. We took a rapid survey of the Armoury and of the Grand-Master's Palace. The knights, to judge from their armour, cannot have been very tall men. There is not one suit of armour that stands more than 5 ft. 10 high. One old fellow, if he filled his armour, must have been quite a Jack Falstaff.

I had my hair cut, bought light jacket and trousers, and ate ices. It was extremely hot. We saw some oranges growing, but they were quite small and green. Melons, plums, peaches, apples, and apricots were sold in the marketplace. I saw less of Malta than I might have seen, because the captain told us that we must be on board again in an hour and a half. The island, seen from the sea, appears very barren; it is almost of a uniform reddish-brown colour. The doors of the houses and shops are very strong and well supplied with locks and bolts. This does not say much for the honesty of the Maltese.

Three things struck me as being very remarkable in Malta: first, the cats are of a most extraordinary breed—they are spare, thin, and active-looking, very much like polecats; secondly, the quantity of beggars that there are; thirdly, the large proportion of the population who squint and have eye-diseases.

Ever since we left Malta sailing has been delightful. I have had a bath in a large tub every evening, and this increases the soundness of my sleep. Yesterday morning, July 21st, Cape Matapan came in sight, and towards the evening we were sailing between the coast of Greece and the island of Cerigo. To-day we have been sailing among the islands of the Archipelago. The scenery reminds me very much of the west of Scotland. A fine fresh breeze has been blowing in our faces at the prow of the boat. It is rather tantalising to see these beautiful countries and not be able to land and explore. On the island of Zea we could distinctly see a small town some height up the mountain, composed of very similar white houses which appeared to have no roofs. I hope some day that I shall be able to come and examine these islands more closely. We saw two flying-fish in front of the steamboat this morning while Bader and I were enjoying the beautiful scenery and fine sea-breeze in the front of the vessel.

July 26th (Thursday).—On Monday, 23d, we entered the Hellespont, and about three o'clock P.M., after first going to the consul at Dardanelles, we found ourselves before Renkioi. Dr. Parkes and some others came to meet us, and about half an hour afterwards we came on shore and took a general survey of the hospital. Our quarters were not ready for us, consequently we had to live in tents. Playne, Dix, and I live in a tent along with a Mr. Hall. It is extremely comfortable compared with our sleeping apartment on board of ship. The tent is double, and we keep it open at three places. All night long we hear a continual hum of grasshoppers and various insects. Sometimes a jackal comes and howls close beside our tent, and every now and then the English sentinel howls out "Bono," to awaken the Turkish guard who have been appointed to keep off some "Bashi-Basouks" who have rebelled against their English general at Dardanelles, and threaten the surrounding country. Yesterday, early in the morning, we went up the hill to the village of Renkioi, which is about two miles up the hill. We met with a nice-looking Greek café-house keeper, who gave us a lesson in Greek, cups of coffee, nuts, bread, and water, for fourpence. Afterwards we called on Dr. Robertson, who is comfortably settled in Mr. Calvert's house in order to be near some cases of cholera which he is attending. There have been twenty-five deaths from cholera in the village during the last ten days. It is passing off now.

July 28th.—Yesterday Bader and I got up in the dark of the morning and walked to Dardanelles. By this we avoided the heat, which is tremendous here in the middle of the day. We arrived at Dardanelles about eight o'clock and went to an Italian café. We took a survey of the town, made a few purchases, and brought the letters home in a caïque.

Dardanelles, I am told, is a good specimen of a Turkish town. The streets are narrow and full of shops. Very few women are to be met with, and those that one does see have their faces covered, all excepting the eyes, with white cloth. At one end of the town we saw some very nice Greek girls. Lots of Bashi-Basouks were galloping about, looking very fierce. Last night we had a great thunderstorm, but about eight o'clock this morning the rain ceased. Bader and I bathed in the rain, running naked into the sea from our tent; I enjoyed it very much. We feel it a great convenience to have our tent so near to the sea. Fox and Playne went off to Constantinople in the Bacchante yesterday; Bader now occupies Playne's bed.

August 21st, 1855.—So few incidents have occurred since I last contributed to my journal that I have considered it not worth while putting pen to paper for the last few weeks. I have now given up living in a tent, and have taken up my quarters in No. 9 ward, along with Bader and Dix. With the exception of a few walks to the village, I spend every day about the hospital, reading, sleeping, smoking, bathing, and endeavouring to learn the zitter. For a week I have been laid up with a sore finger, caused by the loss of a nail while working in the boat. I have been trying to learn Greek also, but find great difficulty for want of proper books. Nevertheless Polychron and I can carry on a tolerably intelligible conversation, for he knows about as much of English as I know of Greek, and the two languages, being joined, made some considerable vocabulary. I am intending to go to the Crimea and Constantinople on Friday along with Mr. Jenner and Dix. It is very pleasant being paid by Government to amuse myself in travel, etc. The weather is now getting quite cool; at night a blanket is necessary. The nurses and orderlies are beginning to get discontented for want of occupation and amusement. The place is certainly very dull for persons without resources. The cook calls it "a damned low place." The other night one of the nurses called Dr. Parkes a billy-goat, and for this and boisterous conduct was put in a strait-jacket. The new mess-house has been occupied by us now for several days. We find it much pleasanter than the tent; there is plenty of room, and we have each the luxury of a plate, knife, spoon, fork, and glass. One Sunday I saw the inhabitants of Renkioi dancing, which is customary with them every Sunday afternoon. They have several different dances, most of which are very slow and simple. One that I saw struck me as being very picturesque. It was composed entirely of young men, each of whom performed a sort of hornpipe, not singly but all together. The colours and form of their dresses are very picturesque, and most of them are elegant figures, and have tolerably handsome faces. The maidens had very little to do with the dancing; they merely took hold of each other's hands and sidled slowly round in a circle. All the time they kept their eyes modestly fixed on the ground. It is very seldom that I can have any communication with these young ladies; sometimes when I meet a few alone I find them tolerably affable: I fancy it must be the presence of their brothers or lovers that makes them so reserved and timid. Some of them looked very charming while dancing. They carry adornment of person to a very high extent; many of them wear necklaces and forehead bands of gold pieces, and this seems to be the chief use of money in this country.

On the 22d of August Dix and I left Renkioi in a screw steamer (the "Esk"), the captain and owner of which had offered us a free passage to Kamiesh. The next morning we found ourselves aground on the coast of Dardanelles opposite Abydos. There we remained thirty-six hours, until we were lightened and dragged off by another steamboat. On account of this we did not arrive in Constantinople until the evening of the 26th. We entered the Golden Horn by moonlight, and I was very much delighted with my first view of Constantinople. The "Esk" was freighted with a number of French deck-passengers, who were carrying goods, and intended to set up as shopkeepers at

Kamiesh. Six of them were women; one was a pretty young Italian. I practised French by conversing with them, and found them the most extraordinary set of people I had ever met. Next day, Sunday morning, went in a caïque to Scutari. The hospital in very good order, sweet and clean. Saw Fitzgerald; Cumming. 27*th.*—Left £5 note in an Italian's shop; returned and received it all safe. Polychron pleased to see us. All together went on an exploring expedition and got a little insight into Constantinople life. Returned to our ship about two A.M. Everybody asleep on board. Dix had a small row with an English sailor. 28*th.*—Steamboat obliged to stay at Constantinople. Wet day. Went with Jenner up Galata Tower. Smoked cigarettes and drank coffee all the afternoon. Remarked a lot of jolly little Turks who seemed to be very much beloved by their grandfather. Sailed at seven or eight P.M. and had a splendid moonlight view of the shores of the Bosporus.

29*th.*—Black Sea. Mate taken ill with cholera in the morning, died in evening, and was buried half-an-hour afterwards by moonlight, Dix reading service. Sea looked steely black, excepting one quiet streak of moonlight. Body went in feet-foremost, bent almost double, and steamboat pursuing its course steadily.

30*th.*—Sea rather rough, wind contrary, passengers sick. One of French passengers seized with cholera. In the evening, light in direction of Sebastopol, which Chapman told us was the reflection of the firing guns.

31*st.*—High coast near Balaklava in view; 12.30 A.M., Kamiesh. Went ashore alone about four, and walked to Harris's tent. Was shown part of the way by a vivandière, who spoke despondingly of the condition of the army. Arrived at Harris's tent in the dark, much tired with my long walk. *September* 1*st.*—Rode along with Harris to meet Dix; found he had set off alone. 2*d.*— Dix and I rode to Kamiesh to settle with captain and steward; nothing to pay. On our way back came near the French batteries, and had a splendid view of Sebastopol.

September 3*d.*—Looked about camp, walking with a serjeant over the field of Inkerman, and obtained tolerably clear ideas of the valley of Balaklava and the valley of Tchernaya. *Sept.* 4*th.*—Balaklava with Dix; saw Jenner. *Sept.* 5*th.*— In the morning, heavy cannonading, continuing steadily all day. Harris and I went to the monastery of St. George, where there are a few monks and their wives, a Russian officer and some rather nice-looking daughters. Went into the chapel, which is much gilded and rudely ornamented. At night, from the picket-house, we could see the harbour of Sebastopol beautifully lighted up from a burning ship. Shells and rockets flying about in all directions. *6th.*—Balaklava again with **Dix** and Harris. *7th.*—Called on Worthington and saw the **General** Hospital and Scott behind the 14th regiment. Firing continuous. Informed of intended attack. *8th.*—Set off to obtain a good view of the attack. Could not pass the Lancers, which were drawn up to prevent people from passing. Circumvented them and got to a hill opposite the Malakoff. On our way saw the French advancing in thousands; English soldiers drawn up hearing a speech from the colonel, and cheering. At twelve o'clock precisely saw the French rise out of the trenches and cover the hill like ants; French banner advancing slowly to the top of the hill and planted in the centre of the battery. Then the English commenced to fire, making a tremendous noise, and were soon hidden from sight by the smoke. Strong smell of powder. A few balls and shells fell not very far from us. Balls look very pretty hopping along the ground, and appeared almost as innocent as cricket-balls. Day was extremely cold. Watched the fighting for about an hour or two, then went towards the 88th. On our way met Russian prisoners conducted by the French, some of them severely wounded. Lots of soldiers and officers getting carried on stretchers. Felt anxious to afford assistance, and to take a more active part in the grand fight. When I arrived at the camp my services were very gladly accepted by the surgeon, and I continued at work until twelve at night operating and dressing wounds.

9th.—Heard that Sebastopol was in our hands. Was thanked and treated considerably by the officers of the 88th. The General got me an order to enter the town, and told me that he had taken the liberty of sending in my name to the General of the division, Sir W. Codrington. Passed into the town; viewed the trenches and Redan; soldiers getting buried in the deep trench outside of the Redan. Ground difficult to walk over, being so much ploughed up by shell and shot. Walked about the part of the town to the east of the bay. The other part was all in flames, and continually exploding. French soldiers plundering. Took a Russian dog prisoner, and picked up some trophies. *10th.*—Rode off with my trophies and dog to Balaklava. Stayed for a day with Jenner.

11th.—Sailed in the "Orient" hospital-ship, towed by the **Imperador**. *12th.*—Black Sea; heavy swell—**Dix** sick as usual. Could not sleep at night for holding on. *14th.*—Constantinople, six P.M.

15th.—Went ashore, and on our way met with captain of Bacchante, who invited us on board to dine and sleep. Called on Swan, who lent me money and invited us to come and see him.

September 23*d.*—I have now returned to Renkioi after being absent for one month.

October 2*d.*—215 patients arrived by the Imperador. Veal exerting himself much, and getting excited. No serious surgical case. Only thirty-two surgical cases.

Patients to be seen standing about the hospital. Probably they will all recover. Miss Parkes walks about as usual, but no doubt doing a great deal of work without making any fuss about it.

December 29, 1855.—Before the year ends I must put a few words in my journal, which has been rather neglected of late. It is true that nothing particular has occurred, with the exception of a journey to Smyrna about a month ago. I sailed along with Holland, Dix, Armitage, Stretton, etc., on the 24th of November, and arrived early in the morning of the next day in the harbour of Smyrna. Holland, Dix, and I put up at Madame Gion's, where we were made very comfortable. We only remained one day in Smyrna, and during that time visited the hospital, which we found very much inferior to Renkioi. Saw silk-mills, fig-packing, and cloth-dyeing. The streets of the town are much cleaner than those of Constantinople, and altogether the town has a much more European and less interesting appearance than Constantinople. A very large number of pretty girls are to be seen walking about the streets. One silk-factory that we visited was full of Greek girls. All of them had beautiful eyes, and most of them fine features and a lively expression. They are much more free and coquettish than the girls of Renkioi. They seemed much amused to hear me talking a little Greek with them.

On Christmas Day we had a family dinner-party, and a dance in the evening.

Two days ago the orderlies and nurses gave a ball in one of the wards, and on Monday we are to have a ball in our mess-room. The married officers are giving parties, and people generally are endeavouring to make Christmas appear like England.

March 26, 1856.—I left Renkioi on the 18th of this month, and am now stationed at Abydos as medical officer to the Convalescent Hospital. As far as I have seen as yet, I have reason to consider myself better off than at Renkioi. It is true I am very solitary here, and my living is more expensive, but on the other hand I have more time to myself. My rooms are more comfortable, and my duties are more important, for I am the only English doctor within eight miles of Dardanelles. My house almost hangs over the sea. The Hellespont is very narrow here, consequently the ships and steamboats pass quite close, so that I can see their numbers. The villages of Maitos and Cestus are distinctly visible from my windows; altogether, the view is much more lively than that at Renkioi. It is delightful to sit smoking with my windows open, listening to the small waves quietly rippling on the shore. Towards sunset the wind generally lulls, and the sea becomes like glass thrown into small broad waves, which, when rendered purple by the light from the setting sun, have a delightfully soothing effect on one's spirits. The hospital is about two or three hundred yards from here. Just now the piers there have a very animated appearance. A few hundred mules are getting embarked and landed there every day. They are very fine strong animals, some of them fifteen hands high, but so unmanageable that it is impossible sometimes for five or six men to hold one. They tumble overboard occasionally and cause no end of a confusion. The mule-drivers are about the most picturesque and curious set of men I ever saw: they are collected from all nations,—Turks, Arabs, Negroes, Spaniards, Genoese, Greeks, etc. Some of the Arabs are very fine strong men, and their dresses are extremely picturesque and very gaily coloured. I often wish I could take photographs or pencil-sketches of them to carry back with me to England. There are no evident remains of the old town of Abydos here, but the ground is thickly strewn with pieces of pottery-ware and marble, which have probably at one time helped to form an ancient city. Just behind this house there is an abrupt little hill which is called Xerxes Hill, because Xerxes is supposed to have surveyed his troops crossing the Hellespont from thence. I was told yesterday by an Armenian that there are about 2500 houses in Dardanelles. Of these, 500 are Greek, 300 Armenian, 200 Jewish, and the rest Turkish and Frank—about 100 Frank. Dardanelles is situate almost on a swamp. To the south of it there is a river about as large as the Derwent between Derwentwater and Bassenthwaite. To the north the ground is very low and swampy. On both sides there are slaughter-houses, and round about there are heaps of dead cattle getting devoured by dogs, crows, and vultures. To the west is the Hellespont, which is very narrow at this place. To the east the country is level and cultivated for about five miles, and then it becomes mountainous and very picturesque. The town is called by the Turks Chanak-Kalessi (or the Castle of the Pots), because there is a strong fort pointing its guns towards the Hellespont, and the chief manufacture of the place is earthenware pots. There are four doctors, an abbé, and two papas.

May 14, 1856.—Since I last wrote in my journal, I have been going in regularly to Dardanelles every day to see my patients at the Land Transport Corps. I am exceedingly well pleased that I have this work to do, for besides the practice which it enables me to see, it also enriches me by 15d. per day, and gives me an opportunity of learning Turkish. I am also fortunate in being thrown much in contact with Crawford, whom I have found to be a most honest and straightforward fellow. His plain, truthful, clear way of speaking and dealing is a wonder and puzzle to the Levantines here, who never can do anything without scheming, planning, and tricking until they overreach themselves. ———, who has been considered a favourable specimen of a Levantine, is exceedingly un-English. He never looks one full in the face, and he does things that honest Englishmen would feel ashamed of, such as supplying many things to the Land Transport Corps here at extravagantly high prices, but never in his own name. The English Government allows him three per cent. on the expenditure, consequently it is to his advantage to spend as much money as possible, and in this way he gained £10,000 last year. I think he will probably be hauled over the coals for all this some day. Last Wednesday there was a grand review of the Land Transport Corps animals on the road to Renkioi. About 2000 animals were reviewed, and all, thanks to Crawford, in splendid condition. A tent was pitched, and a good lunch provided, after which the Arabs were made to go through their exercises, throwing the jeri, etc. Some of the gentlemen rode races, which were watched with great interest. One party went off to dig for old pots at the site of Dardanus.

Yesterday a party, consisting of La Fouche, Basilgate, Windsor, Preston, Capt. Freeland, W. Parkes, and myself, formed a picnic to the Genoese castle, a place about seven miles inland from here. The scenery is very wild and grand about this old castle, which now merely consists of a number of strongly built round ruined towers perched on the top of a rocky hill at the entrance to a valley, but at one time it was probably very extensive. Nothing appears to be known of its history, but it is supposed to have been built about the same time as the castles at Smyrna, Balaklava, etc.

For the last two days the Land Transport Corps animals have been selling by auction. The Renkioi people have been selling their goods and chattels to the natives of Dardanelles, and have been casting lots to decide who has to go home first.

In about another two months I suppose I also will be thinking of leaving this delightful country.

June 18*th*, 1856.—On the 6th of this month, Mr. Crawford, Marescaux, Van Lennep, and I set off on an expedition into the interior for the purpose of selling mules and horses. We took with us about 100 animals, and a number of Arabs, etc., to look after them. Of our servants the most prominent were Papa Sojolo, Mustaffa (cooks); Mustaffa the fietan; Hussain Hassan, Selim, Mahmet, Dowood, etc., body-guards; Ali, Marescaux's servant. On our first day we rode from Dardanelles to Cham, passing the Genoese castle and following the river Rhodias almost to its source, then crossing the mountains, which are thickly and beautifully wooded to their summits. About mid-day we reached the village Tamankioi, where we found the animals that had been sent forward the day before. There we ate eggs, milk, etc., and having rested ourselves, proceeded on our journey. Two or three miles farther on we came to an encampment of Turks, and drank coffee with them. After this we lost our road, and in trying to find it again the party got separated. We passed several very pretty villages with tiled roofs. At one of these villages there is a hot mineral spring and baths. The population of this country consists almost entirely of Turks, and they are a very fine healthy race of people. It was dark long before we reached the little village of Cham. The first thing we did when there was to light a fire, cook a supper, consisting of lamb, eggs, coffee, youart milk, etc.; then we ate it, smoked narghelies, made our bed in the open air and went to sleep. In the middle of the night I awoke drenched through and through with dew, but soon slept again hydropathically, and in the morning was perfectly dry.

When we got up we all went down to the river Granicus and bathed. Then, as there was to be no fair that day, we took a ride down the river to a place called Bazaar Kioi. There we called on the chodar, who was very civil to us. Some of the party bathed in a naturally hot chalybeate bath—too hot to hold the hand in until it got accustomed to the heat. There is a large ruined mansion here, picturesquely situated, and commanding a splendid view of the winding of the Granicus and high mountains in the distance. This night we slept in some of the bazaar booths at Cham, and in the morning bathed again in the Granicus. This day the sale commenced, and the horses brought such good prices that Mr. Crawford determined to go back to Dardanelles for more, and accordingly about four o'clock he and I set off with a body-guard of six Arabs. We reached Tamankioi, where we changed horses, at seven, and Dardanelles at about half-past one.

The next day, Wednesday, about three o'clock P.M., Crawford, Windsor, and I left the yard and went slowly up the Rhodias. On our way we overtook the animals which were sent off a few hours before. Freeman, second assistant, was riding at the head instead of the foot of the procession, consequently there were many stragglers. By the time we reached the foot of the mountain it began to be dark, so that the animals were stopped and encamped for the night, and Freeman along with them, while Crawford, W., and I rode on to Tamankioi. Selim was left behind with the animals, and was sent to a neighbouring village to look after provisions for the men. Every one whom he asked at the village for eggs, milk, etc., replied "Yok," until at last, his patience being exhausted, he drew his sword and demanded the agha of the village. This man being presented, Selim threatened to cut off his head instantly unless he brought forward eggs, milk, etc. This threat had the desired effect, and the provisions were rapidly produced. Then Selim demanded ten men for a guard, and promised them that if a single animal were missing in the morning, they should all be executed forthwith. This request was also complied with readily. On Thursday morning we waited at Tamankioi until the animals overtook us about mid-day.

Freeman came a short distance with us and then returned to Chanak. About five P.M. we arrived at Cham, where Marescaux and Van Lennep were anxiously expecting us. They had been told that we had been robbed and murdered on the way the night before, and were glad to find that they had been misinformed.

Early on Friday morning, after bathing as usual in the Granicus, we set off for Baghashere. On our way we stopped at Bazaar Kioi, where I tapped a woman with a quill and some of us bathed in the hot baths; then in the afternoon we pursued our journey along the banks of the Granicus. The country here is as beautiful as any I have ever seen;—mountains forming amphitheatres covered with wood, and verdant valleys with a fine rapid river running through them. The trees were many of them overgrown with the wild vine, which, forming festoons on them, produced a very beautiful effect. As we approached Baghashere we came upon some very large trees, which are rare in this country. After finding a place for encamping the animals, we all rode to the Pasha's house, where we found Van Lennep, who had ridden on in front. The Pasha was very kind, gave us dinner and offered us the use of his house for as long as we might stay, but we preferred encamping with the animals out of doors. In the morning we came into town to a house that the Jew had hired for our use. After breakfast the sale commenced. Marescaux and I went to call on the Pasha, who wished me to see his wife, who was extremely ill. His harem was separate from his house, within a large courtyard. I prescribed some medicine, etc., and promised to see her again the next day. In the morning I was received very kindly, and the old Pasha, after telling me that his wife was much better, said that I had been sent by God to save her life, and that his daughters had expressed all sorts of kind wishes, among others that I should have a nice wife who would make me happy. I was also kindly and gladly received in the harem. The little girls especially were glad to see me, and repeated their kind wishes in person. They were all exceedingly pretty and pleasant-looking.

On our way to this place we got in front of our baggage and commissaries, and lost sight of them. The consequence was that they nearly missed us, and if they had not heard the pistol fired off, we should have been obliged to go supperless and blanketless to bed. The next morning we were up and away by five A.M. The sky was cloudy, and there were a few drops of rain. At twelve A.M. we came on the shore of the Sea of Marmora. The wind was blowing pretty strong from the north, and the waves were dashing furiously on the shore. The Arabs, who were a little in front of us, as soon as they saw the sea, set up a shout, "El Bahr," and commenced singing joyfully. We rode by the Sea of Marmora until we came to the Hellespont. Then it began to rain. We encamped for two hours and got some dinner. For the rest of the day we were riding through the rain, and got thoroughly wet. At six P.M. we arrived at Chardak, where there is a large khan, which received all our horses comfortably. It is apparently built of ancient stones, and supported by Doric, Ionic, and Corinthian columns. We hired a house for ourselves, and here, after drying our clothes, we spent the night very comfortably. Windsor was strutting about very proudly in some Turkish clothes which he had bought at the fair. The next day we passed through Lampsakia, which is a considerable-sized village, partially Greek and partially Turkish, situated prettily on the side of a hill. We then rode by the banks of the Hellespont until we came to Abydos.

November 1856, **Paris.**—I shall, now that my Oriental travels are terminated, try to complete my journal from a few notes which I have scribbled in my pocket-book, and hope to spend an hour or so very pleasantly in trying to recollect and picture to myself the beautiful country which I have left, I am afraid, for ever.

July 22d, 1856.—"Bacchante" sailed with Parkes, Pigott, Humphrey, etc., on board. I rode to Renkioi, saw them on board, and watched the vessel steam away.

August 23d.—Set off with Abbott and Varley and 250 mules

for Gallipoli. After some trouble with the Turks at Chardak, we managed to get forty mules across to Gallipoli before dark; Varley and I slept in a cemetery along with these forty.

24th.—Rose at four; no caïques till six. Mules very restless, causing great difficulty in getting them in and out of the caïques, and giving me some idea of the difficulties that Alexander and Xerxes must have encountered in crossing the Hellespont. About three o'clock P.M. left Gallipoli and travelled for one hour to a flat piece of ground near the sea, where I bathed, got the tent pitched, and went to sleep. After sunset Crawford arrived.

25th.—Got up before sunrise, bathed, went ahead with quartermaster's serjeant to a village called Pleiare to provide rations for the men. Rode between the Gulf of Saros and the Sea of Marmora. Sea visible on both sides; country arid; no trees; Gulf of Saros beautifully smooth; banks mountainous on the far side. A few small wooded islands near the shore. Encamped near a village called Tugla, on account of salt springs. Crawford and party did not arrive.

26th.—Rose at half-past three A.M. Found Crawford encamped about half a mile on the road. Crossed some highish sandstone hills beautifully wooded with fine trees and oak shrubs. The road had been recently traversed by the French artillery, which had left traces, such as French names carved on the stones by the roadside. From the top of the pass on one side we had a splendid view of the Gulf of Saros and Sea of Marmora; on the other a very extended view into European Turkey; in the foreground, wooded hills, in the distance mountains, and between a broad dry plain. These hills are said to be infested by robbers, and my guide has just given me a hint not to ride on alone.

As we passed along the plain to our right was a Greek village prettily situated on the hill-side. Farther on we passed another Greek village called Mavris. Then I rode on to find a place for encampment. This I found on the far side of a town called Rishan.

27th.—Set off again in front early in the morning. Afterwards was overtaken by Varley and Crawford. Road rather uninteresting; country fertile, but uncultivated. Passed a few villages, all Greek. Journeyed eight hours until we came to a town called Onumkyupry. On the Adrianople side of the town there is a long stone bridge composed of nearly 200 arches; a river runs under one of these arches and turns a water-mill. We chose this place for pitching our tent, and bathed in the mill-race.

28th.—A long journey, nearly nine hours, to Adrianople.

For the greater part of the way we rode by the side of a broad, swift, but muddy and running shallow river called Maryitza. It runs from Adrianople to the Gulf of Saros. About four hours from Adrianople we could see its mosques and minarets quite distinctly, and the air was so clear that it appeared only a few miles distant. Long before we came to the city we passed through groves of mulberry-trees carefully cultivated. The city chiefly stands on rising ground in the angles formed by the junction of three rivers. For miles round about the country appears rich and verdant from the number of trees, mulberry-bushes, etc., which flourish by the side of the rivers. The three smooth broad winding rivers, the multitude of minarets, bright-domed mosques and trees, mixed up everywhere with the dark sombre red-coloured roofs, give the city a peculiarly grand and picturesque appearance. We found a place for encampment by the river-side before arriving at the town.

29th.—Called on the Pasha, an old man, who can speak both French and Greek. He is said to be like most Turks, very apathetic, and to spend the greater part of his time in the harem, and his appearance certainly did not belie this report. He told us that 600 English horses were coming to be sold the next day, and this rather made us fear for the sale of our mules. After taking leave of the Pasha we went to the telegraph-office to send a despatch to Constantinople, and then amused ourselves by riding about the town. The streets are broad and clean, and the town altogether appears much cleaner than any Turkish town I have seen. The principal mosque, built by Sultan Selim, is a fine piece of architecture. The decorations and architecture appeared to me purely Turkish. When inside, the dome appeared higher than St. Paul's, and the effect was grander; the minarets are very high, said to be the highest in Turkey. From the top of one of these I had a splendid view of the town, but the ascent was no easy matter, and before we reached the top our legs ached severely, and we were heated in no slight degree.

30th.—Began selling mules, but got no good prices. Only six were sold. Went to the sale of the 600 horses. They were not fetching good prices.

31st.—Tried to sell again, with less success than before.

August 1st.—To-day we took a ride on mules to a village about a mile from Adrianople where all the Europeans have their country houses. We called on the two brothers Wiltshire, who are the only Englishmen resident here. They trade in silk, and this year appear to be doing well, in consequence of the failure of the silk-worms in France and Italy. We saw some

Frenchmen who were buying eggs. They were giving £10 for about one pint measure, and they had bought about 150.

Raw silk this year costs 140 piastres, about £1 the oke (= 2¾ lbs.).

Aug. 9th.—Crawford set off alone by post for Constantinople; Abbott, with 112 men, mostly Italians, for Dardanelles—men rather mutinous at being obliged to walk; Varley, Harding, and I with the remaining mules for Stamboul. Our first resting-place Rulalee, about seven hours from Adrianople. Neither meat nor cheese to be bought. Our road lay by the side of the telegraph-line all the way. The wire at times passes for miles through a perfectly desert country.

August 10th, Sunday.—Encamped, mid-day, at a place called Burgas, the prettiest Turkish village I have ever seen. There is a fine mosque with marble floor and pillars, built nobody knows when. The streets are clean, in places arched over by vines. Post passed us on the road. Arrived late at night at Charisteran.

Aug. 11th.—Arrived at Chorla, mid-day; three men sick; obliged to carry them in the cart. Travelled all night. Great difficulty with the sick-cart, constantly stopping to get them better packed. Just before sunrise we arrived at Silivria, a very old town, with ruined walls, castle, and two ruined churches; one with a minaret had been used by the Turks. The floor paved with marble, and polished marble pillars. Left Silivria after sunset. About midnight met Crawford and Brack near Buyuk Chockmedjie, where we encamped. Left our sick men at Silivria.

August 12th.—Returned to Silivria in order to accompany the sick by steamboat to Stamboul; stayed with a Greek gentleman named Panar. One of the sick men was dead when I arrived.

13th.—Waited in vain all day expecting the arrival of the steamboat.

August 14th.—Embarked with three patients. One extremely rough; sea rather rough; wind contrary. Arrived at Constantinople about three P.M. Put Garland in hospital.

Jardin des Fleurs, Vasilouec, August 15th.—Set sail for Dardanelles about four P.M., in the "Norwood" sailing ship. At Dardanelles the command of 200 Spaniards on board the ship was given me by Mr. Calvert, and I sailed with them for Gibraltar.

Finally arrived in England, Sept. 28th, 1856.

Part II.—Letters.

TO HIS SISTER.

Bay of Biscay, near the Spanish Coast,
July 8, 1855.

I FELT very sorrowful at parting with you. The ship tosses so much that it is with the greatest difficulty I am able to write. The bottles at dinner-time will not stand on the table. All the nurses and ladies are sick, and all the medicals except myself, and another who is an old sailor. Notwithstanding all this I am not in the least sick. We bade farewell to England off the coast of Devonshire. I cannot say I felt happy to part with her; I am afraid it will be long ere I see her again. The sun is now shining, and the sea looks beautifully blue and fresh; there are only a few little white waves, but there is a fine broad swell (probably produced by some wind near America), which first lifts us high into the air, then sinks us deep into the sea. The nurses are lamenting their folly in ever thinking of going to the East, and cursing the day on which they set sail. . . . Lady Canning, it is said, chose them on account of their plain features. It is not easy to write on board ship. If you receive this you may conclude that I have arrived at Gibraltar. I shall write to mother.

TO HIS BROTHER.

Renkioi Hospital, *July 26th,* 1855.

WE called at Gibraltar and Malta on our way, and stayed for three or four hours at each place. I shall not say anything to you about either place, for you have often heard all about them. Gibraltar pleased me most. The scenery there is very splendid, and I felt it a great relief to put my feet on land after sailing for so many days; a bath, which I took in the evening, was very delightful. The sea was quite warm and full of phosphorescent animalcules, which spangled about me in all directions when I splashed. All sorts of queer people were to be seen walking about the streets in strange costumes, which I will talk to you about some day when we meet again. At Malta we remained about three hours, and during that time I managed to see the greater part of the town, and to bathe twice. The bathing was extremely delicious, and almost necessary for my existence, because the chimney of the steamboat had been smoking on us for the last three days, and our skins had got dried up with the heat of the sun, which on deck was burning, and reflected on our eyes from the sea. I should recommend no one to travel in a steamboat that can get a passage in a sailing vessel. We entered the Dardanelles on July 23d, Monday. On the Sunday we were sailing amongst the Greek islands. The sea was quite smooth, but there was a pleasant breeze blowing against us. The scenery reminded me very much of the west of Scotland, but it is not nearly so beautiful (at this time of the year at least), for all the mountains are of a uniform dusky yellowish-brown colour, produced, I suppose, by the sun burning up the grass and all vegetables. It was very delightful to stand on the deck at night and see the islands and ships by moonlight, with the moon and stars reflected on the sea, forming paths of light in different directions. Some of the sunsets were extremely splendid—one in particular, where the sun set close to Sparta over Mount Elias. Our hospital is not on the Plains of Troy as I expected; it is about five miles from the entrance of the Hellespont, on the south side. We can see the land on the opposite side very distinctly (it is about five miles across); and if we climb up the hill, the Plains of Troy are just beneath us, and we can see Tenedos, also the coast of Asia Minor as far as Mitylene. Mount Ida, too, is close beside us. The English Government has bought about 300 acres of land for us. It consists of a nearly level plain, projecting into the Hellespont, and bounded behind by hills 900 feet high, inhabited by pigeons, eagles, wild boars, jackals, etc. There is plenty of water, which rises to the surface in different places, but does not form any stream on account of the porous, dry nature of the soil. It is a very healthy place, and well suited for an hospital. As yet we have no patients, although Dr. Parkes has reported the hospital ready to receive 500. There is no possibility of my having anything to do for a month. About seven of the hospitals are erected. Each hospital has to contain fifty beds, and they are going to erect enough to hold 3000 patients. Our quarters are not finished yet. In the meantime we inhabit tents, which we find a great deal more comfortable than our cabins on board the "Bacchante." Four of us sleep in one tent, which we take care shall have a pleasant breeze through it all night. It is pitched only a few yards from the sea, and I very frequently have a swim. It is very easy to stay in for an hour, because the water is so warm. I did not sleep very well the first night, because every now and then I was waked up either by a jackal howling, or by a locust buzzing past my ear, or by the English sentinel shouting out "Bono" to awaken the Turkish guard. I have now got used to these slight annoyances, and sleep soundly from nine till half-past four A.M. Yesterday morning I walked to the village, which is about two miles up the hill. Three of us got coffee, tchibouks, bread, water, and meat, together with a lesson in the Greek language, for fourpence. Some of the Greeks that I have seen are nice-looking, honest, good-natured fellows. Those about here are very innocent, elsewhere they have a different character. Mother will forward this letter after she has read it.

TO HIS MOTHER.

RENKIOI HOSPITAL, *August 4th*, 1855.

I WISH to give you as clear an idea of our quarters and mode of life as I can, and therefore I will draw you a kind of plan of the arrangement of the hospital tents, wash-houses, etc., and enclose it with this letter. The land on which the buildings stand is very flat, but there are mountains 900 feet high close behind us. There is no distinct stream of water, but there are wells and fountains of beautiful water scattered over the ground, —water that rises among the hills behind and sinks into the sandy soil before it reaches the hospitals. No patients have as yet arrived, and we have nothing to do but read, bathe, and enjoy the climate. We can only get pears and mulberries to eat for fruit, but the grapes will soon be ripe. Two or three days ago I rode with the superintendent of Smyrna hospital and two or three other doctors to the plains of Troy; although the temperature was 90° in the shade we did not feel the heat much. When we began to get warm, we put our horses into a canter and so fanned ourselves. Our ride was chiefly over grass-land, sprinkled over with bushes a few feet high. We crossed the Simois and saw the source of the ancient Scamander. At the source of the Scamander I fell in with a pretty little Greek girl, and we soon became friendly. I made use of all the Greek words I could muster, and we managed to keep up a sort of conversation. When I took leave of her she bowed her head almost to the ground, took my hand and kissed it, and wished me goodbye in the Greek tongue very prettily. I find that the modern Greek does not so much differ as I expected from the ancient as taught in England, excepting in pronunciation, and what I know of the ancient helps me in acquiring the modern.

TO L.

RENKIOI HOSPITAL, *August* 17, 1855.

WE have not any patients yet, and judging from the English papers, which we see here, it appears probable that we shall not have any for some time yet. I have accordingly applied for leave of absence to go and see the Crimea, and it is most likely that I shall set off with Mr. Jenner on Friday week (in eight days from the date of this letter). I think it better to go off now, before I am settled in quarters, because I am not spending my time very profitably here. The tent which I live in is so infested with insects of various sorts, that when I am in it almost my whole attention is taken up in warring with them. This life suits my health remarkably well; the heat is never so great as to prevent me from taking exercise, even in the middle of the day. The nights are very agreeable and cool. Last night I was awoke by a strong wind having blown off my blankets and sheets. I spend one hour at least every day swimming about in the Hellespont. This, I think, takes all my fat away, but gives me muscle instead, which is far better. The village of Renkioi is up the hill behind this hospital about two miles; it is said to contain 4000 inhabitants, but I rather doubt this, for it does not appear to be so large as Keswick. It supports two papas or priests, and a cavash or Turkish constable. The rest of the inhabitants are all Greeks, most of whom come down to work at this hospital. They are not fond of working, and seem to care little about money, for they sometimes refuse to work although they get paid well. When such is the case, the cavash and some Turks go to the village and bastinado the papa until he sends his parishioners down.

The Greeks appear to be as fond of dancing as their forefathers are reported to have been, and some of their dances are very picturesque. Every Sunday they have a great turn-out at the village. The young men come out in their best clothes, which are remarkable for brilliant colours, and the maids adorned with gold about their forehead, rings on their fingers, and long white gowns, very much like those that you see depicted on ancient vases. The girls do not join actively in the dance, never advancing at a quicker pace than a walk, and always keeping their eyes modestly directed towards the ground. As a rule, they are very much prettier than English girls, and some of them are exceedingly beautiful; but it is remarkable that there appears to be no intermediate stage between a girl and an old woman. The common Greek men and servants are nearly all good-looking, have elegant manners, and appear much quicker and more intelligent than our workmen and orderlies. I suppose all this is given them by nature, by means of the warm climate, for they do not work at all, and seem to have no desire to improve their condition. Upon the whole, they appear to lead a very happy existence. They live mostly on black bread and onions, and all the money they get appears to be spent in adorning themselves and their families. They are extremely fond of music, songs, and stories. In the evening I often hear one man repeating verses for about half-an-hour without stopping. At present I do not understand enough of the language to know what it is all about. All the land in this part of Asia Minor is very fertile, but in consequence of the misrule of the Turks it is almost uncultivated, and is consequently valueless. The land on which the hospital is built was bought at the rate of £1 per acre.

I do not regret in the least that I came out here as surgeon. It is almost certain that I shall see much more practice than if I were a physician, and in three or four years I expect I shall return to London, and become a student once more. Until that time I hope to employ myself in studying languages, music, and history, and seeing a little of this part of the world. My salary will more than enable me to do all this, which is much more satisfactory than if I were doing it at mother's expense.

TO HIS MOTHER.

MIDDLE OF THE BLACK SEA, *August* 29, 1855.

I LEFT Renkioi last Wednesday in a steamboat called the "Esk," the captain of which was kind enough to offer me and a friend of mine a passage to Kamiesh. The boat is freighted with a great number of French deck-passengers from Marseilles. We are the only cabin-passengers. Our voyage up to this time has been rather unfortunate. First, we ran foul of another ship. Then we got aground opposite Abydos, and remained there two days. We were obliged to stay three days at Constantinople, of which I was very glad, for it enabled me to see the town. Last night, by moonlight, we buried a sailor who died of cholera since we left Constantinople. The ceremony was very simple. My friend read the service; only a few sailors were present; the moon was full, and the sea perfectly black, except where the moon was reflected. The corpse slid from the plank, fell with a heavy splash, and the vessel pursued its course as before. None of the passengers were aware of the fact. I have taken every precaution to prevent the cholera from spreading, and the rest of the crew are as yet tolerably healthy. We shall probably arrive at our destination early to-morrow morning, and then I shall make my way to Balaklava, where I expect to meet with friends who will entertain me.

Sept. 1st.—I have arrived safely before Sebastopol, and am staying with Harris, 88th regiment, in a bell-tent. There is continual firing of bombs, night and day.

P.S. No. 2 (*Sept.* 3*d*).—I have not been able to send my note off yet, so I shall just say a word or two more. I have been fully engaged every day seeing the camp and the battle-fields in the neighbourhood. The Crimea is very healthy at present, but about fifty men are disabled in the trenches daily. I shall tell you all that I have been doing when I arrive at Constantinople.

In the meantime I enclose you a flower from the field of Inkerman.

TO THE SAME.

Hospital-ship " Orient,"
Black Sea, *September* 13, 1855.

When I last wrote I promised that I would let you hear from me again when I arrived at Constantinople, but as I have an opportunity now (the sea being very calm) I shall not put off writing longer, but will endeavour to give you a slight account of what I have done and seen in the Crimea. On the 31st of August, about five in the afternoon, I landed at Kamiesh alone, and after a good deal of trouble and walking about in the dark, I found the 88th regiment, and my friend Harris, the surgeon. I walked through the French camp with a vivandière, who was kind enough to offer her services as a guide. She was very polite and communicative. Every now and then she burst into tears, at the same time telling me that the English and the French in the Crimea were all miserable and dying; but she very quickly dried her tears, and appeared to derive great consolation from the thought that the English and French are " Frères." I afterwards found that all the Frenchwoman said was perfectly true; every one to whom I spoke replied in the same strain. This state of feeling was produced by the trench-work; not at all by disease, or want of food and clothing, for the Crimea is very healthy at present, and the army is well supplied with all necessaries; but the English army alone, at the time of which I speak, was losing daily fifty men, killed and wounded. Harris, as I expected, was very glad to see me. My arrival in the dark took him very much by surprise, as you may well imagine; nevertheless he had no difficulty in accommodating me with a bed on the floor of his tent, where, notwithstanding the continual firing of the cannons, I slept as soundly as if I had been in my own bed at home. In the morning Harris and I rode back to Kamiesh to look after my friend who came with me from Renkioi, but we missed each other on the way, for when we returned we found him in the tent. Harris managed to get him a bed in a new hut, and thus we were comfortably settled in the Crimea. The next day my friend (Dix) and I set off on a walking expedition to take a survey of the camp, and get some idea of the position of the different regiments. The complete desolation of the country struck us very forcibly. Nothing but dust and tents in all directions. All the vines have been cut for fire-wood, and the ground so trodden over that nothing will grow. We walked to the top of a hill where we could see down the famous valley to Balaklava in one direction, and also up the valley of the Tchernaia to the mountains in the interior. Even this valley is desolated, though not so much as other parts of the camp. In this direction, as far as the eye could reach, we saw encampments of Sardinians, Turks, and Russians. One Russian battery was firing at a group of soldiers in the valley, and we could distinctly see the balls as they fell and dispersed the soldiers. We then walked round the hill and looked into the valley of Inkerman, which is still green and refreshing to look upon. Many poplars and oaks still grow there, and there are a few houses, which give a homely appearance to the valley, although they are deserted, and no doubt much injured by cannon shot. One day Harris and I took a ride to a Russian monastery on the sea-coast, near to Balaklava. The Russian monks are allowed by the English to pursue their religious duties unmolested.

The sea-coast by the monastery is very high, rocky, and extremely picturesque. The monks too have been careful to beautify their home with terrace-gardens reaching to the sea, about 500 feet below them. They have a well of beautiful cold clear water. A French doctor was mixing some nasty stuff that he called "absinthe" with it. It tasted to me very much like compound tincture of camphor, and I preferred drinking the water pure. I got admission into the chapel. There were several Russian monks walking about. The walls of the chapel are covered with thin golden ornaments and bad pictures of Christs, Virgins and Saints. The monks were continually bowing to each other, and behaved in a manner which appeared to me very absurd. I saw several pretty young ladies; I was told they were the daughters of a Russian officer, a prisoner there. During the whole of this day the English and French kept up a very heavy fire on the Malakoff and Redan, and into the town. In the evening we could see the town well lighted up by a large ship which was burning in the harbour.

Rockets, shells, and red-hot balls were flying about in all directions, making a deafening noise; it was a sight well worth beholding. I watched the fire until the powder-magazine blew up, with a tremendous explosion and blaze, and then I went to bed. This firing continued two days. On Friday night we were told that it was the intention of the Generals to storm the Malakoff and Redan at twelve o'clock the next morning. On Saturday morning I went to look for a position where I might see the fight, but I found that the heights were all occupied by Lancers, who were keeping the people back. However, by going round about some distance I managed to elude them, and to get on a hill between them and the Malakoff, where I had a splendid view of all the batteries and trenches. The French began early in the morning to march down to the trenches in thousands. Punctually at twelve the firing commenced, and fortunately for me the wind was strong enough to carry away the smoke quickly. I could distinctly see the French advancing up the Malakoff hill and planting their standard in the middle of the battery. The taking of the Malakoff was effected very easily. The English, I could see, did not get on so well with the Redan. The musketry and cannonading went on for about an hour, until I was tired of hearing it. I knew that some must be suffering fearfully, and thought I might be more useful in the camp than on the top of the hill. What I saw on my way back horrified and disgusted me with war. I met many Russian prisoners, some of whom were wounded severely, and many English and French wounded being carried to the hospitals. When I arrived at the 88th the surgeon was glad to see me, for he had more wounded than he could manage, and his assistants were at the front. I had several operations, such as removing bullets, cutting off fingers, etc. I cut off one arm by the shoulder-joint, which is considered a capital operation in England. Several officers in the regiment afterwards spoke to me and expressed their thanks for the trouble I had taken. The General personally did the same, and also told me that he had taken the liberty of sending in my name to the General of the division (Sir W. Codrington). During the night I heard many explosions, and when I awoke in the morning I was informed that Sebastopol was in the hands of the Allies. I applied for a pass to enter the town, and in consequence of my exertions the day before I had no difficulty in obtaining one.

On my way to the town I passed through the Redan, and saw the scene of the previous day's havoc. The dead soldiers were getting buried by their comrades in the trench of the Redan. Some of them were mangled terribly, and presented about as horrible a sight as one can well imagine. The interior of the

Redan is large enough to hold a considerable army, but as far as I could see it is not commanded by any battery, excepting the Malakoff, so that being taken, it must yield. The waste of English life on Saturday appears to have been totally useless, as has since been proved by the evacuation of the battery when the troops had ceased to attack it. When I arrived in **Sebastopol** I found scarcely any English in the town, but many French were hard at work plundering. I think I must have been one of the first fifty English who entered the town. All the houses and public buildings were in a frightful state of dilapidation. The shells had penetrated their walls in every direction, and a large portion of the town was in flames, and every now and then powder-magazines were exploding. I have a young dog with me now, which I took prisoner in Sebastopol. After the taking of Sebastopol I determined to make my way as soon as possible to Constantinople. Consequently on Monday morning I rode off to Balaklava; slept in one of the old broken-down houses all night. In the morning I bathed in a rough sea, and got dashed against sharp rocks. I then climbed up to the old Genoese castle of which you have heard, saw through all the hospitals, and came on board this ship, which is now getting towed across the Black Sea by the steam-ship "Imperador." The opening of the Bosporus is in sight, and I expect to arrive in Constantinople to-morrow morning. As I shall not be able to write to Allie or L. for some time, perhaps you will be so kind as to send them this letter.

TO HIS SISTER.

RENKIOI HOSPITAL, *September 29th,* 1855.

I AM at last settled quietly in my 12 ft. by 15, having made it exceedingly comfortable by converting packing-cases into sofas and divans. I quite enjoy having a home of my own after travelling about, sleeping in steamboats and on the floors of bell-tents for so long. Certainly the camp in the Crimea is uncomfortable even in summer. The tents must be frightful in winter. You must not let L. go there, I am sure he could not bear it; nevertheless my excursion has done me a great deal of good. Every one remarked when I returned that I had grown quite fat, which was true, and I attributed it all to the amount of exercise which I had taken. There is not a soul in the Crimea who does not wish to return. When a man gets wounded they say he is a lucky fellow, for the sick have all that they desire now, and are made extremely comfortable in hospital. Some hospitals are in first-rate order. For instance, in the Castle Hospital at Balaklava, although full of wounded, the air is as fresh as in your drawing-room, which certainly is not the case with any other hospital I was ever in. There is another good hospital at the Monastery of St. George, and there are hospitals connected with each division, besides separate hospitals for each regiment. The condition of these last depends altogether on the regimental surgeon. Some are well managed; others are not. When I was in the Crimea I was staying in the camp of the 88th regiment, which was severely engaged in the attack on the Redan, and I consider myself very fortunate in having had some operations to perform. The General told me that he had taken the liberty of sending in my name to the Brigadier-General, and I am told that I shall probably receive a medal and clasp in consequence. But without that I am quite satisfied, and well pleased to have been present at the taking of *Sebastopol* (for the town is all on the south side of the harbour); on the north there are only one or two batteries, and a few houses, which I think will soon be in the hands of the Allies. We have no patients yet, consequently some of our men, who cannot employ themselves, have volunteered for service in the Crimea. I prefer remaining where I am, as my services are not required there, and because I do not like to do anything that may interfere with the promotion of the assistant surgeons, who have gone through so much hardship. I am very fully employed here, carpentering, fencing, swimming, riding, reading, and studying languages. I see a little practice among the Greeks and sailors. Nevertheless, I should like to do a little more for my pay. On my way down from the Crimea I was obliged to stay for a week in Constantinople, which I was not sorry to do, for to me it is the most interesting city I ever visited. It is capitally situated you know, and from the sea it looks splendid, with all its mosques, minarets, towers, and cypress-trees. But on entering it I was at first disappointed, for the best street is not so broad or so well paved as the Low Street, North Shields, and the smells are powerful; but after a time I got over these annoyances, and then I was highly entertained with everything I saw. The inhabitants at present seem chiefly French soldiers and Armenians. The Turks, I should say, form a very small proportion. Besides these, there are Greeks, Persians, Albanians, Arabs, English, Italians, and, I should say, one might find specimens of almost every nation. The best time to walk is early in the morning; it is then that one can see the Greek and Armenian young ladies going to church, with their prayer-books in hand. They are nearly all pretty until a certain age. The finest collection of girls that I ever saw was in an Armenian church that I entered one morning, the anniversary of the birth of the Virgin Mary. Their faces, excepting the eyes, were covered with veils. Fortunately this was sufficiently transparent to allow their beauty to shine through. During my excursion I met old friends wherever I went, and this of course added greatly to my pleasure. I was recognised once by my voice, not by sight. People out here look so different that you may easily pass your most intimate friend without knowing. The other day we had a party in our mess-house, which was decorated for the occasion with flags, myrtle-branches, and armoury. The Pasha and English Consul were present, and a host of young English ladies, English officers, and Bashi-Basouks. The artisans entertained them with racing, singing, and various games. The Bashi-Basouks also showed a little lance-exercise. These Bashi-Basouks are about as fierce-looking a set of men as I ever saw. We sometimes have visits from them which frighten the ladies and some of the doctors. They are continually deserting, and it is feared that they will come here for plunder; but I think we are far too strong for them. They are extremely passionate and fierce, but they are not sufficiently firm to oppose cool Englishmen. If they come they will try to carry off our nurses. They have expressed a wish to have them for wives.

TO HIS BROTHER.

RENKIOI HOSPITAL, *October 3d*, 1855.

YESTERDAY 215 patients arrived here from the Crimea. They were in their beds one hour and twenty minutes after the arrival of the ship. These are the first patients that we have received, but it is thought that during the winter we shall have plenty to do. The hospital is in splendid order, and is situate in the most healthy neighbourhood, so that I think our patients will very rapidly recover. Of those that have just arrived, I don't expect that more than one or two will die. This morning they look exceedingly comfortable and happy, and seem delighted with their new mode of life. My Russian dog was pleased to see them; I think he recognised the red jackets. He is not patriotic enough to hate the enemies of his country. My life here is quite as profitable to me and much pleasanter than it was in London. I have a very comfortable little house (12 ft. by 15), well furnished with books, etc. Looking out from my window I have a fine view of the Hellespont, the Ægean Sea, Samothrace, Tenedos, and many other little islands. I have a horse, a boat, and a Greek servant called Θεωδωρις. With all these it would be extraordinary if I could not make myself happy. The climate is splendid; there has only been two or three days' rain since I came out, and there is always a pleasant breeze from the sea. During the hot weather I used to spend a considerable part of the day in the water, and in consequence I have become a tolerably good swimmer. I would like very much to hear of the welfare of you and your family, if you can find time to write to me. It is a great pleasure to a person so far away to receive letters from home.

TO L.

RENKIOI HOSPITAL, *October 30th*, 1855.

ALL your letters have arrived, and have been always received and read with great delight. You can only have some idea of the pleasure of receiving letters from home that have travelled so far. I have nothing new to communicate, excepting Henry's arrival and stay here. He was with me for eight days, during which time we rode, walked, and talked a great deal. He thought that fleas and pains in the bowels were sufficient to make life miserable, and did not envy my life in the least. I saw him on board of the steamboat at Dardanelles. Parting with him had rather the effect of making me home-sick, and I am sorry to say I have scarcely succeeded in recovering myself yet. To-night I am orderly-officer, and have to sit up and look after patients and orderlies all night. There is a hot wind blowing from the south, which has filled the Hellespont with ships and compels me to throw off all but my shirt and trousers. I think it is most likely that I shall spend this winter in the Crimea, or somewhere in the front, but as I am not certain, I prefer acquainting you alone with my intentions, as I know that you are best able to appreciate my reasons. When I am about to set off I shall write and tell mother also. I am fully aware of all the miseries of spending the winter in a bell-tent, but the advantage of seeing service and being of use counterbalances all these. It is not likely that we shall have many patients here for several months, and General Storks has written to ask Dr. Parkes for volunteers. As yet I have heard nothing official, but as soon as I do I intend to offer myself. I am hoping to be sent on some fresh expedition to the Perekop, Circassia, or Nicolaieff. When I hear more I will write again.

November 6th.

I HAVE heard nothing more yet about going to the front. It is said that Scutari is to be no longer used as a hospital—if so, we shall have plenty to do this autumn.

You must not believe half what the *Times* correspondent says about Renkioi.

TO HIS MOTHER.

RENKIOI, *Nov. 7th,* 1855.

THE weather here still continues to be quite warm, which leads one to suppose that the winter here must have a very short duration. Yesterday was a grand feast-day with the Greeks, called the Feast of Saint Demetri. On this day, every year, compacts, betrothals, and agreements of all sorts are made. The young women and men come out in their best clothes, and have dancing and music all the afternoon. Although they are all, comparatively speaking, poor people, their dresses are of a very costly description. I think many of them must carry their whole wealth about themselves. One young lady had upwards of 100 pieces of gold, about the size of sovereigns, hanging about her. All those who are betrothed may be distinguished by a band of gold pieces surrounding their forehead.

P.S.—If you have an opportunity, will you send me my Greek Homer?

TO HIS SISTER.

RENKIOI HOSPITAL, *Nov. 21st,* 1855.

THE sick and hospital stores from Smyrna are at present being conveyed to Renkioi, and I am offered a passage back in the ship which is employed in conveying them. Although the weather is not very favourable, I think I shall take advantage of the offer, for it is uncertain how long it may be before I may again obtain leave. Smyrna and Scutari are both going to be abolished, consequently all the work will fall upon us this winter. I have not heard anything more about volunteering for the front, which makes me fear that I shall not be allowed to go.

I saw a splendid Greek wedding up at the village on Sunday. I was not present at the beginning of the ceremony. When I arrived at the Ecclesia (church), it was full of people, and smelt strongly of incense. The couple who were getting married were standing in the centre of the church wearing crowns made of tinsel, Vasilicon, pasteboard, etc. Behind them stood the bridesman, who held candles, fixed in two other crowns over their heads. The priest or papa stood in front of them with a great book in his hand, out of which he mumbled something, and occasionally howled, but this latter performance was chiefly done by another man, who kept up a continual howl during the whole ceremony. Nearly the whole congregation, after paying a small sum of money to the priest, went up one by one, the men before the women, and kissed first the top and then the bottom of both of the crowns. The children were lifted up by their mammas to do this. The bridegroom was dressed in a very simple style, but the bride was arrayed in a most gorgeous style, in satin and gold. Her face was covered with the white of egg, and her eyelids bound together with the same. This gave her skin the appearance of wax. Throughout the ceremony her face remained totally expressionless, and her body perfectly still. After the kissing was accomplished, the priest, bride, and bridegroom performed together a very slow dance as they proceeded out of the church. In going home they formed a sort of procession, with the bride at the head and the whole congregation following. Musicians played on fiddles and guitars, and guns were continually being fired in all directions. When they arrived at their house the old father came out to meet them, and made a speech, the purport of which was that he gave the bride two cows and a flock of goats. Somebody else, probably an uncle, shouted out from behind, " Cocks and hens into the bargain!" This was considered very witty, and made them all laugh. I enclose you Vasilicon from the bride's crown.

TO HIS BROTHER.

RENKIOI, *Nov.* 25*th*, 1855.

WILLIAM and I spent a very pleasant week together, riding to the Plains of Troy, and visiting many small Greek and Turkish villages. I have capital opportunities here of observing the manners of the Turks and Greeks. Here they are in a natural state, uncorrupted by contact with Europeans. The race is much purer, and is not, as at Constantinople, mixed with Circassian, Arnaut, and Nubian blood. I have been told that nearly all the persons in high places have been themselves, or are descended from, slaves. There is a Turkish village about two miles from here, high up among the hills, called Cashkioi. It contains a mosque and about forty or fifty houses. The inhabitants are farmers, and lead a very peaceable respectable life. One or two old gentlemen there keep harems, which generally consist of three or four ugly old women, but most of them are the husband of one wife. They are extremely religious and moral, reverencing God and goodness. They never tell lies or cheat; because their religion does not allow it. Here is certainly a practical result of religion! They are also extremely hospitable and good-natured; but the most remarkable thing about them is their innocence and ignorance. They did not know until very lately that the Russians and Turks were at war, and never took the trouble to inquire why this hospital is being built. Most of them are rather good-looking. All have good (rather large) noses, dark eyes, and shaggy eyebrows. However, they are not sufficiently clever to live in this country, and are gradually getting turned out by the Greeks. All their former energy and fierceness have been destroyed by the peaceable life they have been leading for so many years, and they are not able to compete with others in the arts of peace.

The cold weather has come at last, and I am happy to say I am well fortified against it; with a nice stove in my room. In the middle of the day, if we see the sun it is still very powerful.

P.S.—All the patients from Smyrna and Scutari are coming here. We shall have plenty to do this winter.

TO HIS MOTHER.

RENKIOI HOSPITAL, *Dec.* 13*th*, 1855.

I HAVE just received a letter from L., in which he says that you are now at Derwent Bank, and intend to be there during Christmas. I am writing this letter with the hope that you may receive it about that time, and read it with L., Allie, and William round your Christmas fire.

I have not heard from William since he left Smyrna, but I conclude you have heard from him, for L. tells me that he expects to see him at Christmas. When I was at Smyrna a little French girl, who seemed rather to have taken a fancy to him, talked of him to me, and told me that he had enjoyed himself there, and had left in good health. It is rather curious that when she first saw me she ran and told her mother that William had come back again. The resemblance between us had struck her so much! The weather here still continues remarkably fine. I still feel it quite hot when I go out of doors, with nothing but my nightshirt, and fence, which I do for a quarter of an hour every morning directly I get out of bed. I still bathe occasionally, when it is not windy. A great many ships have been brought ashore here lately by a south wind. The hospital lights are partly the cause of this, for the captains, in the night, mistake them for ships, and, expecting to get good anchorage, sail right on to the shore. A few days ago I had a delightful ride with my servant along the shores of the Hellespont. I take him with me to interpret Turkish. He knows no English, but I now know enough Greek to ask for anything I want, and am able to hold an imperfect sort of conversation. Every yard of the road appeared to me to have been covered with buildings at one time. The ploughed fields were covered with pieces of tile and marble, and every now and then we came across excavations, walls, and ditches. At one place on the top of a little hill, near the mouth of the Hellespont, there are some remains of an old castle with an underground passage which goes about fifteen feet into the ground. The people here do nothing in the way of excavation—the Turks because they do not think it worth while, and the Greeks because they are frightened. The Greeks here are extremely superstitious. They firmly believe in ghosts, vampires, and in the churches they have crying pictures, and the same superstitions as the Romish Church. Last Sunday I was shown by the papa, a crying picture of St. George. The papa told me that if I were a good man and held a piastre against the picture it would be held there by St. George. The piastre was held by some gum which the papa, I suppose, had placed there. The people must be very foolish not to understand this simple device of the papa's.

TO HIS MOTHER.

RENKIOI HOSPITAL, *Dec.* 28*th*, 1855.

CHRISTMAS-DAY has passed very quietly with us. We invited the lady nurses and military men to dine with us, and in the evening we had a little singing and dancing and music. Last night the orderlies, artisans, and nurses had a ball in one of the wards. It was extremely amusing, as you may well imagine, to see some of our old fat nurses dancing the polka. In a few days we are going to have a very grand ball in our mess-room, to which a large number of Greek girls, and the English young ladies in the neighbourhood, are invited. The Pasha's band is coming from Dardanelles, and the ladies of the camp who have organs and pianos have sent them to us for the evening.

The married medical men are also giving private tea-parties as in England.

The hospital goes on rapidly increasing, and also the number of people connected with it, such as purveyors, paymasters, interpreters, etc., so that we now form quite a little town. Two children have been born here within the last two months. They have both been called Ida, from Mount Ida, which stands just behind the Plains of Troy.

TO HIS BROTHER.

January 10*th*, 1856.

WE had a grand ball in the mess-room the other day. There were about five Greek girls there, some of whom could speak nothing but Greek. I danced with them the whole night. One of these girls had an extremely beautiful face and innocent manners. She had all the beautiful characteristics of a Greek face, and at the same time a very charming expression. She was evidently not much accustomed to ball-rooms, for she always kept my hand in hers when we danced quadrilles. When any one asked her to dance she asked my leave. She lives at Dardanelles, but I have not seen her since the ball. There is only one other girl that I am at all pleased with, that is Theodore's sister "Ellenika." I progress tolerably fast with my Greek, and as I am the only one here who knows any Greek, I have all the medical practice of the village, and have ample opportunity of studying the manners and customs of the natives.

TO HIS MOTHER.

RENKIOI HOSPITAL, *Feb. 8th*, 1856.

THE hospital goes on enlarging, but I do not expect it will be finished for many months yet. Now there are upwards of one hundred and fifty buildings on the ground. Nearly thirty of these are hospitals, each containing fifty beds. Yesterday I superintended the landing of about ninety sick from Balaklava. About twenty of these were in a very bad state, the others could walk. The Land Transport Corps seems to suffer more than any other regiment. We have now a railway by which patients can be carried from the pier to the hospitals in about two minutes. The distance is a little more than a mile. A few days ago I took an excursion with a friend. We were three days away, and travelled south over the Plains of Troy so far as to be opposite the island of Mitylene. Everywhere we were received in a most hospitable manner by the Turks, Greeks, and Armenians. We saw all the ruins of Alexandria and Troas. The ruins appeared to be all Roman. I only saw one inscription, which was Latin. At all the villages directly it was known that there was a Hakim (doctor) present, the sick were brought round about me, and I prescribed and gave medicines. The river Scamander became very much swollen. In going we were able to ford it, but in coming back we were obliged to go round some distance to find a bridge. Some of the Land Transport Corps were drowned the other day in trying to ford the river with their horses. We hear that there are strong expectations of peace. If these be verified, you may expect to see me back in England soon.

TO L.

RENKIOI HOSPITAL, *March 6th*, 1856.

I CONTINUE to live much in the same way as when I first arrived, excepting that I now have much more intercourse with the natives, and associate with them in a more friendly manner. I have a very large practice, among the Greeks especially, but I have also Turkish, Armenian, and Jewish patients. The other day I astonished and delighted some people at Dardanelles by cutting a squint. The boy, who was a Jew, directly he saw himself in the glass, expressed great satisfaction in word and gesture.

The country is extremely beautiful here now, and the weather is cold enough to allow me to take long walks and rides. The hills and ravines are covered with flowers of the gayest and most brilliant colours. I enclose some violets for Allie from the shores of the Hellespont. I am afraid I shall feel very unwilling to leave this beautiful country, and when I get home I shall long to return. If it were not for my friends I should stay here for ever. At times, however, I feel a very great longing to see you all again, and have very much the same sensations which less fortunate exiles (I imagine) experience. Although the Greeks out here are a very happy good-natured people, I should scarcely like to have them for constant and sole companions. They live much like the lower animals, and seem to have little idea of right and wrong. They just do what their inclinations prompt them to do, and yet they are much happier than English peasants.

TO HIS BROTHER.

RENKIOI HOSPITAL, *March 6th*, 1856.

IF a treaty be concluded I think that my agreement with the Government will end very speedily, and I shall either come home or stay out here and buy land, for I hear that a law is passed which allows foreigners to buy land in Turkey. This country suits me so well, and is so very splendid in many respects, that I feel extremely unwilling to leave it. I have now got a tolerable knowledge of Greek, and am learning Turkish, so that I am almost prepared to settle if my friends have no very serious objection. The climate is extremely healthy. There has scarcely been any illness amongst us. I myself have never been ill at all. I know the people of the country now much better than when you were there. I often have long talks with the women, and am frequently entertained at their houses. The girls are not so shy as they were; they even joke and play with me occasionally. I sometimes dance Greek dances or the polka with them. The night before last I was at a party at one of their houses and saw a splendid sight. As there were several other parties in the village we could not get music, therefore five beautiful girls, dressed very gaily with Turkish trousers fitting close over the ankles, got up and danced vigorously to the music which they made by singing Greek airs and Turkish songs. I was reminded of some pictures of old bacchanalian processions—these girls display such grace in all their movements. It is scarcely equalled by the belles of London ball-rooms. These have, naturally, what our English ladies devote so much effort to acquire. I take long walks and rides now every day, climbing up to the top of the hills. I have most magnificent views westward, of the Ægean Sea with its many islands, Tenedos, Mavri, Lemnos, Samothrace, and beyond this on a clear day I can see others far away. Mount Athos by sunset appears very grand, towering up into the sky. It is called here Ἅγιοι, or the Holy Mountain. They think it is called so because the papas all come from thence. Looking to the east I can see Mount Olympus covered with snow, and to the south, as you know, Mount Ida. All the ravines are full of crocuses, anemones of splendid colours, and violets. The wheat and barley are quite short as yet, but in another week I expect the country will be of a bright green colour. I was shocked to hear of the dreadful danger that mother and Isabella have gone through,[1] and I felt extremely glad that they escaped serious injury. Give my love to them and my hearty congratulations.

TO HIS MOTHER.

ABYDOS, *March 20th*, 1856.

I HAVE left Renkioi, and am now appointed medical officer to the Abydos Convalescent Hospital. Yesterday, I, my horse and dog, started early in the morning, and arrived here about two P.M. The wind was blowing furiously in our faces, and filling our eyes with snow and sleet. The distance of this place from Renkioi is sixteen miles,—about one hour and a half. I have tolerably comfortable quarters, but frightfully lonely. The house I live in is quite solitary, and stands close by the seaside: there is a small steep hill just behind (Xerxes Hill), from which Xerxes is said to have surveyed his army crossing the Hellespont. About 200 yards at one side (at the north) there is a French hospital and a Turkish fort, and about as

---

[1] A chimney, built of freestone, had fallen, during a high wind, through the roof, upon the bed on which my mother and sister were sleeping.

much to the south is my hospital, and barracks for 500 men. The house is badly built, and lets wind in in every direction, which at present is by no means agreeable, but which in summer will be very pleasant. To-day I have been at Dardanelles buying cooking apparatus and table furniture, and in a day or two a Greek woman is coming to make divans, cushions, etc. When all this is accomplished I hope to be tolerably comfortable. There are seven rooms in the house, two of which I shall occupy, and two are occupied by a captain, the commandant. All the rest are empty at present. There are only three officers here: this captain, a clergyman who lives at the hospital, and myself. The Hellespont is very narrow here, and as the ships have to pass quite close, it has a much livelier appearance than at Renkioi. I think I am more lonely now than I ever was before, but I am sure almost to be happy, for I have lots of books, and the view from my window is extremely beautiful.

P.S.—I have bought you a Persian Cashmere shawl, but I don't see how I can get it sent to you. I wanted you to get it on the 4th of April,[1] but I am afraid that is impossible. Many happy returns.

TO HIS SISTER.

ABYDOS HOSPITAL, *March 26th*, 1856.

You will have heard from mother by this time that I have left Renkioi and come to this delightful place. I have everything that I can desire now excepting a woman to keep house for me. If you were here we should live in a most delightful manner, but I am afraid that you could scarcely endure to have a soldier for your servant, to cook and do everything for you. I am at present furnishing my room with a sofa or divans. A Greek woman is sitting sewing behind me, and talking to me both in Turkish and Greek. I am obliged to have her husband in the room, because the people in this country are so modest or jealous.

I am just now looking after the sick of the Land Transport Corps at Dardanelles, because the doctor appointed to that Corps has taken fever. I think no doctor ever had a more extraordinary set of patients than I have. There is a specimen of almost every nation in my hospital. I always give my directions in Greek. In requital for my services I can get Arabian horses and Arabs lent to me whenever I like, which at present I find very convenient, for my own horse is ill. There

---

[1] Her birthday.

are a great number of very fine mules just now in the stables. Some of them are seventeen hands high, and enormously strong. The weather has been very cold and disagreeable here for the last month, and we have had more cold weather in March than in all the rest of the year. I hope we shall have fine weather now, for my sitting-room has five windows which let in air in all directions. The house is full of rats, mice, and owls, which at night are very amusing. At present I am happy to say there are no fleas or flies. This is just about the place where Leander and Lord Byron swam across the Hellespont. On a hot day I think it would not be difficult, although it is said the water runs very rapidly in the middle. There are no remains of the ancient town excepting broken pots and vases. Excavations would probably show something, but no one here is sufficiently interested to make them.

TO HIS MOTHER.

ABYDOS, *April* 19*th*,[1] 1856.

I RECEIVED letters from you and William yesterday, a day sooner than you expected, but not at all too soon for me. Now that I am so solitary and so far from home, I am constantly anxiously expecting letters. Sometimes I have friends from Renkioi who stay a day or two with me, for it is too far to go and return in one day. Yesterday two doctors were here, and we crossed over to Europe in a caïque to a Greek village or town with 5000 inhabitants. It is the site of the ancient town (Madytus), which at one time was rather famous. There are no ruins or remains of any sort to be seen now. The Turks have converted all the marble columns into shot for their cannon.

TO MR. POW.

ABYDOS, *April* 23*d*, 1856.

IN your letter you said that you had been reading Homer, and you appeared to take some interest in the Plains of Troy, and in this country generally. I have now often ridden over the Plains, and am as well acquainted with them as I am with the vale of Keswick, nevertheless I have not succeeded in discovering any trace of the ancient city. There are several heaps of stones which are supposed to be tombs, and have received the names of some of the Homeric heroes, but nobody knows anything about them. A little nearer the sea than the sup-

---

[1] He was twenty-three on that day.

posed site of Troy there are some carved stones and broken columns, and this is called the site of New Ilium, a town said to have been built by the Emperor Hadrian. It is astonishing how traces of those large cities should be so completely effaced. I believe that the stones of most of the temples and palaces have been converted by the Turks into cannon balls, and fired into the Hellespont. There is another place here which has the name of Troy, or Alexandria, which I have visited. It was formerly (in the time of St. Paul) a flourishing city; I think it was there that Eutychus fell asleep and the apostle left his cloak; it is distant about a day's journey from Renkioi. There are abundant remains of a very large city, in the shape of walls, arches, columns, and stones, and an artificial port, which at the time was probably furnished with piers. The land is extremely fertile in the neighbourhood, and the soil very deep, but the cultivation is sadly neglected; oak grows in great abundance, luxuriantly, and the cups are sent to England, but this is the only export. It is first-rate for colonists, far superior to America or Australia I should think, for it is only ten days' journey from England, and the land could be bought for almost nothing. The Turks leave this country in a neglected state; they care little about money, and are quite content if they can get enough to eat and smoke, and this they can do with scarcely any trouble. Their agricultural instruments are of the rudest description; the ploughs are made of wood, and they seldom plough more than three inches deep; harrowing and draining are almost unknown among them; nevertheless they are as a rule a good-natured, hospitable people. At first I was disposed to consider the Greeks a superior race, but now from abundant experience I think otherwise. They are larger than the Turks, much cleverer, and their cleverness is generally used for a bad purpose, such as cheating and telling lies. They seem to find a sort of pleasure in telling lies, even without a purpose, and show no shame on detection. The Armenians and Jews are the only industrious people here, but they have nothing to do with the soil, and only employ themselves with merchandise. I am thinking of buying some land here as a speculation, because I think the new laws of Turkey will insure a large immigration of Europeans, and consequently the price of land will rise immensely. I have now a great deal to do, and have a considerable amount of surgical practice with the Land Transport Corps; for this I receive 15s. per day in addition to my 25s., which I consider pretty fair pay for a surgeon of my age.

TO MR. POW.

ABYDOS, *May 7th*, 1856.

I HAVE not quite made up my mind about settling in this country, and in doing anything in the matter I should like to know whether mother and my other friends have any great objection to the project. But I am seriously thinking of investing a little money in land here, so that at any future time, if we like, we may have an opportunity of settling. The most certain way of making it profitable would be for about half-a-dozen to form a colony, and to bring wives out. Several of the Renkioi doctors are half-inclined to do something of this sort, but most of them talk of waiting a year or two. I wish you would write and tell me mother's sentiments on the subject. We had a grand review of the Land Transport Corps yesterday, at which, of course, as medical officer, I was present. The review took place on a flat piece of ground half way between Renkioi and Dardanelles. I had the pleasure of meeting there a great many of my friends from Renkioi, who had come to witness the sight. We left Dardanelles about half-past eight in the morning, forming a long procession, consisting of about 3000 animals and 1500 men, chiefly Arabs. I rode along with the superintendent and one or two ladies at the head of the procession. In front and about us, ten or twelve Arabs were galloping round and round, waving their lances and swords, and firing off guns, reminding me of the pictures of the Sikhs during the war in Afghanistan. When we arrived at the reviewing-ground we were joined by a great number of ladies from Dardanelles, who had come in boats and carts. Three of these young ladies are as delightful girls as you would wish to meet. I find it quite a treat to be able to talk to English girls once more. We had a most glorious day for our review, and the land, sea, and sky were most brilliant. The fields were covered with splendid flowers of all sorts, such as grow only in gardens in England. A tent was pitched, and we had luncheon. Afterwards there were races, in which Dix distinguished himself. Towards evening a party went to dig on the site of old Dardanelles. With little trouble they succeeded in finding two large vases containing a great variety of ornamental pottery. I terminated my day's amusement by dining on board of the "Oberon," a small war steamboat stationed here. I shall probably remain attached to the Land Transport Corps for two months longer. I feel a great desire to see you all once more.

TO HIS SISTER.

ABYDOS, *May* 10*th*, 1856.

I WISH you would consider all the letters you write worth sending; the mere sight of your handwriting gives me pleasure, and the commonest details of your doings at Derwent Bank are interesting to me. You are surprised I should feel lonely here, and ask where the other officers are. We never have any officers for patients here; and on the staff, besides myself, there are only two, the Commandant (Captain La Touche) and a clergyman. Of course we three are on a very familiar friendly footing. But the clergyman lives at the barracks, and the captain is seldom at home. However, I have a great number of friends at Dardanelles, and as I have plenty to do I pass my time tolerably comfortably. For the last month the country has been most beautiful, and the weather delightful. I ride about a good deal, and enjoy it exceedingly. The sun is beginning to be very powerful now, and is drying up the grass and flowers, and the snakes and lizards are beginning to glide about. There are lots of tortoises, varying from the size of a penny to a foot in diameter, crawling about everywhere. The French cook and eat them, and they are not bad. I tasted some the other day. They were also cooking snakes, but I was not tempted to taste. Some of the snakes are horrible-looking reptiles six feet long. The tortoises are very amusing animals; the doctors at Renkioi make pets of them, and put their seals and crests on the shell of the back. A tortoise so marked was found one day four miles from the hospital at the top of a high hill. I am always reminded of the old fable when I see them persevering along in their deliberate sedate manner, and every now and then drawing in their heads, and hiding themselves in their shell at the least appearance of danger. This is the month Ramayan. The Turks neither eat nor drink nor smoke all day, but at sunset cannons are fired off at all the forts along the Hellespont, the mosques are lighted up, and the people commence to enjoy themselves. I was amused the other day at an Arab refusing to take a dose of castor-oil on account of Ramayan. I am He'kim Bashi, or doctor, to about 1000 Arabs. They are the honestest and most faithful set of men in this country. A certain portion, a small number, of them are Christians, but I am sorry to say that they are vastly inferior to the followers of Mohammed. Like other professed Christians in this part of the world, they are always lying, stealing, gambling, drinking, and fighting.

TO L.

We have partings here every day; the Englishmen and Frenchmen are going away by twos and threes. The Frenchmen have all gone, and there are now only a few Englishmen connected with the Land Transport Corps, and some doctors at Renkioi. I went down to Renkioi yesterday, and saw Dr. and Mrs. Goodeve, Mr. and Mrs. Spencer, and Miss Ida Wells off. There are now only eight doctors remaining, and those, as well as Dr. Parkes himself, will probably be off in another week or fortnight. The hospital has quite a desolate appearance now, and it quite makes me melancholy to visit it. I am to be left out here longest of all the doctors, and am appointed to take charge of the artisans at Renkioi, as well as of Abydos and Dardanelles. I shall sleep a night at each place by turns. There are still a thousand animals in the stables, and I think it will be another month before they are all sold. I went on an expedition for the purpose of selling mules in the interior about a month ago, and lived in the open air for about ten days. As I had plenty of servants and horses I was exceedingly comfortable, and enjoyed myself very much. We passed through a most beautiful country, watered by the river Granicus, which was so famous in the time of Alexander. The country-people are nearly all Turks, and extremely hospitable and good-natured. They were particularly courteous to me on account of my profession, and in return I did all for the sick that I could. It was amusing to watch their astonishment when I perform operations. Squint-cutting called forth many maashallahs and gestures of astonishment. I was taken into many harems to see the Turkish ladies and prescribe for them. Many of them are very pretty, and all of them have gentle lady-like manners. The Pasha of a large town in the interior has sent me a deerskin as a present since I came home, and at the same time told me that I have saved the life of his wife.

CHAPTER III.

LETTERS FROM PARIS, STRASBURG, VIENNA, ETC.

"Yearning for the large excitement that the coming years would yield."
Locksley Hall.

ON leaving Constantinople James took the charge of 300 Spanish muleteers bound for Gibraltar. They were a desperate set of fellows, of whom the captain and every one on board the transport ship were afraid. James kept them in good order during the voyage; at its commencement requiring them to give up their arms, knives, and money, in order to prevent gambling, and consequently quarrelling and fighting. Shortly after his return from the East, James went to Paris to study medicine.

TO HIS SISTER.

PARIS, *Nov. 17th*, 1856.

PARIS suits me very well, but as yet I have not seen very much of it, excepting the Latin quarter, which is called "le plus vilain." I have not spoken with a single Englishman since I arrived here, and my whole time is spent in attending the hospitals, and in talking with the students in their cafés. I am getting well acquainted with their life, and at the same time learning French very quickly. The grisettes against whom you think fit to caution me make themselves apparent everywhere, are amusing in the extreme, and at the same time are perfectly well-behaved, as far as one can see. They are very polite, and seem to take a pleasure in instructing strangers. I have made the acquaintance of a Professor of Greek in one of the colleges, and nearly every evening I go to his house and talk to him and his wife, and play with their children. I write exercises in French for him to correct, and in return I give him some instruction in English. After some time, when I can speak French well, and the weather is finer, I intend to explore the other quarters of Paris, and then I shall tell you all about them. Perhaps you will come here, and then we shall explore together. How different Paris is from London! there, after I had been a student for half-a-year, I scarcely knew any one to speak to, but here in a few days I know half-a-dozen without having used an introduction.

TO HIS MOTHER.

PARIS (*no date*).

I WENT this morning to see the interment of the Archbishop of Paris at eight o'clock. His assassination has caused a great deal of excitement here; every one is talking about it, and this morning there were crowds gathered together to the funeral. Notre Dame was filled with soldiers and priests. I am told that there were about 2000 priests present. There were several Capuchins walking in the cold melting snow, with bare feet and hair-cloth shirts. It is said that he was not assassinated for political reasons. I am working in my usual way. Every morning I go to the hospitals till breakfast-time, and in the evening I attend lectures on different medical subjects. In the middle of the day I am reading at home.

TO L.

PARIS, *Feby. 5th*, 1857.

THE fine spring weather which has just commenced to-day, and which I hope will now continue, makes me think of Derwent Bank. I have a very vivid recollection of it as it was three years ago in spring. I remember how green it looked when the snow had just melted off it, the larch with its little red flowers, and all the other trees with their large juicy buds waiting to burst into leaf. Yesterday whilst walking in the Luxembourg Gardens I examined for a long time the little hazel buds with the bright red tops which used to interest us years ago.

TO HIS SISTER.

Feby. 9th, 1857.

EVERY day with me is alike spent in the hospital lecture-room, cafés, and my own chambers. As you have imagined, I study wood-fires carefully, and spend hours in vainly attempting to warm my little room, the tiled floor of which always remains so cold that I am afraid to touch it with my feet, and invent all kinds of stratagems to avoid contact with the floor in passing from one room to another.

P.S.—The other night I was at a bal masqué at the opera-house. The house was crowded with people in the most varied, extraordinary, and elegant costumes; the music was very good, and the dancing excellent. The general effect was exceedingly curious and beautiful. I thought at the time how you would have enjoyed being there, and wished to have you with me.

TO L.

PARIS, *March* 27*th*, 1857.

I WAS just going to write to you when your letter arrived. Certainly that touch of Thackeray's to which you refer[1] is very beautiful, but at the same time I do not feel that it is applicable to us, for I feel certain that when we meet again you will find that the same sympathy which has always existed between you and me still exists, and that we shall together take pleasure and interest in the same subjects. The scarcity of letters passing between us is due to another cause. . . . I have now heard all the distinguished doctors of Paris, and seen them operate, and I would like exceedingly to give you a good description of them, but I am not sufficiently clever with my pen. Every morning now I go to the Hôtel Dieu. The surgeon there is Jobert, who plays very much the same sort of rôle here that Fergusson does in London. He is about the average height of Frenchmen, holds himself erect and firmly, with his head back. His hair is dark, eyebrows bushy, and eyes keen. His nose is largish and aquiline, and all his features well marked. When he lectures he wears a sort of embroidered cap (he is slightly bald). There is an air of confidence and decision in all he does and says, but his language is neither good nor clear, and his voice is husky. He is fond of joking, and looks for applause. His manner of operating is first-rate, although ostentatious. If anything he wishes is not done the noise and disturbance he makes is terrific, and all his satellites, externes, internes, sœurs, etc., are thrown into a hopeless state of confusion and alarm.

Nélaton, the surgeon at Paris who pleases me most, is altogether the opposite of Jobert. He is excessively timid and bashful, an extraordinary quality in a surgeon. His operations are performed quietly, but at the same time with decision, and perfectly. When he lectures there is no attempt at oratorical display, but there is an earnestness of manner which captivates the attention. His language is beautiful, and his delivery without the slightest hesitation. One always knows when he is about to make a joke by a slight blush coming over his brow. He illustrates his lectures with many anecdotes, and these are told in a most delightful manner. The other day he operated

---

[1] *The Newcomes.* The old Colonel finds that he is not fitted to take a place amongst his son's companions, and therefore withdraws.

for cataract. The assistant let the eyelid fall after the knife had been introduced, and thereby caused the discontinuance of the operation. Nélaton did not lose his temper, as almost every one else might. Jobert, for example, would have turned the whole amphitheatre upside down. He appears to study science in a most disinterested manner, speaks against no one, and of his own discourses most modestly. He is not like Malgaigne, who attacks *tout le monde*, as a Frenchman told me the other day.

TO HIS MOTHER.

March 30*th*, 1857.

I AM coming to England in the month of May. I know this will be pleasant news, therefore I put it first. It is for my Easter holidays, and if you like we will spend them at Keswick together. Do you remember this time three years ago what a pleasant fortnight we spent together at Matlock? how we botanised in the woods, examining the wild hyacinth and arum, and the garlic, the juice of which had such a nasty smell? And then the caves of Castleton, Chatsworth Castle, Haddon Hall, and the girl who reproved me so severely? I thought of all this, and of you, the other day, when I was taking a country walk here: the trees were just in about the same stage of advancement, the weather was delightful, and the birds, and everybody else, were showing their joy at the approach of summer. This letter, I expect, will arrive about the 4th of April, the sixty-sixth anniversary of your birthday (I have made your calculation). No one can wish you more sincerely many happy returns of that day than your affectionate son.

TO HIS SISTER.

PARIS, *Wednesday, May* 1857.

MY time in London was short. On Monday morning I was up at four o'clock; had a delightful ride through Kent and Sussex. Everything was fresh, green, rich, and beautiful, from the rain which had fallen the day before. I sat in a first-class carriage, with the windows open, enjoying the fresh air and the green fields. At the same time I was doing what the Turks call enjoying *kef*, i.e. intellectual repose, for I was taking a final farewell to tobacco, and having my Carnival before my Lent of abstinence from smoking. Mother will be pleased to hear that it is now Lent with me. . . . The scenery between Dieppe and Rouen is very beautiful, and reminds one much of that on the other side of the Channel. The coast has exactly the same character, and one would think that the two countries had just been pulled asunder to allow the sea to run between. On this side, the valleys are more clearly defined. In every one of them there is a town, and in many of these towns there are large cotton-manufactories with high chimneys which do not appear to smoke. These manufactories are not at all unpleasant objects to look at. They appear clean, with their curtained windows, and have not the slightest resemblance to those immense square dirty dismal blocks at Manchester. Some of them appear quite grand, standing in the centre of a large verdant valley, and surrounded by tall poplar-trees, which are always a beautiful feature in the valleys on this side. We reached Rouen at seven o'clock, went and saw the Cathedral, and as much of the town as we could in two hours. The Cathedral is magnificent, but I won't say anything now about it. There is another little old Gothic church we entered. It was full of people—chiefly women and girls with nice faces,—some wearing Norman caps, and others coloured handkerchiefs twisted about their heads. A company of girls were singing the most beautiful church-music that I ever heard in my life; the church was illuminated, and the general effect was charming.

TO HIS MOTHER.

July 12*th*, 1857.

THIS morning I have been to see a new hospital (La Riboirière) in the environs of Paris. The arrangement of the wards and ventilation is perfect, and the whole plan of the hospital pleased me exceedingly. In the centre there is a garden, fountains, etc., and everywhere a great deal of taste is displayed. It is a pity that this is not thought of in England, for I am convinced that the sight of beautiful objects, such as gardens, flowers, etc., has a most powerful effect in expediting the recovery of the patient.

TO HIS SISTER.

PARIS, *July* 19*th*, 1857.

. . . Béranger died two or three days ago, and all Paris was at the funeral. Bills, notices of his death, were at all the corners of the streets, "*Béranger vient de mourir.*" The Government feared that his funeral would be the signal for revolt, and consequently the streets and boulevards were filled with soldiers. The crowd was numerous, but there was no symptom of riot. The day before his death, the street was full of workmen anxiously waiting to hear the news. He appears to have been universally beloved. I went to Père la Chaise, but the crowd was so great that I could not see the cortége. A great number of men, especially the workmen, wore immortelles at their button-holes.

TO A.

PARIS, *August 12th*, 1857.

THERE will be a national fête on Saturday, and the whole city will be illuminated. The French people are very quiet, and likely to remain so for some time. The newspapers contain scarcely anything but English news, and the leading articles are composed of ill-natured remarks and predictions of the downfall of England. One or two, the *Siècle* for example, speak in a more sympathising and friendly manner of our misfortunes in India. The journals here must not for a moment be considered as representing the sentiments of the French nation. They are all the organs of parties, and, like barristers, view matters only from the side that suits them.

TO HIS MOTHER.

PARIS, *Sept. 6th*, 1857.

ALLIE is coming to Paris in a few days. I am working hard, and consider it of great importance that I should succeed in November, because if I do not, a whole year will be lost. There is no making sure; slight illness or a little stupidity at the time of examination may make all the difference. I hope for the best, and I am old enough now not to be too much depressed by misfortune. I know I have your best wishes, and I think they ought to be of some avail.

We had a pleasant fortnight together in Paris that September. I and the young friends who had accompanied me thither lodged in the Hôtel des Tuileries in the picturesque Rue St. Honoré. We led a charming Arcadian sort of life, breakfasting often in the sunny Café du Pont Neuf on the banks of the Seine, and dining usually at Janodet's in the Palais-Royal. James came to us every morning, and with him for our guide we would wander through the fair and splendid city. He was our *preux chevalier*, smoothing all difficulties, full of kind consideration for each of us, pointing out and explaining all that was interesting and famous in his usual gentle, simple, courteous manner.

One of our party, who had a highly cultivated mind, took excursions in the neighbourhood of Paris with my brother and me. We went to St. Cloud, Versailles, St. Denis, Fontainebleau. At the latter place, after seeing the château, we had a romantic drive through the forest. It was the time of the *vendange*, and has left sweet memories. My two gifted companions were buoyant with youth and hope and gladness, and in converse animated each other with the bright thoughts and fancies which the sight of these historic scenes awoke in their imaginations. James returned with us to London, and passed the M.B. examination in November.

TO HIS SISTER.

ALBERT ST., LONDON, *Nov.* 1857.

THIS letter is intended for you both. My *viva-voce* examination went off well. Dr. Rigby almost complimented me on my paper; said it was scanty, but contained all that was of importance. He had told us when we were writing our papers that he hoped we would write shortly and distinctly on account of his sore eyes. This accounts for his contentment with my paper, for I had mercy on his sore eyes, and instead of writing three hours like the others, I only wrote one. At the *viva-voce* he only gave me one or two questions, whereas he examined the others for an hour. The other examiners talked and joked with me for a few minutes and then let me go. At the practical examination I had a case of scabies, a case of bronchitis and hypertrophied heart, and a case of phthisis, all of which I diagnosed correctly and commented on. I have heard from good authority that I have passed first-class, and I have not the least doubt on the subject.

TO L.

STRASBOURG, *February* 13*th*, 1858.

EVERYBODY here speaks German, and the greater part French also. The woman who cleans my room cannot speak a word of French, so that I am obliged to speak a little German. Strasbourg is a most interesting old city. The Cathedral is the most magnificent Gothic building I have ever seen. The delicately carved steeple rises higher than any building in the world, excepting the Pyramid, and the stones of which it is built are so finely cut, the arches, buttresses, etc., so thin, that, in the distance, it looks more like lace than solid stone and mortar. The city altogether is most picturesque. The roofs of the houses are high and steep to prevent the snow from resting; branches of the Rhine traverse the city in every direction, and the water is as clear as Derwentwater. There are three rows of fortifications surrounding the city, and large barracks with lots of French soldiers. Strasbourg is one of the French Universities.

Lectures and everything at the hospitals are carried on in French. This morning I went round with M. Sedillot, a surgeon of whom, no doubt, you have read. Scarcely any of the patients spoke French, and the doctor is obliged to make use of an interpreter. The cold here has been extreme, and now, although it has thawed for several days, there are people still skating on some of the branches of the Rhine.

TO HIS SISTER.

STRASBOURG, *March* 3d, 1858.

I AM not going to leave Strasbourg so soon as you think, for I find myself very well here, and it is not very agreeable travelling in the interior of Europe at this time of the year. The equalising influence of the sea is scarcely felt here, and although much to the south of Cumberland, the cold is three times at least as severe. Ever since I came here the canal has been frozen strong enough to bear, and every day I amuse myself by watching the *gamins* sliding in front of my windows. When I leave Strasbourg I shall probably cross the Rhine, and spend some time at Heidelberg, and then the weather will be fine enough to let me enjoy a voyage down the Danube to Vienna. The country in the immediate vicinity of Strasbourg is flat, but the mountains and the Black Forest are within a walking distance. The peasants, more German-looking than French, are extremely good-natured and healthy-looking, and their costume is exceeding droll. The Catholics wear dresses (skirts) of a bright red, and the Protestants of a blue colour; both have most extraordinary head-dresses, which I cannot describe to you. Some have broad ribbons in bows on the top of the head, which, in the distance, look like immense butterflies settled there; others have Scotch caps turned backside foremost, and embroidered with silver and gold. Their shoes have silver buckles and high heels, and their breasts are compressed by triangular plates laced down by their gown. This may be a useful sort of shield, but it quite disguises their form, and makes their chest look as flat as a board. L. asked me about the descent of Louis Napoleon on Strasbourg. Le père Payen, an old militaire of the *grande armée d'Italie*, now half-superannuated, comic actor of Strasbourg theatre, was telling me about it the other day. It appears that Louis Napoleon made friends with a colonel stationed here, persuaded him and sixty men to side with him, then marched towards the garrison, and was in the act of making a speech to the soldiers, setting forth his claim to the empire, when a tambour-major stepped forward exclaiming—" Dites donc farceur pas de ces bêtises-la: je vous arrête au nom de la loi." He then took hold of him by the collar, was knocked down by a cook who stood near. However, as there were 2000 soldiers with the tambour-major on the side of the law, Louis Napoleon and his party were soon overcome.

I subscribe to a library, and take in a German newspaper. My reading relates chiefly to the history of France and Italy, and I advance myself in German by studying this newspaper and a medical book by Dr. Bambeyer you saw when I was at Keswick.

P.S.—I thought it best to leave London immediately, knowing that now is the best time to learn German, and that my love of ease might tempt me to settle too quickly.

TO THE SAME.

Samedi, 13 *Mars* 1858.

JE t'envoie une lettre que j'avais oublié de mettre à la poste; comme ce que je t'ai écrit peut servir encore je te la renvoie. Cela m'étonnait de ne pas avoir de tes nouvelles, mais j'ai réfléchi que ne t'ayant pas écrit tu ne savais pas si j'étais encore à Strasbourg. Ne me reponds pas à cette lettre à moins que tu n'aie quelque chose de pressé a me dire, parceque je vais quitter Strasbourg pour aller à Vienne. Si tu m'écris, mets " Poste Restante," Strasbourg. Aussitôt que je partirai je préviendrai à la poste que l'on me renvoit mes lettres à Vienne.

Au revoir, chère et bonne Alice. Souhaites le bon jour pour moi à mon cher beau-frère.

P.S.—Tu vois j'ai pensé à te contenter en t'envoyant quelques lignes tout à fait dans le style Français.

TO L.

HEIDELBERG, *March 25th*, 1858.

THE weather during the last three weeks has been exceedingly clear and fine, and I have availed myself of it to make an excursion, first into the Department of the Bas-Rhin, then to Baden-Baden, and lastly to come here. My first excursion was altogether out of the way of ordinary tourists, and the peasants told me they had never seen any Englishmen in their neighbourhood.

The country is wild and mountainous, with extensive forests inhabited by wolves, foxes, etc., and numerous old ruined castles on the tops of the lower hills. The peasants are exceedingly hospitable. They seemed to consider it a pleasure to entertain me and give me all their luxuries, and when I left them, always pressed me to stay longer. I passed Phalsbourg, a little town strongly fortified, which Louis Napoleon intended to march upon after securing Strasbourg. If he had succeeded with these two towns, he would probably then have got possession of the whole of France, but his position would not have been so secure as it is now. The soldiers of France are one and all of them in favour of Napoleon, partly because he does all he can to obtain their good-will, but also, in great measure, on account of the dear memory of the first Emperor. The peasants in the east of France do not like him, but they are afraid to speak their sentiments. At Saarburg, near Saverne, a schoolmaster was put in prison for three months to await his trial, for having said something in a café against the Government. A punishment of this sort for a man with a family is very severe, and causes great terror in the neighbourhood. During my stay at Strasbourg three persons of that town were arrested and put in prison. Most Frenchmen with whom I have spoken privately are of opinion that this state of affairs will not last long.

In coming here I spent a night at Baden-Baden. There are two old castles on the mountains which shelter the town. One of these is inhabited during the summer by the Grand-Duke, the other is in ruins. From the ruins, to which I ascended, towards sunset, there is a magnificent view of the Rhine valley. The other castle is exceedingly curious; dungeons of great depth are hollowed out of the rock below the castle. The doors of these dungeons are immense blocks of stone turning on iron hinges. Some of the cells open from above, and the prisoners were let down in chairs. The room of the secret tribunal and the cell and instruments of torture are so dismal and horrid that on seeing them one can scarcely avoid a shudder. What must have been the feelings of the poor victims three or four hundred years ago! The little town of Baden is well sheltered from the north and east winds by an amphitheatre of wooded mountains, and the ground is probably warmed and the climate ameliorated by the hot springs which burst from the earth, and are received into troughs in the street. The water is sulphurous, and hot enough to boil an egg. The season commences in May; until then there is no gambling. At present there are scarcely any strangers. As yet I have scarcely had time to see Heidelberg. The ruins of the castle are most picturesque, and the town is clean and quaint. I have not yet been to the hospital, but I intend going to-morrow morning. There are about 500 students, who walk about the streets in the most extraordinary caps of every form and colour. They are said to be much given to duelling and beer-drinking.

I intend staying a few days here, then I shall go to Munich, and from there to Vienna. On my arrival at Vienna I shall inquire for letters at the Poste Restante.

TO HIS MOTHER.

HEIDELBERG, *April* 3*d*, 1858.

I WRITE to congratulate and wish you many happy returns of your sixty-seventh birthday. (I have added ten, and subtracted one!!) The letter will arrive a day or two late, but I know will be equally prized by you.

In coming here I rested a night at Baden-Baden.

The weather has been exceedingly fine, and the woods and country in general are very much in the same state as the woods at Matlock when we were there. The buds are swollen and ready to burst into leaf, and some trees even show a few leaves. The Neckar (the river of Heidelberg) is a large rapid-running river, like the Tyne at Blaydon in size, but full of rocks and winding at the feet of wooded mountains. The picture in your breakfast-room will give you a very good idea of the bridge, town, and river. There is a good hospital and several very distinguished Professors, but at present there is a vacation for Easter, and consequently there are no lectures. I expect shortly (in a day or two) to be on my way to Vienna. Tell Henry that I climbed to the very top of Strasbourg Cathedral (the highest building in Europe). The last few steps of the ascent were rather alarming, for there is no rail to prevent falling, and the immense height is rather apt to make one giddy. Fortunately there was no wind when I was there, and consequently no danger. The day was clear, and I had a magnificent view of the Rhine valley and mountains. The construction of the tower is very curious, and can only be understood by ascending.

TO L.

May 14*th*, 1858, VIENNA.

I HAVE purposely been rather long in replying to your letter, in order that I might tell you something about my mode of life here, and of the manner in which hospital affairs are carried on. As I anticipated, I came by Stuttgart and Munich, and then down the Danube from Donauwörth. Unfortunately throughout the whole of my journey the weather was cold and wet, but that did not at all prevent me from seeing all that is to be seen in the different towns through which I passed. I was three whole days on the Danube. We were carried rapidly along by the swollen muddy current, through each other. It is also a great convenience to the students when they have some time to wait between the different classes. A certain number of the patients pay for their accommodation, and are in consequence spared the visits of the students. Several of the surgeons and physicians live in a part of the hospital separated from the patients. I have made the acquaintance of two, viz. Professor Sigmund, and Dr. S. Zigmondy. They have both nice apartments. The latter has his wife living with him in the hospital. The teaching in Vienna is in some respects better than in England, but this would take too long to explain in a letter. We will talk over it together at some future time. The German students have one great disadvantage, viz. that their books are all too long and tedious. German Professors don't seem to have the faculty of condensing and arranging their matter, and most of their books are interminable. The Life of Goethe most commonly read here is a translation from the English. In another letter I will try and tell you something of the Professors.

TO HIS MOTHER.

VENICE, *July* 13*th*, 1858.

I LEFT Vienna on Friday morning, and after an eight hours' ride through a mountainous country I arrived at Grätz, the capital of Styria. There I made the acquaintance of Herr Weiss, Professor of History in the University, and was shown by him about the town, and introduced to several gentlemen who he said were very famous poets and romance-writers. There was nothing particularly remarkable about them excepting the quantity of beer that they drank and the number of cigars that they smoked. The Professor himself, however, is a very intellectual-looking man, and awfully learned. He is at present, he told me, writing a book on Wales and the Welsh—an out-of-the-way sort of subject, one would think, for a German Professor in the heart of Styria! My next day's journey was to Trieste, about fourteen hours. The country here is equally beautiful, fresh, and green. The line runs through verdant valleys, and by the side of fresh-looking streams and rivers, and to the right the Tyrol mountains tower high up into the skies. . . .

TO L.

VENICE, *July* 20*th*, 1858.

OF all the beautiful towns in Europe that I have seen, Venice, to my taste, is by far the most splendid. I live in Riva dei

Sciavoni, and from my windows have a splendid view of the Adriatic and several of the little islands surrounding Venice. Gondolas containing fair Venetian donnas and their cavaliers are continually passing my door, and shoot under a beautiful marble bridge to sail about the "sunnier waters" beyond. I spend a few hours every morning at home, making an abstract of a book on Logic. It is the most distasteful to me of all the studies I was ever engaged in. M. Cousin, in his book on Moral Philosophy, clearly proves that nobody almost who has written on the subject knows anything about it. As you may imagine, it is not at all satisfactory in closing a long and difficult book to feel that all your labour has been in vain, and that all your knowledge is negative. It is a curious fact that the two most distinguished logicians in England (Whately and De Morgan) should, the one be a homœopathist, and the other a believer in table-turning. If I were free I would close for ever my books on Moral Philosophy and Logic. As it is, I must still continue to study them for months. It is decidedly warm here, but at the same time very agreeable, for there is always a pleasant sea-breeze, no dust, no dirt, and of course no bustle of horses and carriages; multitudes of people walk silently along the clean well-paved streets. The air is as pure as at sea, for the tide comes and washes through the town twice daily. I was through the hospital yesterday, and saw not a single case of typhus. I am also told by the doctors that fever is very rare. The drainage of Venice is very peculiar, a plan discovered by the old Venetians. With a slight modification I think it might be well applied to London, and would cure the present condition of the Thames. I spend an hour or two every day looking at the palace and churches. This is much pleasanter than seeing sights the whole day long, and the impressions left are pleasanter and more lasting. Venice is more separated from the land than I expected. There is a railway-bridge leading to Verona, but this is so long that looking along it from Venice in the perspective it dwindles into a line, and the opposite shore is quite indistinct, although the high mountains of Tyrol behind can be distinctly seen. Venice does not at all give one the idea of a city built on an island, or rather, as it is said, on seventy-two islands.

The palaces seem to rise right out of the sea, as if their foundations were laid fathoms deep at the bottom of the sea. The green sea-weed clings to the white marble stairs which lead down to the water. Two or three nights ago there was a grand serenade upon the water: thousands of illuminated gondolas, with music, fire-works, etc., passed up the grand canal; many of the palaces were also illuminated.

It is impossible by description to give you any idea of the beauty of Venice. It far surpasses my expectations. The men are handsome and intelligent-looking, and the women beautiful. At the theatre, where one sees them together, the contrast between the Germans and Italians is most marked. One can't help preferring the blood-horse to the dray, although the latter is the more useful animal.

TO HIS MOTHER.

November 1858.

I RECEIVED Isabella's letter this morning. She tells me that you are much afraid that I am going to decide to go to India, and that you have some thoughts of coming to London on Friday with Mr. Pow. Of course, I should be delighted to see you here, but at the same time I should not like you to subject yourself to so much fatigue at this time of the year. Rather than you should do so I would come myself to Shields for a day or two. The examination will be over in a month or six weeks, and then I shall be perfectly free to come and spend some time with you. Don't make yourself anxious about me until I have decided. The passing of the examination, you know, does not oblige me to go. The distance to India is not nearly so great as it was, and when the railway is completed it will be probably only a three weeks' or a month's journey.

TO THE SAME.

December 1858.

I WRITE this letter to-day in order that you may receive it on Christmas Day. Wish all the family a merry Christmas from me, and tell them that I would have liked very much to have spent it with them, if circumstances would have allowed me. I have accepted an invitation to dinner from Mrs. C. It will be some consolation for you to know that I shall not eat my Christmas dinner alone. You will be glad to hear that I have received the Crimean medal; I called on Sir William Codrington, late Commander-in-chief, whom I had met with in the East, and it is through his exertions that I obtained it. He was very polite to me, and kept me for nearly two hours with him, while he hunted through his old despatches, and endeavoured to make out a strong claim for me. There are few military men, I should think, so systematic and careful of every little matter. I know of several instances now in which his good business-like qualities were shown; and I think it would have been much better for our army in the Crimea if he had been Commander-in-chief at an earlier period of the war.

TO THE SAME.

LONDON, *Jan. 1st,* 1859.

I RECEIVED your letter yesterday, and hasten to send you the New Year's gift which you ask for. I wish I could make it kind and expressive of all the love I feel for you. As this is impossible, you must take it for granted, and believe that as I am not demonstrative, I feel an affection for you all the deeper. I am working hard still, but in another fortnight I shall have finished, and hope to be on my way to see you.

CHAPTER IV.

LETTERS FROM INDIA AND CHINA.

> " And through a lattice on the soul
> Looks thy fair face."
>
> *In Memoriam.*

WHAT a grief this going to India was to us! When he had bid farewell to his mother, and all the rest of the family, he and I set forth together, travelling by night to London. We had three or four days there, days of unrest and sadness, of preparation for the voyage, of bidding good-bye to friends who were never more to greet him, who lamented the loss of his companionship. Dr. Parkes of Netley knew his worth, and especially regretted that one so promising should leave this country.

It was an early grey February morning when he began his long journey to the far East. I alone went with him to London Bridge. As we drove through the squares and streets, we talked of what was nearest our hearts, and we mingled our tears. He sent kind messages to those who were dear to both. He said that it was not ambition which induced him to go to India, that he liked a quiet life, not contention or struggle. Then we parted; a sweet tender smile was the last look he gave me, and he went on his way, and I knew that I should see his beautiful youthful face no more—except in dreams.

Eleven years afterwards, when parting from his little girls, he recalls the bitterness of that hour, showing how greatly he had shared in the sorrow.

TO HIS MOTHER.

CHARLOTTE SQUARE, *Friday night.*

I AM just going to write you a few words of farewell before leaving England. I am going to-morrow morning early, and Allie will accompany me to the train, and then set off herself for Shields. Since I left you I have been very busy, but now

I have got my business tolerably satisfactorily accomplished. I am at present, and probably shall be for some time, in rather low spirits, and totally incapable of writing a pleasant letter. When I arrive at the Mediterranean I feel that I shall be better. Whenever I have a good opportunity I shall write to you, and let you know all that I am doing in India. You shall hear as frequently from me now as you ever did, and this will make the distance which separates us appear less. You will soon begin to look forward to the time when we shall meet again.

TO THE SAME.

HARBOUR OF MARSEILLES, *Feb.* 28*th*, 1859,
ON BOARD THE "PANTHER."

WE are waiting in the harbour of Marseilles for the English mail, which has been detained by bad weather. As the sea bids fair to be very rough, I think it well to begin my letter to you now, while the ship is steady.

We took our time passing through France, and stayed at three places by the way,—Montreux, Chalons-sur-Saone, and Avignon.

I was particularly delighted with the last of these, Avignon. It is a fine old town, surrounded by thick walls, protected by many square stone towers. The houses are old, but substantial, built of dressed pleasant-coloured stones. There is an old cathedral (eighth century), and the palace of the Popes, large, and built like a fortress of immense strength. The view from a terrace behind the cathedral is exceedingly fine;—in the distance high snowy mountains, and near at hand the Rhone and the Durance dividing, forming islands and winding about. There are several bridges. One ruined bridge for foot-passengers is very beautifully formed.

TO THE SAME.

BETWEEN CORSICA AND SARDINIA,
Feb. 29*th*, 1859.

WE left Marseilles at 5.30 P.M. yesterday. The wind blew furiously from the north, but as that was directly behind us we went along famously and without much motion. I slept well, and as yet have not had the least feeling of sea-sickness. There is a Dr. Murray in the same cabin with me. We knew each other at Balaklava in 1856, and as you may imagine were rather surprised to be thus thrown together again. He has been ten years in China, and is now on his way to Hong-Kong as surgeon to the Embassy. We are on board of a very fine vessel, and the accommodation for passengers is exceedingly good. There are about thirty passengers; but there are not many going all the way to Calcutta. Several of the passengers are French, and there is one very nice old Turkish gentleman, who belongs to the household of the Viceroy of Egypt, and is probably ambassador or something of that sort at Paris, for he tells me that he has made the journey from Alexandria to Paris about forty times.

I forget to tell you yesterday that I received a letter from Allie at Paris. I did not inquire for letters at Marseilles, not expecting to receive any. To-day the sea is tolerably smooth, but the wind is rather against us. The weather is fine and sunny, and the snowy mountains of Corsica and Sardinia look very brilliant, contrasting with the dark blue sea. The passengers are walking about on deck, standing in groups making each other's acquaintance, and trying to pass away the time, which is already beginning to hang heavy. I put down all sorts of things in this letter, hoping that something may interest you, and feeling sure that the very fact of its coming from me will make it readable to you. I have got out my books of Hindustani, and shall learn a little every day. I already have learnt to write a little, but the characters are very difficult.

March 1st, off the South Coast of Sicily.—Yesterday evening we went sailing close to the shore of the northern part of Sardinia. The country is rugged, mountainous, and unfertile, and, I am told by a Frenchman, is chiefly inhabited by robbers of Corsica, who are avoiding justice by living there. It is however said by the French that the Corsicans have such a strong sentiment of patriotism that they all return sooner or later to get themselves hanged in their fatherland.

TO L.—(JOURNAL.)

Saturday.—We arrived at Malta early on Thursday morning. I went ashore early, looked through S. Giovanni Church to pass the time, and then called upon my friend Dr. Edwards, and spent the whole day with him and his friends, among whom I found the chief purveyor Pigott, who was formerly at Renkioi Hospital along with me. We were detained at Malta in consequence of the letters having been wet in crossing from Dover to Calais. If they had not been dried at Malta they would probably have been rotten before arriving at Calcutta. Edwards and I walked about Malta together. From the fortifications we had fine views of the harbour. The sea was of a dark blue, and the houses and rocks of Malta of a glaring light yellow. A Russian fleet, consisting of four large ships, was just leaving the harbour. We visited the military and naval hospitals. The naval hospital is delightfully situated on the side of the harbour opposite to the greater part of the town. It is on a highish promontory, with sea on both sides of it, and I should think is always well supplied with fresh air. In connection with it there is a nice garden, with palms, orange-trees, and aloes growing luxuriantly. The wards are large, high, and well ventilated, and the beds, etc., clean and in good order. Edwards and his friend treated me very hospitably, and I enjoyed very much getting ashore, feeling myself on *terra firma* and among friends once more.

The weather is fine and sunny, and we can just see the coast of Africa. We expect to arrive at Alexandria early on Monday morning. I do not enjoy my voyage at all. Time passes with me very slowly, and the end of my journey (Calcutta) seems very far off in the future. We took five passengers on board at Malta. At Suez we shall join the mail from Southampton, and then our numbers, I am told, will be increased three times.

TO HIS SISTER.

STEAMBOAT "NUBIA,"
THE RED SEA, NEAR ADEN, *March* 13.

I RECEIVED your letter at Paris. I travelled very comfortably through France. As you have probably seen my letters to L., mother, and William, it would be useless giving an account of the voyage. The heat here is very great, and is much complained of. It increases daily, and I am told will have reached its acme when we arrive at Aden. As yet I find it agreeable. There is scarcely any motion. At night it is most delightful to sit on deck. The sky is always clear and the stars seem brighter than in the north. We are close to Aden, therefore I must finish my short note to you. *Ma sœur bien aimée.*

P.S.—All the sailors are Indians, and most of them are active and good-looking men, but not powerful. The agility of some of them is surprising. They run up and down the rigging just like monkeys. Some of them are almost naked. Some of the passengers have black servants, and these are exceedingly handsome men, with beautiful eyes and fine mild expressions. One who stands beside me at dinner is dressed in pure white Hindu clothes, and is perhaps the finest-looking man I ever saw, but there is something about his expression which tells me that he would not exert himself for the world, and which also shows a sort of stoical indifference to men and things, perfect content, but no delight in life.

TO HIS BROTHER HENRY.

ON BOARD THE "NUBIA," RED SEA.

I PROMISED to give you an account of a Turkish Bath, but the one which I took at Alexandria did not appear to me exactly the same as the regular Turkish Bath; however, I will describe it to you. First, I was shown into a large room of an irregular shape, lighted from the top. In connection with the room there were several little rooms, with a few mattresses lying on the floor of each of them. I was ushered into one of these, then my money, watch, etc., were taken from me and given to the master of the bath to take charge of for me. One of the attendants helped me to undress, twisted a white towel round my head, a blue one round my waist, and then threw a white sheet over my shoulders, and put wooden shoes on my feet. In this costume I was conducted through several rooms full of naked bathers, lying on their backs on marble slabs, and being soaped by Hummungees, until I arrived at a little hot room with one small trough, into which ran both hot and cold water; in this room there was also a large bath. The floor was of marble, and the room was full of steam, and its temperature seemed to me to be under 100° Fah. When I entered, the Hummungee was already engaged in the same room with another bather, and consequently I had to wait a little. The Hummungee commenced his operations on me by throwing very warm water on my arms and breast, then he put on a linen glove without fingers, smacked his hands together with a flourish, and passed the gloved hand firmly but slowly over my arms, breast, back, and legs, and succeeded wonderfully in peeling off a large portion of my outer skin. Then he soaped me all over, using tow instead of a sponge. He then took my turban off, and soaped my head by the same means. After that I had water poured over me, and was told to get into the bath, which was just like an old Roman bath in shape. After remaining in the bath for about ten minutes I was reclothed and conducted back to my clothes; then the shampooer made his appearance, and began first to wear off the thick skin from my feet with a piece of stone that looked like lava. Then he began pressing my muscles and cracking my joints. His method of cracking my back, which he did at three places, is too complicated to describe, and I am not even sure if I quite understand how he managed it. It was a most extraordinary sensation, and I do not think I could resolve to subject myself again to the same operation. My chibouk and coffee were then brought, and I was left to enjoy *kef*.

TO L.—(JOURNAL.)

RED SEA, *March* 10*th*, 1859.

WE were only at Alexandria from nine in the morning till five at night, but that was quite long enough to see and get a good idea of the town. It is a dirty place, with all the confusion and dirt but none of the beauties of Constantinople. I rode about the town on a donkey, visited Pompey's Pillar and Cleopatra's Needle, which is very like the obelisk at Paris. We set off from Alexandria by train at five P.M., and travelled through a flat country by the sea-side for a long distance. At nine o'clock we had to leave our carriages and get into a steamboat to cross the Nile, which at this place is about the width of the Thames at London. The night was dark, but we could see that the country was flat, with few trees, and the Nile looked like a large canal, about fifteen feet below the level of the land, with abruptly sloping banks. About two in the morning we arrived at Cairo, and went to the hotel. As we had to start again for Suez, I got up by daylight, took a donkey, and went full gallop through the town, followed by an Arab, who used various means to induce my donkey to go faster. Cairo is, according to my idea, the most thoroughly *Oriental* city I have ever seen. It is full of mosques, minarets, baths, curious old houses with flat roofs, narrow winding streets with overhanging windows. Round about the city there are large plantations of palm-trees, and in the city itself there are solitary palm-trees, which harmonise well with the Oriental architecture. I had a ride right through the city; my object was to reach the mosque of Mohammed Ali, which stands on a hill and commands a full view of the city and the valley of the Nile. The morning was clear and fresh, and I was delighted. I was some height above the other buildings of the city. The valley of the Nile was green, and wooded in parts. Several clusters of pyramids were easily seen—in all, I should think, about a dozen. When the sun shone on them they looked like snow mountains, except in form, for in the distance their points and angles appeared perfectly sharp and defined as if they had been recently cut.

Since I arrived in Egypt I have enjoyed myself exceedingly. The sight of the Arab faces and costumes reminded me of old times in Turkey, where I spent such a pleasant year of my life. I regret, however, that I had not more time to wander about Cairo. The other passengers were too tired in the morning to see anything, so that I was more lucky than they. We set off again by railway for Suez at eight A.M., and in a few minutes were right in the desert. Fortunately the heat was not great; I even was scarcely warm enough, and kept my great-coat continually. We came to a station every now and then, where there were a few Arab tents and huts, and a water-tank for the engine. At each of these stations I used to take a little walk, examine the sand and stones of the desert, and inhale the delightful fresh cool air. The sand is of a brownish yellow colour, and very stony. The stones as it were form a sort of crust on the top, the sand having been blown away and leaving them. The stones that I picked up were all flint; some of them were evidently pieces of petrified wood, petrified with silica, not with carbonate of lime; at some parts there is not a trace of vegetation, but generally there are here and there small tufts of apparently dried-up plants. We were five hours in going from Cairo to Suez. At Suez there is nothing interesting; the shores of the sea are dry, and in parts rocky. In going down the gulf some of the mountains are very high and precipitous, but I saw no signs of vegetation. The tops of some of them were covered with snow. To-day we are in the middle of the Red Sea, out of sight of land. The ship is going steadily and fast, with a fair wind. We have four times as many passengers as in the other steamboat. They are all well, but very hard up for something to do. Many of the gentlemen play at whist, even in the day-time. There is a prayer-meeting every morning. One or two of the ladies quarrel, but the majority of them are happy and good-natured. Sir C. Trevelyan, Governor of Madras, is among the passengers. We have had some talk together, and he is very polite to me. I forgot to tell you something of the *mirage*. There seem to be two kinds. The horizon sometimes appears like a wavy sea, and the effect is produced by the heated air rising from the hot sand, just as you see it rising from a heated stone; at other times there is an atmospheric effect (more difficult to understand) by which you see a lake, with shore, islands, etc., in the distance, and can with difficulty be persuaded that it is an illusion. The line of the horizon when I crossed the desert was always indistinct, and it was impossible to distinguish the little inequality from the clouds. Long before we reached the sea, we fancied over and over again that we saw it, till at last we became incredulous. When we saw the ships, then of course we were satisfied. When we first saw them we were twelve miles off, yet they were quite distinct, and their hulls appeared lifted high out of the water. The weather is decidedly warm to-day. Passengers are complaining of the heat, but I enjoy it. We are going along steadily and rapidly through the middle of the Red Sea, with a clear sky and a deep blue sea, and a breeze which just whitens the tops of the waves. At dinner and breakfast the punkahs or fans are kept constantly going by Indians.

TO HIS MOTHER.

SHIP "NUBIA," INDIAN OCEAN, BETWEEN
ADEN AND CEYLON.

WE arrived at Aden on Monday morning, and stayed there all day. The captain of the "Cassibelaunus" came on board and lent me a carriage to go and see the town of Aden, which is about 3½ miles from the port. I had always heard nothing but ill of the town, and was prepared to dislike it, but as my expectations were not great I was more than satisfied. There is no grass or vegetation to be seen, with the exception of a few small trees, which have been recently planted, and are almost dried up. The rocks are high and rugged, of a brown colour, and are of a hard trap, which when broken up makes a very good soil, but this for want of water becomes like unfertile sand. The forms of the mountains and rocks are very picturesque, and the sea runs in among them, forming beautiful little bays, the clear bright blue water of which contrasts beautifully with the arid sand and brown rocks. All that is wanted to make Aden a perfect little paradise is a plentiful supply of fresh water. In the olden time (many hundred years ago), when the Arabs were a more cultivated and civilised race than at present, there were large tanks which collected the water which ran down from the sides of the mountains and rocks. Sometimes for a year or two not a drop of rain falls at Aden, but when the showers *do* come they are so heavy that if the water were collected it would be sufficient for the interval. The present Governor of Aden, R. L. Playfair, R.N., has discovered some of the old tanks, and had the sand with which they were completely concealed cleared away. Six of the tanks are already fit to receive and hold water. They are immense basins, fantastically shaped, but it is said of a form remarkably well suited to resist the tremendous force with which torrents of water occasionally come down from the rocky ravines. The lining of the tanks is composed of a cement called chuman, which becomes very hard, and has a surface smooth and polished like marble. I had a nice bath in the sea at Aden, but I was afraid to swim on account of sharks.

TO THE SAME.

NEAR POINT DE GALLE, CEYLON,
25th March.

WE have had a very smooth passage from Aden. The weather has been very hot, so much so that at night we are obliged to sleep without clothes. Time passes very slowly, because we have nothing to do, and the interruptions are so frequent that it is impossible to read anything serious. We try to make the time pass more quickly by means of singing, dancing, and theatricals. The piano is taken on deck every night, and that with a fiddle and a drum makes very good music to dance to. The rolling of the ship makes dancing rather a difficult and hazardous proceeding, and the slight accidents which occur in consequence cause a good deal of laughter and fun. One night there was a theatre, with stage, foot-lights, etc., rigged up on deck—this was a grand pastime.

TO HIS MOTHER.

BETWEEN POINT DE GALLE AND MADRAS.

It seems now such a long time since I left England; the voyage is dreadfully tedious, but yet endurable. It is some relief to write a few lines to you, and to think of your reading them, as I know you will do, with pleasure. I begin now to look forward to my arrival at Calcutta, when I expect I shall shortly receive some letters from home. The receipt of them will give me greater delight than you can imagine, for I am sure I shall feel very lonely on my arrival. The few acquaintances I have made on the voyage are going to leave Calcutta. We spent a very pleasant twenty-four hours at Galle on Thursday and Friday. We arrived there at mid-day. The weather was decidedly hot, but yet there was a pleasant breeze, sufficiently strong to make the waves throw up their white foam upon the rocks. We anchored in a beautiful little bay, the shores of which were wooded to the water's edge with plantains, palm-trees of all kinds, many tropical plants and trees of which I do not know the names, some of them bearing most magnificent flowers, and all looking fresh, green, and beautiful. The town of Galle is not large, and there is nothing of consequence to be seen. The Custom-house has the date 1658, and so has the Mansion-house. There are several good hotels, cool and clean. Lord Elgin is living at Galle for a short time. He invited Sir C. Trevelyan and all of us to a ball at his house, which I did not leave till two in the morning. One can dance quite as well in hot as in cold weather in this part of the world, because it is not considered improper to appear in light clothes. After two hours' sleep I got up, hired a carriage, and drove to a place called Wach-Walla. The country looked most beautiful in the early morning. The drive was sometimes through a forest of palms, which were often covered with creeping plants, which formed festoons between them and bore quantities of enormous brilliant-coloured flowers. Many of the plants are very aromatic. The cinnamon plant is very common; its wood, leaf, and flower have all the well-known smell, and I therefore easily recognised it. I enclose you a little piece of grass which has a strong smell of lemon. From Wach-Walla we had a splendid view of mountains, a fine fertile valley, and a winding river, giving off canals for irrigating the rice-fields. The inhabitants of Ceylon are most of them ugly and effeminate-looking. The men wear their hair long and held back with a comb like Wilhelmina's.

TO THE SAME.

CALCUTTA, *April 4th.*

I SHALL write you a few lines to-day, as it is your birthday, but I shall not be able to post this letter until the 8th. May you have many happy returns, and may we spend many of them together! From Ceylon hither was not particularly interesting. The weather was calm and hot, and the steamboat went monotonously through the water for nine days. We stayed for a few hours at Madras, but we had no time to go ashore. We were a day coming up the Hooghly. This river, from its mouth to very near Calcutta, is very like the Thames from the Nore to Greenwich. The waters have the same colour, and the shipping and tug-boats are just like those one meets on the London river. But as we approach Calcutta the character of the river alters much. The banks of the river are seen on each side more distinctly, and then, instead of oaks and chestnuts, we see palm-trees and bananas, with their large light-green succulent leaves. By the river-side there are lots of nice houses, square, with flat roofs and broad verandahs, and surrounded with large gardens, laid out like English parks.

I have first-rate quarters here, about the coolest in Calcutta. I have a large room in the upper story, nicely furnished. My two windows open on a broad balcony, shaded with thick walls, arches, and pillars. I spend the greater part of the day on this balcony, reading, smoking, and enjoying the air and prospect. I spend several hours daily studying Hindustani. A native teacher is with me for an hour every morning. I am obliged to have three servants, who have almost as easy a life as their master. This very agreeable but rather lazy life that I lead will not last long, for I shall probably be sent into the interior shortly. I shall not be sorry to leave Calcutta, for I feel rather ashamed of drawing pay merely for amusing myself. The time is not lost to myself, for I manage to get through a great deal of reading and study. The climate at present suits me remarkably well. The heat is delightful to me, it makes mere existence a pleasure. From what I hear I imagine that in a month it will be rather too hot. On Sunday I went to the cathedral and heard the Bishop preach. The cathedral, like all the rooms here, was hung with punkahs or fans, which were continually kept going by native servants. The monotonous movement of these punkahs has a peculiarly soporific effect, and half of the congregation were asleep. Yesterday I went to the river-side and saw the burning of some dead Hindus. It is done without any ceremony, and is not so revolting a sight as one would imagine. Pariahs, or outcasts, stir up the fire, and see that everything is properly burnt. The body is placed on a heap of wood, about four feet high, and then a little more wood on the top. In about half an hour or an hour nothing is to be seen. The city of Calcutta, although large and full of good comfortable houses, is not particularly interesting, for all the buildings are very much alike, built of brick and stucco, and painted white. The flat roofs, verandahs, balconies, and large rooms make houses very pleasant to live in. There is a large park, called "The Maidan," where people drive about and ride in as great style as in Hyde Park. I already know a great many people in Calcutta, and am going to dine out three times this week. Yesterday I was astonished to meet one of the young ladies I knew at the Dardanelles. Neither of us knew that the other was going to Calcutta. I am living at the General Hospital.

TO HIS SISTER.[1]

I RECEIVED my first batch of letters by the last mail, and was delighted to find one from you and L. among them. Since I received the letters, the distance which separates us does not appear to me so great. When I was in the Crimea the feeling of distance from home was stronger. I am so accustomed to travelling now that I should think nothing of the journey back again to England. I like India quite as well as I expected. People complain of the heat, but I find it nothing more than pleasant. I enjoy the evenings exceedingly whilst sitting on the balcony looking at the palm-trees, and the curious birds and the animals of the country. The crows here are very queer-looking birds with long grey necks and wise faces. They are exceedingly audacious, and often come popping into the rooms. One perched on my bed this morning. They take a particular pleasure in riding on the back of goats and cows, who don't seem to mind them at all. The little court-yard of

---

[1] By the mail, 22d April 1859.

the hospital swarms with life, and all the different animals are on as good terms as the London "happy family." The little black babies are most delightful little creatures; they are quite as well-behaved as little puppy-dogs, and never cry except on very strong provocation. They are carried about perfectly naked, *à cheval*, cross-legs on the hips of their mothers or brothers, or left to roll about and amuse themselves on the ground. The Hindu men here are exceedingly gentle and harmless-looking. They remind one of antelopes or some timorous animal of that species, and one is not surprised that a few Englishmen should put hundreds of them to flight. They get terribly knocked about by many of the Englishmen who have arrived here since the mutiny. They bear it all meekly, don't look, and I fancy don't feel, revengeful. I saw yesterday the (charak) festival at which Hindus torture themselves by putting hooks, etc., into their skin, and being swung round. The ceremony is more absurd than horrible, for there is little or no suffering. The two hooks are only through the skin of the back, and the sensibility of this is previously deadened by pressure. The weight of the body is supported not by the hooks, but by a band which goes over the chest. Those that I saw were not drunk, their faces did not give the least evidence of pain. Whilst swinging in the air they laughed and joked, kicked about their legs, and threw down presents among the people.

I have just received an order to proceed to Hong-Kong to be attached to a regiment of Sipahis stationed there. So you see there is not much chance of getting to the Punjab yet.

TO HIS BROTHER HENRY.

CALCUTTA, *April* 21st, 1859.

I WAS at Mr. Knowles's country-house the other day, and stayed all night. The house is close to the river-side, and is surrounded by grounds beautifully laid out, and planted with all kinds of magnificent trees. There are several immense banyan-trees (the tree, you know, which has pillars supporting its heavy lateral branches) and one or two very large india-rubber trees with beautiful dark glossy-green leaves. Mr. Knowles and I got up at five A.M. next morning, and rode to Barrackpore and back, a distance of about fifteen miles. We galloped nearly the whole way, and the horses did not seem anything the worse for it. The morning was delightfully cool and fresh, and the scenery exceedingly beautiful, although the road was perfectly flat. Every now and then we caught a magnificent view of the fine broad reaches of the river through luxuriant foliage, such as you do not see in Europe. On returning we put on our loose clothes and breakfasted under a tree by the river-side. I am going off to China to-morrow or the next day, and scarcely know whether I am glad or sorry to go. I like India so much that I am sorry to leave it, but at the same time I am delighted at the prospect of seeing Java, Penang, and China. I fancy I shall not find the Chinese so pleasant to look upon as the natives here. Most of the Chinamen that I have seen, and there are a good many here, are exceedingly ugly, and there is something to me particularly unpleasant and insolent about their expression. The Indian men, women, and children are nearly all good-looking, and exceedingly well dressed. Some are not dressed at all, and yet look well. I am getting on tolerably fast with Hindustani, and as I am to be with a native regiment in China, I shall continue learning it there. I shall give you my experience of the Chinamen when I have seen them in their own country. People always appear to most advantage in their own country. The half-caste here are a very strange lot. A certain number of them are well-made, strong, handsome, and honest; but the majority of them are thin, pale, cowardly, and deceitful. There seem to be two classes of them quite the opposite of each other. They are almost entirely out of society here. How strange the difference in the treatment they receive here and in England must appear to them.

I enclose you my portrait. For mother's sake I kept the sword out of the picture. My uniform is not that at which we appear at mess.

TO L.

"THEBES," BAY OF BENGAL, *May* 3*d*, 1859.

I LEFT Calcutta on the morning of the 27th. Three steam-boats started within a few minutes of each other, all filled with opium. The "Thebes" is now behind the other two, but the captain still hopes to make up. The steamboats which leave Calcutta always run after the opium sales,—always race to convey information concerning the sale as early as possible to their master-merchants at Hong-Kong. We had a delightful voyage down the river. In England I have always heard the Hooghly spoken of as such a poor river, but for my part I think it is the finest river I have yet seen. It is broad and winding, and every now and then in passing along, wide reaches like lakes open out. It is true that the lands and banks round about are perfectly level, but the flatness is completely relieved by magnificent solitary trees, little lawns, and thickets. There are also many picturesque little villages by the water's edge. It is a long journey from Calcutta to Hong-Kong, but it seems nothing to me. I packed up my things in an hour, paid my servants, and embarked. I wished my bearer to accompany me, but his religion would not allow him to cross the sea. He came with me, however, to the boat, and directly he was beside the river he washed himself and took some of the sacred water in his mouth. Natives are continually washing in the Hooghly, men, women, and children. There are most stringent rules against Europeans bathing, on the grounds of decency, but natives here are scarcely looked upon as human. Sailors think nothing of murdering them, but that is not allowed at Calcutta. I hear continually of frightful atrocities committed by the naval brigade up country. Cooper's execution, which appeared so horrible to us, is thought nothing of here (the natives not being looked upon as human). In the upper provinces, where the natives are a superior class of people, the feeling of the English towards them may be different. I am merely speaking of Calcutta. I am not sorry to leave Calcutta, for it is soon seen, and although a pleasant enough place to live in, ceases to be interesting when known. The people are fond of display, and ride and drive about in splendid carriages in a place called "The Maidan," very like Hyde Park and Rotten Row. Every evening this drive is crowded with carriages with beautiful but awfully lazy-looking ladies. We have had a fine passage across the bay; so hot that I slept every night on the boards of the deck in my shirt and white trousers. We passed by the Andaman Islands, but too far off to see them well. Several times we have passed little solitary verdant islands in mid-ocean, uninhabited excepting by monkeys, who eat their cocoa-nuts undisturbed from year to year. There is only one first-class passenger beside myself. He is a Cockney who kept an old curiosity-shop in Piccadilly, and is now on his way to collect curiosities in Japan. There is a young German second-class passenger who has been nearly everywhere (among other places, the interior of South America) gaining a living by playing the accordion. He has his wife and a little baby born in Calcutta with him. We shall stay a few hours at Penang to-day, and in two days we shall be at Singapore, where I intend posting this letter.

STRAITS OF MALACCA, NEAR SINGAPORE.

I must finish my letter in order to post it at Singapore. I got on shore yesterday at Penang, and walked about the town for an hour. It is an exceedingly pretty place. All the shops are kept by Chinamen, and, in fact, the population seems chiefly Chinese. There are a few Malays and a regiment or two of

Madras soldiers. The Chinese houses and shops are delightfully neat and light, and very tastefully decorated. The little Chinese boys looked very droll running about the streets; many of them had tails reaching almost to the ground. Penang is very picturesquely situated. There are many high mountains on the island, and also on the mainland opposite. The island seems to me very fertile, and nutmegs, spices, and fruits of many kinds, the productions of the island, abound in the bazaars. I enjoyed feasting on pine-apples and mangos after my six days' voyage. We had a magnificent thunderstorm the other night. As many as sixty flashes of lightning in a minute I counted. The rain came down in torrents, and the thunder-claps were sudden and sharp, like the report of a cannon when you are standing close to it.

TO HIS MOTHER.

CANTON, *June 2d*, 1859,
70TH REG. BEN. INF.

I AM very glad to have been sent to China; it is very amusing and interesting to see the Chinese. I have nice cool quarters, and the weather is not hot enough to prevent one from taking exercise. Living is very expensive in China, but as I have money besides my pay, that does not much affect me. Most things here cost two or three times as much as in India. The Chinese at first behaved rather badly, and assassinated a great number of Sepoys and English soldiers when they caught them walking alone. The country is overrun by thieves and robbers, who oppress the people very much, and commit all kinds of enormities. Now that the people of Canton see that they are protected from these robbers, they are disposed to be very friendly and amiable towards us. They are most anxious to learn anything that we can teach them, and are very far from being an obstinate, sullen, unimprovable race, as they have sometimes been called. Their industry and skill is astonishing. The gardens in front of my window, from constant care, irrigation, etc., are made to produce six crops annually. There are shops in the town where you can buy patent locks and complicated mathematical instruments, accurately copied from English models. The whole country is either cultivated or built upon, and the population is so great that many thousands are obliged to live continually in boats on the river. They are not a particularly religious people, but they are very tolerant of all other religions, and are easily converted if they think any advantage can be obtained. The Mussulman Sepoys have made several proselytes since I came, and every now and then Chinamen are to be seen up to their middle in the tanks getting baptised by Baptist missionaries. All Chinamen who have got any money cause their children to be very carefully educated. Filial duty and industry are the two virtues most carefully insisted on, and the works of their two great authors, Confucius and Mencius, are venerated in China as much or more than the Bible is in England. I am inclined to imagine that the Chinese at one time were a very great and powerful nation, but that they are now much degenerated. The laws and institutions seem perfect, and one would think admirably suited for maintaining order and justice in the kingdom, but practically they do not seem to answer, for there is much more thieving and plundering going on here than in any other civilised country. People are being continually executed for very slight offences, but they seem not to care anything about it. A man being carried in a basket to execution does not excite any attention in the streets, the people are so much accustomed to it.

TO HIS SISTER.

CANTON, *June 12th*, 1859.

IN your letter you ask me to tell you all I can about the Hindus, Mussulmans, etc. I have already told you something, but as yet I have not had good opportunities of observing them. When I get into the interior of India I will try and give you a fuller account of them. The regiment I am with is partly Mussulman and partly Hindu. The majority are Hindus, and remarkably fine handsome men, from the neighbourhood of Oude. At the commencement of the mutiny they were asked to volunteer to do service in China, and were probably thus prevented from joining the mutineers, although some of the officers will not allow that they were at all disaffected. By coming to China, *i.e.* crossing the sea, they have lost caste, and have in consequence got over a great deal of their absurd objection to do things which they used to think degrading to them, but I am told that when they get back again to India they will regain their caste by paying a few rupees at some temple, and then they will resume all their old prejudices. The campfollowers, of whom there are numbers, are of all religions and castes. The different religions appear to me to have little to do with the character of the people. The Mussulmans and Christians that I have met with are not at all like European Mussulmans and Christians. They are just like peculiar castes of Hindus. Notwithstanding the hatred of idols that the founder of their religion inculcated, the Mussulmans here are in the habit of paying money to have prayers said for them in Hindu temples.

I see a good deal of the poorer class of Chinese, shopkeepers and tradesmen, but the mandarins keep out of our way. The people are disposed to be very friendly. They seem particularly unprejudiced for Asiatics, and disposed to learn anything or do anything that they think will advance their interest. I fancy that they do not believe in, or care much about, their religion, although they have a great number of temples full of gilded and painted idols before which they burn long sticks of somewhat the same composition as the pastilles we sometimes burn in England. (These joss-sticks, as they are called, are very convenient for lighting cigars. I keep one continually lighted in my hut.) The burning of these joss-sticks I believe is the only religious duty that they perform, but I cannot say so positively. The most remarkable peculiarity of the Chinese is the respect and love they bear towards their parents. After their death they almost worship them, and have most superstitious ideas about their graves. The Comprador (furnisher) of our mess since we came here has buried his father three times, each time erecting a more costly monument than the preceding one. The cemeteries are always on the side of a mountain or hills, and most of the mountains round Canton are covered with graves and monuments. There is a small society of Mussulmans in Canton. A few days ago I paid their mosque and minaret a visit. These are said to be about 800 or 900 years old, and they certainly wear that appearance. In several there are time-worn granite stones about the mosque with Arabic inscriptions. The minaret is so dilapidated that I had some difficulty in ascending it. I remarked among the Mussulman Chinese children who were playing in the neighbourhood of the mosque, several without the usual Chinese caste of feature, but with slightly prominent noses and large eyes. Near to this mosque there is a very ancient pagoda, which towers grandly to a great height. It is elegantly but substantially built of brick, and has stood probably 900 years. The Chinese building seems to be very good; most of the houses are built of brick and tiled. Both the tiles and brick are superior to those used in England. They make use of lintels and pillars of granite, varying from ten to twenty feet in length, in building their bridges and temples, and for placing over their doors. The oldest houses in Canton have their walls built of mud, which is cast into large square blocks, and makes a good perpendicular well-squared wall, which hardens in time and may last hundreds of years. I feel that it is impossible by description to give you a good idea of the construction of the houses, but I will try and get some drawings, and when I have an opportunity send them to you. The Chinese have a good way of watering their gardens, which I think might be advantageously adopted at Derwent Bank. They water with two pails at the same time. These two pails are very large, but are easily carried, because balanced on one shoulder with a piece of bamboo; they are emptied simultaneously, so as to maintain the balance. The water is made to come from the spout in a fine thin broad film by a very simple arrangement. The end of the spout is closed, but on its upper surface, close to the end, a notch is cut for the water to rush out at.

I lead a very quiet sort of life here. There are no ladies, consequently there is little quarrelling among the officers. They are quite tamed down by the heat, fevers, etc., and a good many of them do nothing all day long but yawn and smoke cheroots. Others are sufficiently industrious and energetic. I have a great deal of time to myself, which I spend in studying German and Hindustani, and in reading books on China and Hindustan. I find the Chinese language rather too difficult to learn with pleasure, and as we shall probably be only a short time here, I think it scarcely worth my while seriously to attempt it; by degrees, however, I may learn something of it. For the last week rain has been pouring down in torrents, and in consequence the air is much cooled, and the country looks fresh and green, but when the sun shines one feels as if in a vapour-bath. I like China very well, but constantly feel desolate at being so far from every one who cares about me.

TO HIS BROTHER.

CANTON, *June* 1859.

I HAVE had a very pleasant voyage from Calcutta to Hong-Kong in sixteen days. In the Bay of Bengal it was exceedingly hot, but I kept on deck night and day, and was very comfortable. On this side of Singapore, however, it was once actually rather cool. We spent a day and a night at Singapore, and it was a great treat to me to get a walk on shore and a fresh-water bath. Singapore is a perfect little paradise. The harbour is surrounded by numerous little islands covered with cocoa-nuts, palms, nutmegs, plantains, etc., richly green, and growing in the sea at high-water. The town reminded me somewhat of Venice; the sea makes inroads and canals which intersect the city, and these are covered with Chinese boats busily plying about in all directions. A large part of the Chinese population live entirely on the water. The women there as well as here help their husbands to pull, and one often sees them standing like Venetian gondoliers, and working the boat along. Their back-and-forward motion at the same time serves to rock to sleep a little baby strapped to their back. Their dress is neat and clean, perhaps not so graceful, but more decent than that of the Hindustani women. There is a wonderful amount of activity and life among the Chinese; the contrast between them and the Indians struck me most forcibly. The Indian rarely laughs, and I think never jokes. The Chinaman is full of fun and jokes. The Chinaman has not the politeness of the Indian, he is continually showing the Europeans with whom he deals that he looks upon them as barbarians, and despises them. I was a day at Hong-Kong, which time I spent in calling on various friends whose acquaintance I had made on my voyage to Calcutta. Early in the morning I got on board a Peninsular and Oriental Company's boat, and was at Canton the same evening. The body of old Yep or Yeh came up in the same steamboat with me. He died rather mysteriously at Calcutta just before I left. A young interpreter had charge of the body, and told me a great deal about the habits of the old man. He seems to have been remarkably clever and intelligent. The interpreter said he was an awful liar, and had many disgusting vices. He told the interpreter that he was made Commissioner of Canton on account of a treatise which he had written on a passage in Confucius, "Dew falls in autumn." On this passage he succeeded in establishing a new system of taxation, which was highly approved of by the Chinese Emperor. I cannot vouch for the truth of all this, but still I suspect it is tolerably correct. We had a very pleasant journey up the river. The scenery is fine, diversified with mountains, valleys, islands, and highly-cultivated plains. The river is crowded with junks, flower-boats, and craft of all kinds. The city of Canton is very much destroyed, but still one can form a very good idea of what it has been. During the last week I have been much shifted about, and have been living in temples and all sorts of queer buildings, curiously decorated with paintings, china-work, and remarkable-looking gilded gods. Now I am finally attached to the 70th Bengal Infantry, and am quartered in a little hut on the wall of Canton. From my window I have a fine view of the high White Cloud mountains; it is the healthiest and most windy part of Canton.

TO HIS BROTHER.

CANTON, *July 2d*, 1859.

ALLIE said that mother was going to send me a box of clothes —a few books would be more acceptable. The Chinese are excellent tailors; they make my uniform, which I am obliged to wear out of doors. In the house I wear Chinese clothes, which are by far the most comfortable and convenient ever invented. I wish I had an opportunity of sending you a suit. If you do send me a parcel, it had better be addressed to Calcutta, for my stay here is very uncertain. I am still living in the same sort of way as when I wrote to you last. Black men are living all round about me in huts and small houses. A Sipahi looks after my house and clothes, and a Chinese boy with shaven head and pigtail waits upon me at mess. Every morning the drums and fifes begin to play at five o'clock. This of course wakens me, and I get up and watch the rising sun while taking my coffee and cheroot. Till breakfast-time I study Hindustani, read and visit the hospital. Sometimes I take a walk into the city, but this is often very unpleasant in the early morning on account of the buckets of poo-poo which are generally at that time carried out to fertilise the fields. Poo-poo is a Chinese word, so expressive that I think it unnecessary to give you a translation. The Sipahis (Hindus) have a great horror of these buckets. I have seen an advancing column at review completely broken by the sudden upsetting of one of them. A fort composed of these instead of gabions would most effectually repulse all Sipahis. I made an excursion the other day to Whampoa, a town about ten miles down the river. I dined on board a man-of-war steamer, and after dinner had a delightful sail with some of the officers. The river at Whampoa is composed of a great number of channels separated by little hilly granite islands. The scenery is most beautiful, and as we approached the steamer the sunset was magnificent, reflecting a rich purple colour in the water, through which we were slowly and quietly gliding. Between Canton and Whampoa the banks of the river are low; in some places the river is somewhat above the overflown rice-fields, being separated from them by low embankments planted with rows of plantains, peaches, and lichens. The last of these is a delicious fruit, very abundant in China. The trees bear each four or five crops annually. The plantains can be made to bear fruit at any time of the year simply by cutting them down to the ground four months before the time the fruit is wanted. They always grow up and bear fruit in four months. This kind of husbandry would suit the Bow-begum[1] nicely. There is some talk of this regiment being sent to Aden, but I am afraid that it is not true. If I am sent there it will suit us splendidly for our projected excursion. I should only be a fortnight's distance from England. I am always longing to see you all again."

[1] Our sister Isabella.

Mother is always in my thoughts. I am sorry I have no portrait of her. Could you get one done on paper, and send it me in a letter?

P.S.—I shall write to mother next mail, but she must consider other letters that I send home as equally intended for her. Give kind messages from me to John, George, and their families. Wilhelmina's portrait decorates the wall of my hut. I enclose you a drawing of Chinese tracery used for window, brickwork, gratings, etc.

TO HIS MOTHER.

CANTON, *July* 21*st*, 1859.

I HAVE scarcely time to write you a letter, but I must send you a few lines. The post leaves unexpectedly to-day, and I have only three-quarters of an hour to write my letter, and carry it to the post, which is a mile from here. We have just heard bad news from Pekin. The ambassador has been fired upon, 400 of his men killed and wounded, and several gunboats destroyed. The war in China has therefore recommenced. Fresh troops have been sent for from India, and I shall no doubt remain in China a year or two longer. We are expecting that our small force here will be shortly attacked, but I do not think the Chinese here have any chance of success. It is sad to think of the terrible slaughter of Chinese that must follow their outrage on our ambassador. As in all wars, the poor innocent people suffer most, whilst the rulers, who by their stupidity have brought on the war, escape.

TO L.

July 31*st*, **1859.**

I HAVE received by the last mail letters from William and Allie, announcing the death of our old friend Mr. Pow. We have all lost a sincere friend, and the thought that I shall never see the good kind man again is very depressing to me. I felt on leaving England that I was bidding him a final farewell, and with that feeling wrote him a letter from London; but still I did not realise the loss so vividly as I do now. Mother must feel it very much, and Etal Villa must be very different now that he is no longer there. I lead a quiet solitary life here, and I fancy think more about you all than if I were actually living with you, and I sympathise very fully with all your sorrows. The Sipahis are very healthy, as a rule, and at present I have only ten patients in a hospital not fifty yards from my hut. You may imagine how much time I have to myself. I am contented with my life; there is much to interest me, and the scenery is beautiful, but I feel that I am too far from home. I have nothing to annoy me in the way of practice, and the officers of the regiment seem all glad to have me with them. You have no doubt read of the disaster at Pekin. It affects us considerably, and will probably detain us a year or two longer in China, as nothing more will be done this year unless the French come in force from Cochin-China. I hope I may go with the next expedition to Pekin, but I am afraid the Sipahis will not be sent, as they suffer so much by the sea-voyage. Their religion does not allow them to cook at sea, and they consequently live entirely on uncooked rice, and a grain like dried peas. When they get ashore after a fortnight's voyage they are like skeletons, and perfectly helpless. I do not think that the feeling of the Indians towards Europeans is at all altered by the mutiny. The charm which old General Benson used to talk of is simply fear, and they dread us as much now, if not more, than formerly. They have always been slaves governed by tyrants, and I fancy they will always continue to be so. They have many good qualities, but are quite wanting in boldness and determination.—easily excited, and, like women, capable of doing most horrible deeds when their passions are roused. I have just received orders to proceed and take charge of the hospital at Stanley, Hong-Kong, and as I have very little time to pack up my things and prepare for my journey, I must conclude this note and write you more fully another time. I enclose two pairs of Chinese slippers for Allie.

TO HIS MOTHER.

STANLEY, *September.*

My life is very unvaried and solitary here, and as I have no friends to talk to you about, have already described the place and spoken of the character of the people, I find some difficulty in getting material to fill up a letter. It seems superfluous to send loving messages so far across the seas. You know well how I love you, and may feel sure that my solitary life here intensifies my affection for you by giving me so much time for thinking of the love you have felt and shown to me from my birth. I know you would feel unhappy if I did not send a letter to some of you by every mail, and therefore I have carefully done so. . . . This short note had better be allowed to wear itself out along with the old vinaigrette, pencil-case, etc., in the depths of the old pocket so familiar to me.

TO HIS SISTER.

STANLEY HOSPITAL, *August 27th,* 1859.

... You are mistaken in thinking me unfortunate in being sent to China. It has always been my wish to see as much of the world as possible; and now you see I am getting it gratified, and, besides, I am better off here than if I were in India. I have a large hospital entirely to myself, for there is no other doctor here, excepting a native, who executes my orders. I assure you this kind of practice suits me much better than private practice in England. I am far removed from that wicked place (as you call it) Hong-Kong, or more properly Victoria, which is the only part of the island inhabited by English. There are about 1000 Chinese huddled up together in a small village here by the sea-side, but the greater part of the island is uninhabited and uncultivated—not because it is so very barren, but because the Chinese as a rule only cultivate very fertile flat land. The hills are generally made use of for burying the dead, and the spots are chosen which command the finest views. The village of Chuckchu, called by the English Stanley, is exactly like all the Chinese villages I have seen. They all consist of one narrow flagged street, with others running at right angles from it. The houses have generally only one story, and are all alike, but the street walls of adjacent houses are never in the same line, on account of some superstition. The temples or joss-houses are generally outside the villages. Chuckchu stretches along the sea-beach, and the waves absolutely wash the foundations of the houses. There are two very pretty joss-houses built among the rocks by the sea at some distance from the village, which, seen from the exterior, are very picturesque objects, but they are full of ugly gods and all sorts of rubbish put there by the villagers as votive offerings. Generally, on a sort of altar, one finds a few cups of tea, spirit, and edibles put there for Buddha, but generally eaten by the priest. The villagers and common people are very superstitious. They are always talking about devils and ghosts, and make most horrible noises with drums and gongs to frighten them off. In remote villages the children really think that we are devils, and directly they see us run screaming away. This is no doubt the effect of their superstitious education, and soon wears off when they become acquainted with us. It will perhaps amuse you to hear what sort of a life I lead here. I have a little bungalow to myself on the top of a hill. From the window on each side I have magnificent views of mountains, islands, and sea. There are two largish rooms, one which I use as a dining-room, and the other as a study and for my bed during the day, and on stormy nights. Generally I reverse the European order of things, and use my house only in the day-time. Besides these two rooms, I have a bath-room and servants' rooms. A broad verandah nearly surrounds the house; the kitchen, stables, etc., are outhouses detached, but only a few yards distant. In the way of servants, I have a Chinese boy and cook, and a few Sipahis to look after my rooms and go messages. The Sipahis I employ rather for their good than for my own. They have nothing besides to do, and they like to wait upon me, so I consent to be waited upon. I do not give myself up entirely to laziness, as you were afraid I should do, but take plenty of exercise—swimming, walking, etc. While in the house, however, I fully appreciate the luxury of being waited upon. If I had a wife with me to talk to, and enjoy life along with me, I should consider myself among the most fortunate of men. As it is, life often is dreary, and being always with Chinamen and Indians is almost the same as living in a desert island.

Sept. 11th.—The weather of late has been tremendously stormy, and I have often feared that my little house was coming down. One typhoon carried away part of my roof. At these times of the year the Chinese Sea is very dangerous. The steamboat in which I came from Calcutta went down the other day, and among others the captain, a very nice man, was lost. His wife and family are in the Isle of Man, and he was expecting to realise a fortune shortly, and to return to them.

It is reported that troops from England are to be here in February, and in that case we shall be sent to India, for the Sipahis do not bear this climate well. The climate of Hong-Kong seems to have a very bad effect on the health of most people. Persons rarely stay here more than five years; many die, and the most look pale and sickly. It suits me, however, remarkably well. I am as well now as ever I was in my life. After I had been at Canton a month, I had fever and became very thin, but since I came here I have got strong and healthy. The sea-bathing, I fancy, has a great deal to do with this. You people who live in cold climates can have no idea of the luxury of bathing and washing in the tropics. It is a misfortune that on account of the sun we cannot bathe in the day-time. I always bathe before sunrise and after sunset. The sun, even immediately it rises, has tremendous power at this time of the year. I am now very careful not to expose myself unnecessarily, for I believe that my slight fever at Canton arose from my exertions in catching a very beautiful butterfly when the sun was straight over my head.

I am very desirous of going to Japan while I am in this

neighbourhood, and am in hopes that if I stay here five or six months more I shall be able to do so. At present there is no one to take my place, so there is no means of obtaining leave. None of the English army doctors can speak Hindustani. I am glad to hear that you find my letters interesting, for I considered they were rather dull productions. You never speak of Fanny, Wag, and Romulus,[1] in your letters. It is pleasant to hear about everything in any way connected with home. I have two little Chinese dogs, one black and one white, called respectively Quei and Chou, who are amusing companions to me.

P.S.—I should like the *Revue des Deux Mondes* sent to me by post. Will you order it of Williams and Norgate? Read it yourself and then send it to me.

TO HIS BROTHER.

STANLEY HOSPITAL, *Oct.* 18*th*, 1859.

YOU ask me in your letter if I think that the weakness of the Chinese Government has been caused by the English making it contemptible in the eyes of the people. This may possibly be accelerating its downfall, but independently it has for some long time been declining, and appears to be doomed. I have a suspicion that the lying and thieving that goes on everywhere in high quarters may be the result of choosing merely very clever men for judges and high official posts throughout the land. The chief qualification, and what often decides the result of a competitive examination, is good handwriting, and consequently no end of pains is spent in attaining perfection in this. Their religion, like the old Brahma religion of India, was originally excellent, but, like the Indian religion, has become of none effect —obscured and almost drowned in superstition and absurd ceremonies.

The Chinese have one great fault, and that is their exclusivism and contempt of foreigners. This feeling, which is fostered and encouraged by the Government, is the cause of the English thinking much worse of the Chinese than they deserve, for foreigners are treated most unjustly by them, and Chinese who are connected in any way with the "foreign devils," as they call us, are treated equally badly, and are looked upon as traitors. The consequence is that most of the English out here only remark this injustice, and don't care to observe the manner in which the Chinese deal with each other. If they extended their observations further they would form a better opinion of Chinese legislation and manners. I have been much pleased by watching

[1] The pony and dogs at Derwent Bank.

the behaviour of the poorer classes towards each other. On the river at Canton, which is crowded with boats of all descriptions, continually jostling each other, one sees feeble old women and children pulling about, and everywhere, notwithstanding the bustle, meeting with the greatest courtesy and consideration. I have scarcely seen any quarrelling, and that little never extended beyond words. Since I came to China I have never seen one man strike another. I do not believe there is any country in the world where the ties of relationship are so strong,—where there is so much paternal, filial, and brotherly affection. Much is done, and with a certain amount of success, to make this family feeling, as it were, extend throughout the whole empire, and so to bind all the people together into one great family, of which the Emperor is the head or father. Probably if the Emperor were a pure Chinaman, and not a Tartar, this idea would be more realised than it is at present.

With respect to intercourse with the English, I am disposed to think that, notwithstanding the bad conduct of some of our countrymen, they are beginning to respect us more than formerly, and as they get to know more of us this respect will increase.

The mass of the people have been kept in the dark, or rather misled regarding us. Lying accounts of us and our actions have always been published, and any more enlightened Chinaman venturing to question the truth of these has been looked upon as a traitor. Books on Vaccination and Astronomy, published in Chinese, have been immediately secured and republished by Chinese governors without acknowledgment, in order to keep people in the dark as to the attainments of the English, and to extend their own reputation. The Emperor in his edicts has been in the habit of calling us devils, and saying that it would be absurd to administer justice to us in the same way as to Chinamen. Notwithstanding the way in which they have been incited to behave badly towards us, many Chinamen have been most particular in keeping their word, and have often acted most honourably. Religion is in almost the same condition as in Italy. Perhaps the common people may be a little more superstitious here. The Buddhists here have a Queen of Heaven, a species of Trinity, say their prayers in an unknown language, count them with beads, tinkle bells, go through numberless genuflexions; the priests practise celibacy; many women become nuns, and live in convents. Indulgences are granted for money and meritorious acts, and a purgatory is anticipated after death. The better educated despise all this, and simply revere Confucius, who confessed that he knew very little about the gods or a future life; but recommended men "to do to others as they would be done by," to reverence their parents and governors, to look with respect on learned men and farmers, and to tolerate manufacturers and merchants. The mere possession of money does not command so much respect as in other countries. The missionaries here, I am sorry to say, are not prepossessing. I often see them riding about in Hong-Kong, carried in chairs by coolies. The Roman Catholic missionaries are bolder and more energetic. Some of the Protestants are, I believe, most industrious, sincere, energetic men, but their labour is lost.

TO HIS SISTER.

STANLEY, *Nov.* 10*th*, 1859.

SOMETIMES I am afraid that you may find inconsistency in my letters when I speak of the Chinese and people about me. This arises partly from my opinions becoming modified as I become better acquainted with the people. Sometimes perhaps the inconsistency is only apparent, and might be made clear by a fuller explanation, which would be tedious in a letter. We have just received news from England *via* Bombay. The Peiho disaster seems to be causing some excitement, and I suppose now troops will certainly be sent to march on Pekin. I am satisfied now to stay in China to see the end of the war, although I am sorry that England is in such a fix that she is almost obliged to undertake the war. I see that the *Times* says the war must be pursued vigorously for the "interests of commerce and humanity." No doubt the interests of Jardine, Dent, and other rich Chinese merchants will be much promoted, but I cannot see how the interests of humanity will be furthered by causing anarchy in an empire where 300,000,000 enjoy at present, in tolerable security, the fruit of their labour. Thousands of innocent people will be killed before we reach Pekin, and there will be devastation and misery of families to a terrible extent. There is no knowing what may be the result of taking Pekin. A bad, though the best of Asiatic governments, may be destroyed thereby, and China may become another turbulent Hindustan, infested by robber chiefs. All that we shall gain by taking Pekin will be a quantity of booty for our soldiers, and a treaty which will be broken as soon as the army leaves China. The expenses of the war will be for ourselves, for the Chinese neither can nor will pay. I am tolerably well now, and feel that I have got safely through my first year, for the weather is quite cold, and at night I am obliged to use blankets. We shall not now have any rain, damp, or heat for five or six months. At present the climate is delicious, like September in England. You see I am still at Stanley, and am hoping that the hospital may not be broken up for some time yet. I felt heartily sick of the East about a week ago, when I was passing a sleepless night with no one to keep me company. How I longed to be at home, and how I thought continually of Shields, Derwent Bank, and you all. With health all my determination has come back again; I must try India before I return.

Nov. 13th.—I was hoping to have seen some letters from you before finishing this, but the mail, from some reason or other, has not yet arrived, and the homeward-bound mail is going off. Two European regiments have just arrived from India, and I am afraid my patients will be turned out to make room for them, and I shall be sent back again either to Canton or Hong-Kong.

TO HIS MOTHER.

STANLEY HOSPITAL, *Nov. 27th*, 1859.

I AM still at Stanley, and possibly may remain until the expedition starts for the north, which it will not do probably before the end of February. The climate of Pekin is excessively cold during winter, much too severe for campaigning. Lord Clyde has written from India to recommend that the native regiments be sent. Of course I shall be glad to go, but I doubt the prudence of sending native troops, for while on board of ship the Hindus are forbidden by their religion to eat any cooked food. They eat nothing but uncooked rice and peas, and in consequence some die, and the rest when they arrive at their destination are so thin and feeble that it is a long time before they are fit for duty. It takes a long time for a Hindu to recover his health, for they eat nothing but vegetables, and make but one meal in the twenty-four hours. Their religion interferes very much with my treatment of them when they are sick. Many of them, even when dying, will persist in cooking for themselves, and this with them is a very long process. In the cold weather they strip themselves almost naked, then wash, and without drying or putting on their clothes, set to work to make a fireplace of clay, which must be made afresh every day. You may imagine of how little use it is to give medicines to patients of this sort. They are not all so unmanageable. I have induced some of them, by giving extras such as sugar and sago, to take an extra meal. These take wine, under the name of the red medicine. The carefulness and economy of the Hindus surpass anything I ever heard of. They starve themselves for the sake of saving, and delight in continually talking to each other of their dollars. I have a very honest, simple Hindu to look after my things. He has my keys in his possession, and keeps everything clean and in the most perfect order, keeping a sharp look-out that the Chinese boys and other people coming about steal nothing. His especial delight is polishing my sword and gun, that being connected with his own profession. He is a Sipahi. The lower castes are much given to drinking and other vices of Europeans. Lest you should be anxious about my health I will tell you exactly how I am. For the last two months I have had attacks of remittent fever every fortnight at regular intervals, but they have been becoming each time less severe, and it is now a fortnight since I had my last attack, and I have only a slight feeling of illness with headache, which makes me think I have got over the fever.[1] The weather is now occasionally quite cold, and there will be no more hot weather for months.

TO HIS BROTHER.

HONG-KONG, *Dec.* 29*th.*

THE *Free Press* and Mr. Attwood's speech arrived all safe. Certainly opinions about the Chinese are very contradictory, but assuredly no one who has studied our dealings with the Chinese can come to any other conclusion than that we have acted disgracefully throughout, and if anything worse than the Chinese, who are not altogether without blame, but they always have the excuse that they warned us to keep off them, and never wished to have any dealings with us. At one time, there can be no doubt, the Chinese were a very grand nation. Not all the trickery, lying, and degeneracy, together with the bad government of modern times, can annihilate the good works of the ancients. The good foundation laid by these still holds together the vast empire. But there is no doubt that everything is degenerating. They cannot now make the porcelain, nor colour it, as they did formerly. The absurdities of Buddhism have very much taken the place of the good moral practical religion of Confucius and Mencius. Still there is hope for them, for they practically acknowledge how they have fallen by the value they set upon old works of art, and the immense respect they pay to their ancient authors. The common people about here are much given to lying and deceit in their dealings with us, and although this cannot be carried on to the same extent as in their dealings with each other, still I believe in honesty and straightforwardness they are much inferior to English peasantry.

---

[1] How lightly he tells of these wasting fevers! How sick and lonely he must have felt in that hospital, without a single European near him, he that was so loved and longed for at home!

But China is an immense country, and it does not do to judge of the whole by what one sees in the south, any more than it would do to judge of Europe by what one sees of Greece. I should like you to give Mr. Pow's legacy to me to whatever charity or public object in Shields you think most worthy, or to the encouragement of art.

TO L.

STANLEY, *Dec.* 7*th*, 1859.

I AM much pleased with the portrait of Wag. He seems to have aged a great deal since I saw him last, but this may arise perhaps from the photograph rendering his yellow and tan whiter than they really are. I have exactly the same feeling as yourself about writing what has to be read three months afterwards, and that I am at such a distance from home, that as far as concerns my friends I might as well be dead, but still I have the consoling reflection (which buoys me up) that it cannot last long, that sooner or later I shall return to India, and that there it will only require a fortnight to send a communication from one to the other. Within a few years perhaps communication may be much more rapid.

I should enjoy being along with my friends, English society and comforts, much more perhaps than living this solitary life; but still when I am free from fever I lead a tolerably happy sort of life, and have the satisfaction of feeling that I work for my pay, and in a humble way am of some use to the world. At present there is no one in China to take my place here, so that if I applied to return I should not get leave for a month or two at least. Besides, now that I am in China, I think it would be a pity to sacrifice the chance of seeing Pekin, and perhaps other places. From what I hear I shall like India as a residence better than China. Here there are no good horses or roads, and no plains to ride over. The narrow paths are all flagged, slippery, and only fit for foot-passengers. It is also very unpleasant to be obliged to carry a revolver, and to be continually on the look-out for Chinamen coming to chop off your head, which they do as a pure matter of business, without any revengeful feeling, but merely for the sake of the reward offered by the mandarins.

I find plenty to occupy me. I have ninety patients in hospital, and these, with reports, official letters, etc., take up a good deal of time. The rest of my time I spend in studying Hindustani, and in translating a German book. The weather occasionally feels very cold now, although the thermometer has not as yet been below 57°. I keep a fire burning, and have two blankets over me at night.

Dec. 12th.—I am just going to walk to Victoria where I have to attend a court-martial, and where I shall put this letter in the post.

TO HIS SISTER.

Dec. 27th.

I RECEIVED a letter from mother by the last mail. The sight of her dear handwriting was a great delight to me in this remote solitary place. You can scarcely imagine with how great a longing I look forward to the arrival of the mails. You are a capital correspondent; continue to write at least once a month, and remember that a short letter is better than none at all. Remember to give my love to mother, Isabella, and all the children.

TO THE SAME.

STANLEY, *Dec. 27th*, 1859.

It is to be hoped that our difference with China will be arranged soon, and therefore the letter of introduction to Sir Hope Grant will arrive too late. But letters of introduction are of little use here; one easily becomes acquainted with whomsoever one wishes, and in the course of conversation one easily finds out about mutual acquaintances. Many of the officers are expecting that we shall all be sent to India as soon as the Sikhs arrive, but I doubt that. Both officers and men are anxious to return; the men especially, because many of them are uncertain as to what has become of their wives, children, and property during the time of the mutiny. Probably many on returning will find all gone—a terrible prospect, which you people in England can scarcely realise.

The little village of Chechii here has been in a state of great excitement, and very gay for the last few days. A large theatre has been erected with bamboos and matting close to the principal joss-house, and a company of actors 100 strong, has been performing to the great delight of the inhabitants and of visitors who have come from neighbouring villages and islands. The performances have been kept up continually from morning till late at night, only allowing a short interval for dinner. I of course went once or twice to see what sort of performance it was. The scenery was rude and very simple, after the nature of the by-play in the Midsummer Night's

Dream. Chairs, tables, etc., were made to represent doors, walls, etc.; their intention being intimated to the public by notices stuck upon them. The pieces performed were something like operas; they seemed to me to be in verse, and were sung in a sort of way with a clanging brassy (I cannot say musical) accompaniment, and every now and then a letting off of gunpowder crackers. The pieces that I saw seemed to be historical, for the magnificent satin and embroidered costumes of some of the actors clearly showed that they were taking the part of Emperors, judges, and high dignitaries, and these were followed often by long trains of soldiers and standard-bearers. Occasionally there were fights and battles, and these opportunities were taken for showing the acrobatic skill of the actors. I found the performance rather tedious, but the Chinese spectators seemed highly interested and delighted. They could not understand what was said, for the actors spoke in the Mandarin dialect, which is quite distinct; occasionally, however, a few words of explanation were given in the regular tongue, and sometimes a joke, which set the house into ecstasies of delight. The theatre was arranged somewhat like an English one, with a raised stage, pit, and gallery on each side—right for women and left for men.

TO HIS MOTHER.

HONG-KONG, *Jan.* 31*st*, 1860.

IN my letter by the last mail I said that I would write next time to you, so I now set to work to perform my promise. In writing all my letters to William, however, I have felt that I was at the same time writing to you, and that you would read them with as much pleasure as he. The English mail has not yet arrived, so that I have had no news from home since I last wrote. I have been at Hong-Kong with the 47th regiment B. N. I. for a fortnight. I like my quarters very well. All the officers live together in barracks, and from morning till evening are continually playing, laughing, and talking. I lead a very different life from my quiet one at Stanley. The change is rather pleasant, and does me good. I have medical charge of the 47th and of a portion of the 65th regiment, *i.e.* of all the black troops at Hong-Kong. There are about twelve officers, whom I like very well. We hear that the whole of the Bengal brigade is going back to India in about a fortnight. It is to be relieved by the troops from Bombay. Thus I expect to be back again at Calcutta about the end of February. I would much rather stay in China a little longer, but shall be obliged to return with my regiment. If the Sikhs arrive before the

Bombay regiments, I shall try to exchange with some one so as to try to accompany the Sikhs to Pekin, but I scarcely hope to be able to do this. You had better address my letters now to Calcutta, but at the same time send a short note to Hong-Kong to let me know that you are all going on well, in case I should still be here. The weather here is exceedingly changeable just now. Sometimes it is so warm at night that I sleep without clothes; at other times it is so cold that we sit comfortably warming ourselves over the fire. The sun is always very powerful. I enjoy being able to take plenty of exercise, rowing about the harbour, which is very picturesque and beautiful, surrounded on all sides by high rugged mountains, and full of magnificent English ships and curious Chinese junks.

TO H.

Hong-Kong, *March 15th*, 1860.

WE are still in a state of uncertainty here, but there is no doubt but we shall be off shortly, for the regiment is in orders to go to a station about twenty miles from Benares. The whole of the Chinese Bengal brigade has to be stationed in that neighbourhood, so I shall feel quite at home when I get back to India. They say that it is an excellent station, a beautiful country, full of game of all sorts. Send me a gun when you have any ships going to Calcutta. Ships full of troops are arriving daily, and Hong-Kong is now full of soldiers. Sir Hope Grant arrived by this mail, and the French Commander-in-chief by the last. Every one thinks that the Chinese will fight, and no doubt there will be terrible slaughter, and I am afraid for no good result. A coolie corps is being organised at Hong-Kong. Major Temple, a Madras officer belonging to our mess, is at the head of it. They will shortly have about 10,000 men, all Chinese, who will accompany the forces to the north. It is to be hoped that they will not revolt when there, for if they do the army will be left destitute of transport. Horses are not used here as beasts of burden. Immense weights are always carried on men's shoulders, balanced with bamboos.

TO HIS SISTER.

Hong-Kong, *March 28th*, 1860.

... One cannot help feeling sorry for the poor innocent Chinamen who are going to be slaughtered for obeying the Emperor, whom they look upon as a sort of compound of father and God. Here the Chinamen are far from being ill-disposed towards us. Thousands of coolies have been engaged as a transport corps to the expedition. In the north probably the people are more loyal than to aid the foreigners in fighting against their Emperor. Troops from India and France are arriving, and Hong-Kong is now full of soldiers. Two regiments went to Chusan a few days ago, with orders to take possession of the island, and to fight should any resistance be made. The French had intended to occupy that island, and therefore our troops were sent immediately to forestall them. A portion of the mainland on the opposite side of this harbour has also been annexed by the English in order to keep the French at a distance. We have just heard from the north that the Emperor is wishing for peace, has offered to apologise and to allow the ambassador to go to Pekin. I hope the news is true, and that his terms will be accepted, for I cannot see that any good will come from the war. My old regiment, the 70th, has been relieved, and will shortly be on its way to India. The 47th and the 65th go next. Most probably my next letter to you will be addressed from Calcutta. We are ordered to go to Jaunpore and Azimghur, two stations in the neighbourhood of Benares. It is not certain that I shall remain with the 47th, but I hope to march up country with it. I have received the first four numbers of the *Revue*, and read it with interest. I am glad to see that both you and L. read it. It represents the thoughts and feelings of the best and most intelligent Frenchmen, and shows that the two nations are not so antagonistic as many people suppose. It is curious to observe how the reviewers manage to say the most severe things of the Government without rendering themselves liable to prosecution. They always seem to me to be saying to the Emperor: "If the cap fits," etc. The weather here is still cool and pleasant, not too cold to prevent me having my doors and windows open day and night. The officers are all very healthy, with the exception of those given to drink. I never had such a horror of drinking as I have now. Fortunately now it is considered disreputable to drink, and is going quite out of fashion. I think I shall succeed in making one officer here a teetotaler. Formerly one would have been laughed at for attempting such a thing. I have lately been investing my surplus cash in buying Japanese things to send home when I have an opportunity. The things they make are very beautiful; and they have been much sought after by the English to send home as presents.

TO HIS MOTHER.

"DALHOUSIE" STEAMSHIP-OF-WAR,
CHINA SEA, *April 19th*, 1860.

I HAVE been at sea now just one week, and expect to arrive at Singapore to-morrow, when I shall post this note. As yet we have had a very pleasant voyage. The weather has all along been perfectly fine, and for the last three days there has not been a breath of wind. As we pass rapidly through the air we do not complain much of the heat. We all sleep on deck at night without blankets. At mid-day the glare is horrible: the sea being perfectly smooth, like a glass, reflects all the light from the sky. Near the horizon it appears quite white like molten iron, and cannot be distinguished from the sky. Our band plays on the poop every evening, and we sit listening, smoking cheroots, in Chinese easy-chairs, which are about the most comfortable kind of chair that has ever been invented. I have a tolerably good cabin, and enjoy the voyage pretty well, but shall be glad when it is over, for I never feel comfortable or clean at sea. The 47th was the last regiment of the Royal Brigade to leave China. Now the 65th, 70th, and 47th are all at sea. Probably we shall be the first to arrive at Calcutta, because we have the fastest steamer. We may possibly all march up country together to Benares, which will be pleasant, for I have many friends in the other regiments. You remember I have been attached to both of them before my appointment to the 47th. I felt quite sorry to leave Hong-Kong, for I enjoyed my life there very much. I have seen few more picturesque places. The harbour is as fine as any in the world, and the scenery round about, although barren, is very magnificent. Many friends came on board to bid us good-bye. The vibration of the screw prevents me from writing distinctly. I hope you will be able to decipher it, however. Give my love to William, and tell him I approve of his building cottages for the workmen, and of his making use of my money for the purpose.

TO HIS BROTHER.

CALCUTTA, *May 13th*, 1860.

As I sent a letter from Singapore to mother, I shall merely tell you what has happened to me since then. We had to stay for a week at Singapore before we could get coals to supply us to Calcutta. The number of steamers going to China has almost exhausted the supply of coal there. Our Sepoys were delighted to get ashore, for their caste prevents them from cooking on board ship, and consequently they had been even on harder fare than you on your voyage to Barcelona. It was a great treat to me also. The luxuriant verdure of Singapore was delightful and refreshing to our eyes after the long voyage. I enjoyed walking about in the cool cocoa-nut groves, and feasted on delicious pine-apples and cocoa-nut milk. We were about eight days in coming here from Singapore. On arriving we were immediately ordered to occupy tents pitched for us on the Maidan or common of Calcutta. I have a tent there, but the sun is so powerful that I prefer living with Cowan, who has a nice house a little out of Calcutta. The cholera is raging in Calcutta, and as it has also broken out in the regiment, I have a good deal to do. We are expecting to go up country in a few days.

TO HIS SISTER.

RANEGUNGE, *May* 21*st*, 1860.

I HAVE now travelled about one hundred miles on my way up country, and am settled for a few days at this place until the bullock train can be got ready to convey us on to Benares. We came up very pleasantly and quickly by the railway from Calcutta, but still the scenery, being different from anything I have seen before, interested me. The country is very fertile, and mostly covered with a thick luxuriant jungle. Here and there the land is cultivated roughly, and there are lots of populous villages, but the inhabitants seem to be poor, and live in wretched mud huts. The Bengalis are much less civilised than the Chinese. Their boats, houses, etc., are rotten and tumbling to pieces; and the people, although they have perhaps (according to our ideas) finer features, are much less intelligent-looking, and have a less human way of doing everything than the Chinese. Ranegunge at present is the terminus of the East Indian Railway. It is a wretched enough place; everything is dry, burnt up, and dusty; the earth feels and smells like burning hot bricks. In fact, the top of a burning brick-kiln is cool in comparison with Ranegunge. In my house, which is well sheltered, the thermometer stands at 112°. Fortunately the air at present is exceedingly dry; if it were damp the heat would be unendurable. I leave this place to-morrow evening by the bullock train, and expect to be at Benares in a fortnight. We only travel at night, and at an average rate of two miles an hour. I have a fine horse ahead, which I bought at Calcutta, and intend to ride him occasionally by the way. The road between this and Benares I hear is very beautiful. From Ranegunge I can see the dim outlines of mountains through the dust, and long to be amongst them. The water is delicious. I never enjoyed drinking pure water so much in my life as I do now.

P.S.—The sun is so powerful that my whiskers are actually singed and brittle.

TO HIS SISTER.

JAUNPORE, *June* 23*d*, 1860.

BENARES did not come up to my expectations. The cantonments and English part of the town have a barren dreary look from the want of trees and hedges, and from the houses being all alike, and from the compounds being divided off by mudwalls. (The compound is a space of ground surrounding an Indian bungalow, on which stables and outhouses are built.) The English station occupies a great deal of ground; it is about three miles in diameter. Some of the houses are very good, and surrounded by well-kept gardens and pleasure-grounds. The house that Warren Hastings lived in has a fine portico with Doric pillars. In front of it there is a large horizontal sun-dial, which Warren Hastings himself caused to be erected. The pointer is about six feet high, built of stone. The native town is interesting and curious, but there are no fine monuments or temples of any considerable size. The Hindu temples are almost innumerable, but they are all shabby, mean, and small. One that is very famous is covered with gold. The houses are high, and the streets narrow and picturesque, like those of Cairo. Sacred bulls wander about them, and are much in the way. The city has a magnificent appearance when seen in the distance, as from the top of a minaret, but a nearer inspection disappoints. We left Benares about midnight, so as to reach our camping ground before sunrise. The regiment is about 600 strong, and all these went on foot. An advance guard consisting of about thirty men went on about 100 yards in front of the rest. The officers on horseback went between this and the main body, and behind followed the camels, elephants, and bullock-carts carrying the baggage and the sick men. Some elephants were sent ahead to carry our tents, so that they might be pitched before our arrival. The camping grounds by the way are all very much alike; there is generally a village and a tank near, and the tents are pitched in a grove of mango-trees, so that they may be sheltered from the sun. This is the season for mangos, and we ate lots of them by the way. Three days' marching brought us to Jaunpore. The day after our arrival I again commenced marching with 100 Europeans to Azimghur. We were four days on the march;

fortunately the rains were just beginning, and the weather was not very hot, so that I had no sick men. Once or twice we got thoroughly drenched with rain. In a hot country like this one does not care much about getting wet. On arriving at Azimghur I spent a very pleasant day with Captain Robert Peel, and the officers of the 13th, and then set off to return to Jaunpore, where I am now comfortably settled. Jaunpore is the prettiest place I have seen in India. The fields are, many of them, quite green, and the roads are beautifully sheltered by fine large trees. The church reminds me of an English village, but there is no clergyman resident. It is quite a small station; there are not more than half-a-dozen houses, and already I know every one. There are a number of indigo-planters in the district, with whom I suppose I shall soon become acquainted. The native town is very old and picturesque, but I have scarcely had time to explore it yet. There is a fine river running through the centre of it, and a massive bridge, which is proverbial through India for its strength.

TO HIS BROTHER.

JAUNPORE, *July 25th*, 1860.

I HOPE you have not been anxious at home on account of not receiving a letter by last mail. The reason that you did not receive a letter was that I put off writing till the last day, and then I had such a severe attack of fever that it was quite impossible for me to write. The weather this year is said to be very unhealthy. Old Indians say they never felt such heat. Cholera has carried off thousands in Jaunpore, and the European soldiers throughout India have been dying in great numbers, of apoplexy produced by the heat. Two of the officers of the 47th have been delirious from fever, and I myself was verging on that state. Now a considerable amount of rain has fallen, and the air has become cool. At night even I am obliged to cover myself with a blanket, but I am perhaps the only one here who does so, for my fever has made me extremely sensitive to cold. A fever pulls me down very quickly, but I recover almost as quickly, for already I am almost as well as ever. The worst part of the year is over now; we shall have no more very hot weather, and I hope I shall have no more fever. Two of our officers are in Japan. I had letters from both of them the other day. They are delighted with the place, and say it reminds them of England, the vegetables, trees, and climate being the same. The people, they say, are diminutive and ugly, and the women not half so nice as the Chinese. This is rather in contradiction to the glowing reports we used to read of Japan. Now that I have returned to India, I cannot help contrasting the Indians with the Chinese, and they suffer much in the contrast. The Chinese are the independent Englishmen of Asia, and the Indians the mean cowardly Greeks. I believe that the natives of India have nearly the same feeling towards us as before the mutiny. They always did and always will fear and hate us. All the cruelty, which was very great, exercised by English soldiers has not increased their dislike in the least. There is something peculiar about Asiatics, and in which they totally differ from Europeans. It is not an oppressive despotic government which makes them revolt, but a mild, lax one. However good the government may be, if the natives think it not sufficiently strong to resist them, they are sure to revolt, chiefly for the sake of plunder. It is a remarkable thing that all should be so quiet so soon after the mutiny. In travelling about alone here I feel as safe or safer than I would on a lonely road in England; yet there are no Europeans within thirty miles of this, and the Europeans in Jaunpore—magistrates, officers, etc.—are only fifteen in number.

Jaunpore at one time has been a most important city, one of the largest and richest in India. All round about it are ruined monuments, tombs, and wells; some of them beautifully designed, and all much in the same style. The Goomtee (the river of Lucknow) flows through the old city, and is crossed by a large massive bridge, with houses and shops on it. There is a fine picturesque old fort, but this has been nearly destroyed lately. The Rajah or king of this district is a little boy of about thirteen; he is under the protection of the English Government. I went to his palace the other day, and he went all over with me while I inspected all his curiosities and pictures. He is a fine little boy, but swaggers about a good deal, and thinks himself no end of a swell. He is going to learn English, and the Rance or queen, his mother, is in a state of great tribulation, for she says he is going to be made into an Englishman. The house is arranged in shocking bad taste. It is just like an old curiosity-shop, full of pianos, billiard-tables, musical clocks, etc., all huddled up together, and allowed to get dusty and go to ruin. The walls are covered with pictures; wretched Hindu daubs are put next to French and English engravings and oil-paintings.

TO HIS MOTHER.

JAUNPORE, *August* 11*th*, 1860.

... I was delighted to hear from Allie and William that you had returned from Derwent Bank looking so well and so much improved in health by your stay there. Next best to seeing you is to hear that you are well, for I like to think that when we meet again I shall not find you much altered. Get me another photograph of yourself on paper, coloured. Although I prize it highly, I am not satisfied with the likeness I have of you.

TO HIS SISTER.

JAUNPORE, *October* 1*st*, 1860.

I RECEIVE the *Revue des Deux Mondes* very regularly now, and still more regularly a letter from you every fortnight. I prize your letters so much that I am always fearing you may grow tired of continually writing, and so deprive me of one of my chief consolations in exile. . . . Though thousands of miles away from you, I am still always thinking about home, and the pleasure of meeting you again, and some day I hope we shall be together as we used to be.

I am now settled probably for some time at Jaunpore as civil surgeon. I shall in all probability be removed from the regiment, and transferred to the civil list. My pay is very good,—more than sufficient to keep me comfortable. Since the mutiny living is expensive in India, but by degrees I suppose things will return to their old prices. . . . I have to look after the dispensary and the jail, and the indigo-planters and rich natives occasionally send for me. The civilians in India are, as a rule, well-educated and agreeable. Now there are two kinds,—the old ones educated at Haileybury, and the new or Competition Wallahs, as they are called here. At this station we have specimens of each. Generally speaking, the Competition Wallah is not so well suited for his work as the other. The natives, as a rule, do not respect and fear him so much as the other, because he is less tyrannical, and has not the bodily activity which is so essential for the work he has to do.

TO HIS BROTHER.

JAUNPORE, *February* 1*st*, 1861.

. . . I was very much struck with the similarity of the Venetian architecture and that of Jaunpore; some of the arches and ornaments are so much alike that I think they must have been designed by the same architect. The buildings here are of more recent date than those of Venice, therefore probably some wandering Italian has designed them for one of the Mussulman emperors. I expect we shall shortly have a photographic apparatus in the station, and I shall be able to send you some photographs of the temples, etc. You have forgotten to send me the portrait of your wife. I am very anxious to see it. I am afraid it will be long before I see you and her together, but it will be a happy day for me when we all meet.

TO HIS SISTER.

JAUNPORE, *Feb.* 15*th*, 1861.

As you say, we are enjoying our winter. It is just like your summer; the garden is full of roses, mignonette, and all kinds of European flowers, all growing more luxuriantly than I have ever seen them in England; and the barley, wheat, etc., in the fields are just ready for the sickle. We have fires every night, but we shall soon be obliged to leave them off, for the sun is growing more powerful, and the winds are becoming warm. India suits me remarkably well during the cold weather, and a month of it is enough completely to re-establish my health, and make me as strong and fat as ever I was. The heat of summer even is not at all disagreeable when one has a good house; and if it were not for the fevers and the natives India would be a very endurable country. Your conversation with Mrs. S. amused me. She is quite right about the tyranny of the English in India, but I think she is wrong in blaming us for it. The rulers of India, I fancy, must always be tyrants, and it is a great mistake to fancy that India is governed according to the strictly written law. I have heard you speak with horror of the torture inflicted by Lord Clive and Warren Hastings. What would you say if I told you that even now torture is inflicted by Government officials to extort confessions? If you knew all that I know, I think you would be of the same opinion as Mrs. S.; but nevertheless you and she might give an incorrect judgment. The manners and deceit of the natives annoy my wife exceedingly. She cannot take it philosophically, and see that it is as much their nature as their black skin. She says: "Si je savais parler, je leur dirai: Vous êtes des voleurs." By the time she learns to speak their language she will know that such a reproach would be no reproach to them. They know it as well as we do, and are not ashamed. The judge's wife is a cousin of the Bushes, and the joint magistrate was a pupil of Mr. W. in Cumberland. Is it not curious that so many in such a small station should be connected with our friends in Cumberland? The assistant magistrate is a great friend of mine; he was at College with me in London. I like to hear of Wag and Rom.[1] Do you ever make Wag sit up in a pool of water to remind him of his old master? I have a fine large bloodhound that I am very fond of. His name is Jack, pronounced Jaques.

[1] The dogs.

TO HIS MOTHER.

JAUNPORE, *Feb.* 28*th*, 1861.

It is a long time since I have heard from you, but I have heard about you from William and Allie, and am glad to learn that you are bearing this severe winter better than usual. Now, while you are rejoicing at the approach of summer, we are beginning to regret the winter. We can no longer bear a fire, even at night, and soon shall be obliged to have the punkahs again. The winter here is a most delightful season. I wish you could come and spend it with us. You would be delighted to see how comfortably I am settled here, and would enjoy walking about in the garden. The Lieut.-Governor has just paid a visit to Jaunpore. He encamped not far from my house, and his camp was like a little city; he had hundreds of tents; elephants, camels, etc., without number. I dined with him once, and, although he was in camp, he had a magnificent display. He was very polite and amiable to me.

TO THE SAME.

JAUNPORE, *April* 30*th*, 1861.

As I have not written to you for some time, you will be thinking that I have grown lazy, or am becoming indifferent. This is not the case. I think of you as often and as much as ever, and shall never forget all your goodness and love. There are few Europeans in the station, and those few are continually changing. Already I am the oldest inhabitant. I had a great friend here named Young, assistant magistrate, but he has, unfortunately for me, just been removed to Allahabad, and I daresay it will be long before I see him again. In the cold weather he was out in camp about twenty miles from here. I used frequently to go out and spend a few days with him; he too used to come out and stay with me. I have got a good deal to do here, but am not overworked. The dispensary takes up a good deal of my time, and I am very much interested in it. Since I came here the number of patients has increased greatly, and in the last six months I have had more operations than my predecessors for twelve years. I tell you this to let you see that I am not leading a lazy life.

TO THE SAME.

JAUNPORE, *July* 19*th*, 1861.

I am afraid I am too late for the Bombay post, for the rains have rendered the roads very bad, and the post is consequently long in reaching Bombay, and may be too late for the steamer. During the last month we have had a great deal of rain, the river is consequently large and rapid, and much of the country is under water. I rode to Benares the other day (thirty-four miles) and came back the same day. The country was exceedingly beautiful. All the fields that a month ago had been barren and sandy were green and fresh with luxuriant crops; and the sky, instead of being of a uniform hue with a burning sun, as it usually is in this country, was covered with feathery clouds, which reminded me of England, and set me thinking of you and home. I was very glad to hear from Allie that you have been staying at Derwent Bank, and are enjoying such good health; but I was very sorry to hear of Mrs. Young's death, knowing what an old friend she is, and how much you must feel her loss. I drink nothing but water—no wine or spirits or beer, which is rather unusual in India, but suits me.

TO L.

JAUNPORE, *Aug. 2d*, 1861.

I READ the little extract about the Parsee doctor which you sent me; I have also read the discussion in Parliament on the subject. I fancy that you and I differ in our opinion on such a question, and the difference arises from the different atmosphere and people that surround us. In my opinion it would be a great mistake to allow natives of India to be either doctors or judges in this country. An assistant surgeon, a native, who was educated at University College, was turned out of the service for taking a bribe of ten rupees. I have never met a native whose word I would believe, if he could gain anything by telling a lie, and the judge of Jaunpore told me the other day that during the twenty years he has been in India he has only met with one native whom he would trust as he would an Englishman. I do not think that India can ever be governed by the same laws as England. It must either be governed despotically or abandoned. As soon as we have native judges and magistrates, the verdicts will always be given in favour of those who offer the highest bribe, and if Europeans are made subordinate to natives, they will soon cease to fear us; and as it is that fear alone which enables us to hold India, we shall be forced to give it up. The newspapers and people generally in India are talking about the probability of another revolt, but at present there is not the slightest danger, for the country is disarmed; and without arms of course the people can do nothing. The more I see of the natives, the more convinced I am that they thoroughly hate us and completely misunderstand our intentions towards them. This, to me, is the great drawback in India. It is impossible to feel kindly towards them, or to take much pleasure in doing them good, when one knows that their greatest delight would be to torture one to death. You used to teach me never to do good to any one for the sake of gratitude, and to tell me that he who does good expecting gratitude is sure to be disappointed. If this be true with regard to Europeans, it is doubly so with regard to natives of India, and a useful lesson for every one coming to India to learn. Notwithstanding this knowledge of ingratitude, I have a good deal of satisfaction in my practice, especially in surgery. Patients come from a great distance to undergo operations, and I take great interest in their cases. I have just established a branch dispensary about twenty miles from here, and have got an allowance from Government for keeping it up. To-morrow I am going to ride there to see how it is getting on and if there are any operations for me to perform. Two or three days ago I went to see a patient about twenty miles from here. I had to cross three large rivers, two of which were quite dry before the rains commenced. My patient is a rich indigo-planter, and has a very large establishment, which I was pleased to see. The road was so bad part of the way that I was obliged to ride upon an elephant, which was almost as fatiguing as walking. The country was looking very green and fresh from the rain. Every inch of land is cultivated, but there is no great variety of crops just now. Indian corn is more abundant than anything else; it is a very luxuriant-looking crop, standing about five feet high. In another fortnight it will probably be all cut, and the ground sown with either wheat, barley, cotton, or some grain of the pea or bean species. The first crop of indigo is being cut just now; it stands about two feet high, and looks very much like a luxuriant crop of tares. This was sown last year, and will be rooted up as soon as cut. The other crop was sown this year, and will yield again next year. I have sown a little field near my house with Indian corn, and in another month I intend sowing it with some grain for my horses. I have another field sown with grain for my poultry. By degrees I am extending my farming operations. Now I have about eighty Guinea chickens, besides ducks, hens, bullocks, horses, etc., all of which I intend to feed with the produce of my garden and field. This is such a quiet place, and I lead such a monotonous life, that I scarcely know what to tell you in my letters. Jaunpore at last has a clergyman, or a missionary, who preaches at the church. He is rather enthusiastic. He admits that he meets with no success to encourage him, or to assure him that his labour is not thrown away. He told me that he was almost indifferent as to the results of his preaching, being contented with doing what he thinks his duty.

TO HIS SISTER.

JAUNPORE, *Nov. 8th,* 1861.

I SHALL give you a short account of my journey to Allahabad, so that you may know something about travelling in India. Mr. Lind and I started from Jaunpore about two o'clock in the afternoon in a dog-cart, and drove to a town called Muchliohahi, about twenty miles from here. For this distance we had two horses; each horse doing about seven miles. In India people rarely drive a horse more than eight miles. At Muchliohahi we got into palkees (palanquins), and were carried to a place called Badshapore, about twelve miles from Muchliohahi. To carry us this distance we had each eight bearers and a torch-bearer. At Badshapore we put up with the joint magistrate Mr. Jenkinson, who was encamped there. Jenkinson was a pupil of Mr. Webster's at Portinscale. He is a remarkably clever, active officer. Perhaps it would interest Mr. Webster to hear that his pupil is highly esteemed. We passed the night with Jenkinson, and next morning early started on horseback, rode for about ten miles, and then drove the rest of the way, about twenty miles, to Allahabad, where we arrived about ten o'clock. Allahabad is at the angle formed by the Ganges and Jumna; consequently we had to cross the former river—anything but a pleasant business. Just now the river is low, and we soon got across it by a bridge of boats, but the dried bed of the river was the difficulty. This was loose sand, into which the horse sank to his knees, and the wheels up to their axles. It was hot when we crossed. In the month of June this must be a terrible place. The sand here, I am told, in 1857 was strewn with bodies of Europeans carried down from Cawnpore. Now the crocodiles sun themselves on it, and lazily slide into the water when any one approaches. The serjeant who has charge of the bridge told me that a few days ago he saw a native fall into the river; he disappeared at once, and nothing more was seen of him but his blood, which stained the water. He was crunched by a crocodile certainly. The river was running rapidly when we crossed, and straining the cables which held the bridge of boats; the rushing of the water was like a cascade. Shortly after we crossed, an enormous boat containing grain got into the current, and the sailors were quite unable to steer it. The stream carried it at a tremendous pace right down upon the bridge of boats, which of course gave way, and the bridge of boats, etc., was a complete wreck in a minute. In an hour the whole was buried in the quicksands, and the owner of the boat had a bill of £1000 to pay, besides the loss of his boat and cargo. At Allahabad I put up with my friend Mr. Young, the joint magistrate there. We had just time for breakfast and to put on our tail-coats and drive to the Governor-General's tent. There the Governor-General was seated on a gilded throne, looking very regal. The Lieut.-Governor was on his left hand, and the Commander-in-chief on his right. Then came the three Rajahs—Puttiola, Rampore, and Scindia—and the old Begum, all in very "gorgeous array." Lord Canning conducted himself in a most dignified manner, and made a good speech in a distinct, clear voice. His secretary translated the speech very badly into Hindustani, and then each Rajah in turn was endued with the "Star of India."

CHAPTER V.

LETTERS FROM NEW ZEALAND AND INDIA.

"He, the young and strong who cherished
Noble longings for the strife."

TO HIS MOTHER.

SYDNEY, *March* 30*th*, 1862.

WE arrived at Sydney harbour yesterday, and as the mail for England goes to-morrow, I hasten to write a few lines to let you know that we have safely got thus far on our way to New Zealand. Throughout the voyage we had fine weather; once we were on the outside of a hurricane, but the captain managed to keep clear of it. We were also in a gale, which however was in our favour, and carried us through the water at a tremendous pace. We passed our time in reading and playing at chess, but still it hung heavy, and we were very glad when any extraordinary event, such as the catching of a shark or of a large sea-bird took place, to relieve the monotony of the voyage. The most exciting event was the sight of land, as we approached Melbourne. The sea does not agree with my wife, and I am sorry to say that the sea-voyage has not had the good effect I hoped. She is very sick at sea, and the food one gets on board of ship does not agree with her. She has wonderful courage, and did her best to forget and overcome her misery by working hard at English, and with her needle. She can now read an English book with pleasure to herself, and I have no doubt will shortly be able to speak English. We are delighted with Sydney. The harbour, which is like a large lake, is surrounded by bays and inlets, and is exceedingly beautiful. Along the coast there are a number of good houses with grounds well laid out. I should not like however to remain at Sydney, for I fancy it is about as ill-suited for Europeans as India. The grown-up people seem to have good health, but I remarked that the children are thin and colourless.

I am told too that the mortality among the children is great. The town is well built and clean. Some of the public buildings are good, and remind me of Edinburgh. Among the letters I received on arriving here was one from you, which I have read several times and thought over long. Do not despair of meeting me again. **My wife sends her kind love to you.**

TO HIS SISTER.

NAPIER, NEW ZEALAND, *April 30th*, 1862.

... For me the voyage was not altogether devoid of pleasure. I used to enjoy my bath every morning. I had plenty of books which I used to read, sitting quietly on the deck, and when I was tired of reading I used to smoke, and watch the great albatrosses, and other sea-birds, sailing round and round the ship. In this *fainéant* sort of life one leads on board of ship things of small importance become very interesting, and the sight of a log of wood, a shark, or a few whales rolling lazily about in the water caused great excitement and gave rise to endless speculations. The pleasure we had in getting ashore again at Sydney went a long way towards compensating us for the miseries we endured on the voyage. Many of the inhabitants are enormously rich, but very few of them are *comme il faut*. Many of the most influential people are convicts, or the sons of convicts. I heard one of the magistrates speaking very ungrammatically. A member of Parliament, when it was proposed to establish baths and wash-houses, opposed such *lugzuries*, as he called them, and said that he himself had not taken a bath for twenty years. This will give you some idea of the sort of people one meets at Sydney. Directly we reached this place, I took a house, and bought the necessary furniture. It is a little wooden house with three rooms and a kitchen down-stairs, and two rooms up-stairs. The sea is about as far from us as the lake is from you, and every morning after blacking my shoes and lighting the fire, I rush down to the sea and take my bath. I am well pleased with Napier, but in my next letter I shall tell you more about it, and of my prospects.

TO THE SAME.

WAIPAWA, NEW ZEALAND, *June* 22d, 1862.

I HAVE just received a letter from you that has been in India, and followed me to this place. You hope that my face is steadily turned homewards, and therefore you will be glad to hear that I have no intention of staying long here. My wife and I both feel the want of society, and have come to the conclusion that this is not the place for us to spend our lives. I hoped to have been able to buy some land, to obtain the Government grant, and after a year or two to be able to return to Europe, but now I find there are many difficulties which I did not foresee, and am afraid that if I decide upon taking land here, I must settle for five or ten years, and this is a prospect too gloomy for either of us. I am practising here, and enjoy my long rides, but my wife does not at all like being left alone. There are no ladies or people that we can associate with within four miles. The settlers all live in the centre of their respective runs, and as the runs are very extensive, they are necessarily far apart. I have taken a house in a little village which appears to me to be about the most central situation in the district for practice, and have already numbers of patients. We shall stay here for a month or two, and in that time we shall know how the place suits us, but I think it is not at all likely that we shall remain. Many of the settlers here are gentlemen of education, but they are obliged to live like ploughmen, and by degrees adopt the manners of their labourers, and have altogether the appearance of rustics. The children, who swarm, enjoy robust health, but there is a want of polish in their manners; in fact many of them are little boors. I have no doubt, however, as the place becomes popular, and more ladies arrive in the colony, the people will become more polite and live less like savages than they do at present. There is no doubt whatever that this is a splendid country for colonising. The climate is excellent and the land good, and English people and children enjoy better health than they do in their own native land. In a few years the whole face of the country will be changed, and I think much beautified. The native grasses are yielding to English clover and grasses. Whenever English grass is sown, it springs up luxuriantly, and destroys the native grass. All English trees, flowers, and weeds grow well, and overcome the old inhabitants of the country. The English rat has already driven away the native rat, and the English fly multiplies terribly, and will soon have undisputed possession of the country. The Maories are longer in disappearing than their companion vegetables and animals, but yet they steadily diminish in numbers. Many people lament their extinction, but I myself am not sorry to see them replaced by a better race. They are an ugly, brutal, savage-looking people. Many of them are strong and well-made, and they are said to be brave, but beyond this I believe they have no good qualities, but nearly all the bad propensities you can think of.

TO L.

WAIPANA, NEAR NAPIER, NEW ZEALAND,
July 23*d*, 1862.

... This country reminds me of Cumberland, but it is far from being so beautiful. The mountains and rivers are the same, but the valleys are very different. If you can imagine the valleys of Cumberland replaced by the deserts of Arabia you will form a good idea of this country. The grass in the valleys is generally brown, and in the distance looks exactly like sand. The fern-covered mountains and hills are terribly gloomy and desolate-looking. The forests are grand when you are in them, but viewed even from a short distance, on account of the dull colour of the foliage, appear monotonous and gloomy. They are all surrounded by a belt of dead trees, stretching their enormous naked branches into the air, and looking like gigantic skeletons. The effect on one's spirits is decidedly depressing. The scenery of the pass between the vales of Lorton and Keswick is cheerful compared with much one sees here. I have explored nearly the whole province of Hawke's Bay, which is the richest in the North Island, and have taken up my abode in the centre, which is the prettiest part of the province. The village is increasing rapidly, and will, I have no doubt, in a few years be a very pretty place. Gardens are springing up, and the neighbourhood begins to look green, as the European grasses spread everywhere. There is an immense forest near the village, but this will soon disappear, for wherever an opening is made into it, and all around its circumference, the trees are dying. Before this happens no doubt the landscape will be embellished by European trees and hedges. The sheep-run that I expected to have bought is close to this village. It consists of a number of fine limestone hills, picturesque and, I have no doubt, extremely fertile; but at present it is almost in its primitive state, covered with fern. The owner is a disreputable character, a lazy drunkard. He is fast ruining himself. As a rule, settlers here do not make the most of their land. The greater number came here without money, and borrow in order to buy land. For this borrowed money they pay 15 per cent., although they mortgage their land. At first they were not obliged to buy the land, they only paid a nominal rent to Government. As other settlers arrived, the land was put up for sale, and they were obliged to buy or leave the land. Thus many are deeply in debt, and cannot borrow more money to improve the land. Nevertheless, the land slowly improves itself. The sheep tread down the fern, and the European grasses spread spontaneously. Wherever there is a road, or wherever cattle go, clover springs up. The sheep carry grass seeds up to the tops of the hills; the grass springs up there first, and every year descends lower, until the fern has quite disappeared. Some of the settlers enclose the land, plough, sow oats, and then grass. Others merely enclose fields, overstock with sheep, so that the sheep are forced by hunger to eat the young fern, which, once destroyed, does not spring up again, provided grass be sown. The fern must be first burnt. The majority of the settlers, however, are content only to burn the fern, and to sow grass in places. The last plan succeeds, but it is a slow process. People have not yet begun to plant hedges. The fencing is made of very strong posts and rails, which last about ten or twelve years. Some make fences with strong wooden posts and wire. Between this and Napier there are many thousands of acres of excellent land belonging to the Maories that are quite uncultivated. As the Maories are rapidly disappearing, this land will soon fall into the hands of Europeans. The accounts one hears of the Maories are quite incorrect. So far are they from being a fine race of people, that of all the people I have yet seen they are the lowest. They are physically much inferior to many Indians. They are exceedingly ugly, and perfectly useless. They have a sort of animal courage; like dogs, they will attack when they think people are afraid of them, but are at once cowed by determination. Till now they have been successful in their encounters with Europeans, because the soldiers were demoralised by want of activity and determination on the part of their officers and of the Government. Their success has made the natives exceedingly impertinent, and they affect to despise Europeans. The present Governor does all he can to keep peace by making presents, and by yielding to the natives continually, and the more he gives them the more they ask. In disputes with Europeans the natives take the law into their own hands, and it is a general complaint here that the Government will not aid an European in obtaining justice. The decisions in European courts are generally given in favour of Maories, for the sake of maintaining peace. The Governor wishes to keep peace until roads be made throughout the country. If this plan succeeds in maintaining peace for two or three years, there will no longer be any danger, for the Maories will then be less numerous, and the Europeans proportionally increased. Originally the missionaries were very powerful in New Zealand. They traded with the natives, had great influence over them, and were supposed to have supernatural power. They consequently became exceedingly wealthy, and were jealous of other Europeans coming into the country, and did their best to oppose colonisation. One, who still lives in this province, actually refused shelter to Europeans. He was living in state, with Maori servants. His evil deeds were made known, and he has been dismissed from the Church. I think that the reason that the Maories are dying out is that they have contracted some European habits which they are too poor to keep up, and they cannot now live on fern-roots as formerly. They are too lazy to work, and their stomachs can no longer digest fern-roots and cabbage-trees. They do not appear to me to indulge much in drink, but they all smoke.

TO HIS MOTHER.

POINT DE GALLE, *October* 16*th*, 1862.

YOU see by the address at the top of this letter that I have left New Zealand. I am now on my way to Calcutta, but think it not at all unlikely that I may see you again shortly. I have a great desire to come and live near you. I must go to Calcutta before returning to England. When there I shall hear on what terms I can resign the service, and will consider if it be well to do so. As my movements are uncertain, I have thought it best to send my wife on to Europe. When she is able she will pay you a visit, and I hope I may be able to introduce her myself. I was very glad to receive your portrait when I was in New Zealand, but no portrait can equal the pleasing lively recollection of my dear mother, which I can always and do continually call to mind.

TO HIS SISTER.

DINAPORE, *January* 3*d*, 1863.

I HAVE just received letters from you and L., both from New Zealand and from England. The Bombay mail leaves in an hour, so I hasten to send you a few lines. I have heard from Annette, who has arrived all safe at Paris. It was a great relief, for I have been very anxious about her. You may expect to see her shortly after you receive this letter; at all events, she will write and let you know how she is getting on. I have been very busy lately. I have medical charge of a native regiment, and also of a battery of European Artillery. I like the latter charge very much, as I have Europeans to look after. I have some private practice, and might have a good deal more, for many are wishful to have me for their doctor, but I am not at all fond of private practice. Dinapore is a healthy station. The scenery is rather tame, but the Ganges is grand, and on a clear day, looking across the river, one can see one of the snowy peaks of the Himalayas. At present the weather is cold, and one enjoys a fire. I am told that it is never very hot in summer, so you see I have come to a good place to wait for the result of the amalgamation [of the East India Company's and the Queen's troops]. I have a fine Arab horse, one said to be of the purest race and best pedigree in India. He is a beautiful creature, and I enjoy bounding over the sward on his back in the early morning. His name is "Selim." He is as quiet as a lamb, but playful as a gazelle when I am on his back. I sent little presents to you and L. from Sydney to William. I am going to send you a Cashmere shawl by and by. My native regiment is the famous "Royal Lucknow."

TO HIS SISTER.

DINAPORE, *February 4th*, 1863.

I HAVE just received a lot of letters that have been round by New Zealand. You press me to return to Europe, and I feel almost ashamed to remain out here whilst there are so many kind friends at home anxious and longing to see me again. I myself have as great, or a greater, longing to see you all again, and I hope the time is not far distant when we shall meet again. I am afraid to return at present, because I do not know what I could do in England, and it would never do for me to be idle. Here I have plenty of occupation and work that I like; I have operations to perform upon my native patients, and I have a battery of Artillery to look after, and that suits me well. This battery is one of the old Bengal batteries, now amalgamated with the Royal Army, and subject to the same rules. As the men have had their full turn of duty in India, it is expected that they will return to England shortly, and very possibly I may return with them. The Artillery, you know, is the scientific department of the army. As a rule, the officers are of a superior class, and more agreeable companions than other officers. You seem to think that Annette is with me, and yet I remember to have written to say that she was going on to Paris when I was at Galle. I am surprised that you have not heard from her. I suppose she has been busy, and perhaps not well. No doubt you will have seen or heard from her before you receive this letter. I send you my photograph, which might pass for a likeness of George. I do not think I am a bit altered since you saw me. I have no tendency to obesity, but am strong and healthy. People here say I look as if I had just come from England, so you see you need not be anxious about my health.

TO HIS MOTHER.

DINAPORE, *February* 14*th*, 1863.

I HAVE just received a letter from Allie, dated Jan. 19th, from Shields, in which she says that you were moved to tears at the sight of the photograph I sent you from Calcutta. She talks of the haggard features and melancholy appearance which the photograph gave me. Certainly I am not so young-looking as when you saw me; the troubles and anxieties of life must alter one's appearance as one grows older. A doctor too has more to annoy and vex him than other people; nevertheless, I think I am young-looking for my age,[1] and the photograph rather exaggerates any sadness that there may be in my face. Certainly I am not at all haggard. I enjoy excellent health, and am able to work hard; and although I do not enjoy life as formerly, still I am tolerably happy, and satisfied. Now that I have a lot of European soldiers, with women and children, to look after, I take great interest in my patients, and although I have much anxiety, this is compensated for by the pleasure I feel in seeing my patients recover. General Swinley was reviewing the Artillery the other day, and I had a long talk with him. He told me that in all probability the battery that I now have charge of will return to England in a year, so perhaps it will not be very long before you see me.

TO HIS SISTER.

PATNA, *April* 10*th*, 1863.

I HAVE come to stay at Patna for a week. The Civil Surgeon of this place has just gone to Calcutta to see his children off to England, and he asked me to do his work during his absence. I like the change very much. The drives round about Patna are very pretty, and it is a much more quiet place than Dinapore. There are no military here,—none but civilians, opium agents, etc., and every one is disposed to be very polite to me. I have a grand house and garden, with books, a microscope, three or four carriages, and a lot of horses, at my disposal, so I shall no doubt pass my time pleasantly. It is only seven miles to Dinapore, so that I can easily drive there when I feel inclined. I have received many kind letters from you lately about Annette and the baby. I am glad you take so much interest in them. You will find when you come to know Annette well that she has many excellent qualities. You must write and tell me candidly what you think of the baby. Do not be afraid of not praising it; I prefer the truth to compliments. L. hopes that it is not a little Kelt. There is no fear of that; the mother is

---

[1] Not quite thirty.

from the north of France, and has altogether the appearance of a Norman, as by this time you know. As yet I am uncertain when I ought to expect Annette, but I hope she will remain in Europe till October. This is a very bad time for her to come out.

TO HIS SISTER.

DINAPORE, *May 4th*, 1863.

I HAVE just received your letters written after seeing Annette off at London Bridge. I can scarcely tell you what pleasure I had in reading them, and how warmly I felt towards you for the kind way in which you have behaved towards my wife. She has written to me about you, and expresses herself as delighted with her reception from you all. I feel certain that you have saved the life of the little boy, for he would assuredly have died had he remained at Paris. My wife tells me that she has engaged her passage in the steamer which leaves on the 12th of April, so that in a few days I shall meet her in Calcutta.

TO HIS MOTHER.

DINAPORE, *July 28th*, 1863.

I HAVE just received news from Allie, dated Etal Villa, June 10th. The details she gives us of the little baby of course are exceedingly interesting to both of us. She tells us how kind you and Isabella are, and what care you take of the boy; but it is not necessary to tell me that. I know that you will look after him as well and as carefully as you did with your own children, and that he is much better with you than with his mother in India. I am glad to hear that William has a nice healthy little boy. You must have a great deal to amuse and occupy you, with so many grandchildren. Annette is going to write you a letter in English. She often talks about you, and is very pleased with the manner in which you and Allie mention her in your letters. She always reads the letters, and is most eager to make out all that concerns the little boy. She joins with me in love to all.

TO HIS SISTER.

DINAPORE, *September 18th*, 1863.

I AM afraid you think me dreadfully neglectful in not writing to you oftener, and I must say that I scarcely deserve to receive so many kind letters from you. I have very little to say, but I must write for fear that you should get disgusted at continually writing without receiving replies, and, in consequence, stop your bi-monthly letters, the receipt of which is, to me, one of my chief enjoyments in this dull country. My wife is tolerably happy, although she often thinks of her little one, and when she hears of the illness of other young children, is glad to think that hers is far away from this unhealthy country, and is well cared for in England. Annette "distracts herself," as she says, with birds of all sorts, and we already have an aviary consisting of canaries, parrots, mainas, Java sparrows, and other birds of which I do not know the names. We go out riding together every evening, she on my charger, and I on a horse belonging to the regiment.

I do not at all agree with you about Japan. If I can, I shall certainly go there, for it is a fine country, and I like travelling in new countries and seeing strange people. It seems at first sight unjust that we should force the Japanese to associate with us, and there is no doubt that, for a long time at least, our association with them will be rather hurtful than beneficial. There will certainly be war with Japan sooner or later, and the result will be good. The English have improved India, and they are likely to do good in China and Japan also. Whether the war is just or unjust, I have no objection to going there as a surgeon, and doing my best to keep English soldiers alive.

TO THE SAME.

DINAPORE, *Nov. 19th*, 1863.

I HAVE just received two letters from you, one by Bombay and the other by Calcutta. Annette is even more delighted than I am to receive them, and more eager to tear the envelope and read them. The last photograph you sent is very good. I think it is the best photograph of yourself I have seen. The baby is too young to come out well in a photograph, but one can see that he is in good condition, and well looked after. Mother and Isabella are exceedingly good. At first I felt some scruples in leaving the baby with mother. I was afraid it might be a trouble to her. Now I am very glad, since you tell me that she takes a delight in the occupation of looking after it, and that this occupation does her good. . . .

You tell Annette that mother is reading a book on Self-Government in India, and that you are sorry she does not like the natives. I am afraid if you knew all that we think about the natives you would be shocked, but if you were in the country I imagine you would think as we do. They are altogether despicable, and have got more self-government than they deserve. Some natives have entered the medical service, but although they have plenty of talent are not to be trusted. One or two have been dismissed for taking small bribes. I hear that one native also has entered the Civil Service, and I think it a great misfortune that one native should have a responsible situation. We have had news from the Punjab. People generally think that there will be a serious war with the hill tribes. I shall write to you again soon.

TO HIS MOTHER.

MONGHYR, *Dec. 9th*, 1863.

WE are now, as you will see by the date of this letter, at Monghyr. I was sent off suddenly from Dinapore to take medical charge of this station, as the former doctor had been obliged to leave it on account of illness. We are six hours by rail from Dinapore, nearer Calcutta. It is probable I may be stationed here for some time, but not certain. My wife is delighted with the place, and it certainly is very pretty. The houses are all built in a kind of fort, which is about half a mile in diameter. The Ganges runs under the walls of this fort, and the views from the ramparts are magnificent, for the country round about is undulating and picturesque, and in the distance there are tolerably high mountains. My wife and I packed up all our things, and put the whole of the contents of our house in a boat which has just arrived. We ourselves came down by train four days ago, and have been living with the brother of an old friend of mine who is magistrate here. We have taken a house in the country about a mile from the fort, and our things are now being conveyed there. We are glad to hear such good accounts of the baby, and delighted that you are fond of him. Give my love to Isabella, and tell her how thankful we feel towards her for her kindness to our baby.

TO HIS SISTER.

MONGHYR, *Dec. 29th*, 1863.

WE have just received your letter from Derwent Bank whilst mother was staying with you. Annette has been trying to write a reply, but she is afraid that her letter will not be ready in time. She is not at all in a calm frame of mind. The packing, travelling, and arranging our new house in her present state have been rather too much for her, especially as she always will have her own way, and takes the entire management of the household on her own shoulders. We also have friends staying with us, and this gives extra employment. Often in India it is the husband who manages household affairs, because it is difficult for a lady to look after twenty or thirty servants, whose language she can only speak imperfectly; but I leave all to my wife, as she has more capability in that way than I have, and besides I have other occupation.

We both like Monghyr much, but it seems very quiet after Dinapore, which you know is a large military station. Here there are no ladies at all, and consequently no dinner-parties. It is still uncertain how long I may remain here; but if I change, it will probably be to go to Calcutta, which of course will be a good move for me.

Our big dog Jack returned the other day. You know we left him in New Zealand by accident. He jumped ashore just as the steamer was leaving Auckland. I wrote from Sydney to Auckland to have him forwarded. A friend brought him on to Calcutta. In coming round the north of Australia he was wrecked, and taken on in another ship to Batavia, and from thence to Calcutta. His father and mother were with me in China, and he was born in my tent at Calcutta, immediately on our arrival from China in 1860. Is he not a great traveller for a dog? Perhaps you may see him in England some day.

TO HIS MOTHER.

MONGHYR, *April* 12*th*, 1864.

I OFTEN reproach myself for not writing oftener to you, but so little occurs here that can interest you that I scarcely know what to say in my letters. Do not judge of me by my letters, but feel assured that I love you as much or more than ever, that I think of you constantly, and long to see you again. I am glad to say that we have at last got a very nice house, beautifully situated on the banks of the Ganges. The view from our verandah in the early morning is magnificent. Annette is delighted with the house. We have a very charming young lady staying with us, and my wife enjoys her society very much. She is a niece of the Pre-Raphaelite painter Lewis, and daughter-in-law of Sir B. Peacock, judge of Calcutta. Monghyr being on the rail, we have lots of visitors, sometimes several at once, who rest with us on their way up country. Annette sends her love to you and Isabella. She often talks of you, and feels grateful to both of you for the care you take of the baby. We are both glad to hear that he is getting on well, and that he does his best to repay your care of him by his amiability.

TO HIS SISTER.

MONGHYR, *May* 22*d*, 1864.

I HAVE just received your letter dated April 8th, in which you tell me our little boy is staying at Derwent Bank. I hope that he will derive benefit from your judicious treatment. He ought never to be allowed to show temper on any account, or to disobey. I fancy he resembles his mother in disposition, and she tells me that when she was young a little corporal punishment was necessary, "pour faire passer ses colères." Probably the same treatment would be effectual with the son. I have nothing new to tell you of our life at Monghyr. We are both well. Although it is the hottest part of the year, the heat is not excessive. The thermometer is at 87° in the room in which I am writing, but out of doors it is much hotter. We shut all our doors and windows at nine o'clock in the morning, and open them at six in the evening. This we do to keep out the heat, and to allow the cool air to enter morning and evening. About a week ago the heat was very great, but we have had a few dust and thunder storms, which have somewhat cooled the air. I am sitting writing without a punkah, but Annette, who suffers more from the heat than I do, is lying on the sofa in her dressing-gown under the punkah, studying natural history. She has a large English book with pictures, and she is trying to learn the names of all the curious insects that come on our dinner-table, and annoy us by getting into the soup and wine. Annette has a great taste for natural history, and she has so many pets running about the house, that mother, if she were here, would be in a state of continual alarm. She has five parrots, which follow her about like dogs. The latest importation is a chameleon, a most extraordinary-looking lizard, which is continually changing colour. He is very quiet and harmless; he never eats of his own accord, but swallows almost anything we put in his mouth. He will live for a week without eating or drinking, but we give him six grasshoppers daily. The Hindustani word for chameleon means twelve colours, but these colours are only shades of green, yellow, and black. In the house he is generally of a dirty uniform yellow colour; if we touch him so as to make him move, black stripes like the marking on a perch make their appearance, and the grounding blushes green. When placed out of doors on the grass, he assumes the same colour as the grass, and can scarcely be distinguished. He appears to have a great objection to water, and gets very excited (for a chameleon) if any is placed near him.

People in India are glad to have Sir J. Lawrence as Governor-General. I saw him at a reception at Government House when I was at Calcutta. The expression of his face shows that he is energetic, determined, and hard-working. Of the three Governor-Generals I have seen, Lord Canning fulfils most completely my idea of what a Governor-General ought to be. He was more stately and regal in his manners than the others, and appeared more at home when before the public. He spoke well; perhaps his delivery was rather cold and calm for an orator, but this was especially becoming in a Governor of India, where the activity and fire of Europeans is misinterpreted.

May 23*d.*—Your letter dated March 23d has just arrived; thus it has been two months on the way, and there are no marks on the envelope to explain the cause of the delay. . . The expense of living in India is so great that £1200 a year is easily spent. My predecessor at Monghyr made a fortune in seven years (£15,000), but he was very economical, and had better pay than I have. Latterly the pay of Civil Surgeons has been much diminished. Formerly the Civil Surgeon was also registrar of deeds, and this appointment alone was in many places worth £1200 a year. This registrarship is now given to natives whenever a Civil Surgeoncy becomes vacant. This is done to encourage the natives; the surgeons it is supposed require no encouragement, and, having no friends at headquarters, can be hit with impunity. I think shortly the surgeons will be treated with more consideration, for they are very necessary members of society in India, and if they are not better paid, it will be difficult to induce others to come out.

May 30*th.*—To-day I received your letter enclosing Mrs. Stanger's. I feel quite grateful to her for speaking well of the baby.

TO THE SAME.

MONGHYR, *June* 27*th*, 1864.

I AM happy to be able to tell you that Annette has got safely over her accouchement, and that a little girl was born on the 22d of this month at 10 A.M. The little girl promises to turn out well, as far as I am able to judge at present. She is very fair, has good features, and a pretty round head. The day she was born she turned her eyes to the light, and seemed to look about. This, together with the fact that she is very quick in her movements, makes me think that she will be of a lively disposition.

In your last letter you said you were about to leave Keswick with our little boy. I am sure his stay at Keswick will have done him both moral and physical good. I should very much like to hear L.'s opinion of him. I have more confidence in his opinion than in yours, for I know you are prejudiced in his favour.

I have been very busy lately going backwards and forwards from Monghyr to Jaunpore, which is a large railway station, about five miles from here. There are 400 English workmen there, engine-drivers, platelayers, and engine-builders. The majority of them are from Shields and Newcastle (from Armstrong's works). They are a **hard-drinking, disorderly** lot, but I like going among them. It is pleasant to hear the familiar accent of our native country in this remote place. I was called there to consult about a man who had been shaken by a tiger. There are numbers of tigers, leopards, bears, and wolves near Monghyr. This man was rather too bold a sportsman; he wounded the tiger, and went after it into the jungle on foot. Tigers crouch like cats, and you do not see them until you are close upon them. It happened thus to this man. The tiger caught him by the arm and shook him as a dog shakes a rat. The arm was much bruised, and the subclavian artery injured, but this was not discovered until three weeks after the injury, and the case was then hopeless. It was at this time that I was sent for. People seldom recover from injuries inflicted by tigers. The injuries are always more serious than they appear. This man was the best workman in Jaunpore, and a great favourite with the other men. He bore his sufferings and the prospect of death wonderfully. He supported a mother in England, wrote to her regularly, and the day before he died, received a letter from her begging him to be careful of "them savage beasts." He showed us the letter; the tone of it was desponding; she appeared hopeless of ever seeing her son again. The man was remarkably good (not religious), fond of work and sport. He had built himself a hut among the jungly hills, and there he used to spend his Sunday and half-Saturday entirely alone. On showing his mother's letter, he said, "That is why I wish to live, to see her again."

TO L.

MONGHYR, *July 20th*, 1864.

I RECEIVED your very kind letter a few days ago; we were both very much pleased with your description of the boy. Although you say that yours is a quite unprejudiced statement, I can yet see that it is a very friendly criticism; it pleased me and delighted Annette. She does not believe that any one in speaking of the baby is prejudiced, and when Allie praises the little boy to the skies, or mother calls him a "perfect" child, she thinks that they are only stating facts in a kind manner.

I quite agree with you in thinking the prevention of disease the most useful part of the doctor, and should like very much to have some appointment which would occupy me in that way. It is very probable that sooner or later I may get such an appointment, for I heard incidentally lately that it was proposed that I should be appointed one of the Sanitary Committee for India. I quite believe that India may be made as healthy as any country in the world for the English soldier. Many people derive great benefit from a short stay in India, and I think that the army might be rendered more efficient if selections were made in England, and if those soldiers who are likely to derive benefit from the climate of India were sent out. All those who have a tendency to chest diseases should be sent, and those with a tendency to abdominal diseases retained. Another simple way of diminishing the mortality of our soldiers in India would be to send half of each regiment to the hills every hot season. This would give more room to the other half, and control or prevent the epidemics of cholera.

Of course the barracks at the hill stations would require to be enlarged and improved. As the climate there is good, the soldiers ought to be healthier than in England. This plan of sending half of each regiment to the hills every hot season will not cost much money or trouble as soon as the railways are completed. As the soldiers are not drilled much from March to October, the discipline of the regiments would not be much endangered.

Our new Medical Warrant has at last come out to India. It benefits the doctors of the Queen's troops, but the majority of the Indian doctors lose by it. All Indian officers, medical and others, regret that the government of India has been transferred to the Crown. John Company was by far the more generous master.

I have not yet heard definitely when I must join my appointment at Calcutta, but I suppose towards the end of September. I am very glad that I am going to Calcutta, for there is too little society at Monghyr. It does one good to see people round about one working, and stimulating one to do the same. Our little girl is growing very fast, both long and fat. We tried goat's milk mixed with sugar and water at first, but this would not do, so we gave donkey's milk, which answers admirably.

TO HIS SISTER.

MONGHYR, *July* 30*th*, 1864.

I HAVE received your letter, and as the post leaves to-day, I hasten to send a few lines. You ask if I see the *Cornhill Magazine*. We see all the magazines and reviews, and Annette is at present reading Denis Duval, and likes it very much. I have read a few numbers interruptedly of the "Small House at Allington." Trollope writes well, and I admire his novels very much, especially the conversations in them, which are so easy and natural. As there is so little society at Monghyr we have lots of time for reading, and I get through a great deal, both heavy and light. Lately I have been reading much about ancient Egypt and India in the works of Sir W. Jones and Heron. If you meet with either of these books I should recommend you to read them. Since the rains began we have had charming weather, and the country round about Monghyr is beautifully green,—everything is growing fast and luxuriantly. Annette and I drive out every evening in our dog-cart. We have a fine Australian horse, which trots fourteen miles an hour, and is very willing and good-natured. He eats the grass in our compound for a few hours every day, and always when we go out he comes up to us seeking for bread. The dog-cart has wheels more than six feet high, so we are nicely raised, and get all the air that is to be had. The Ganges is rising rapidly, and the plains are getting formed into islands by the filling of the nullahs with water. Last evening we saw about 1000 bullocks and cows swim across a tributary of the Ganges, from one of those islands. You can imagine how curious the scene was. The baby grows more charming every day. She is now beginning to smile. I suppose you would like to have a description of her, but there is nothing particular to describe. All her features are well-formed, remarkably distinctly for a baby. She is as healthy and well as it is possible for a baby to be. The donkey's milk seems to agree remarkably well with her. She is well looked after, for besides her mother and father, she has three ayahs to attend upon her, and a little boy to milk and look after the donkeys. There are two donkeys with little ones, good amiable brutes, who know me and come when I call them. You may be sure they are well fed and looked after; they wander about the compound eating the grass, and have a dish of soaked grain twice a day. We have one excellent ayah, whom we can trust. I hope we may be able to induce her to accompany us to Calcutta.

I am always interested to hear of Mr. Smith, and should like very much to meet him again some day. I am glad that you like his wife. It is not often that our friends marry the persons we should like them to marry. I am generally disappointed with my friends' wives. I am happy to see by your letter that you hear often from mother, and that she is in good health. I hope she may long continue so, and that I may find her little changed when I return from India. Annette sends her love. She intends writing by next post, and will give you a description of the baby.

P.S.—We have just seen some bullocks swimming across the Ganges close to our house. The current must have carried them several miles below the point from which they started, for the water runs at the rate of about six miles an hour. I am astonished that they are able to swim so far. I have had some photographs taken of natives of Monghyr district prisoners. One of the four, whom you will easily distinguish, is a Brahmin. I had him taken to contrast with the others; he is much fairer, but this is not shown in the photograph. The other three are Musaliers, inhabitants of the hills near Monghyr, probably the old race of the country, who were driven to the hills by northern invaders.

TO HIS SISTER.

MONGHYR, *September 10th*, 1864.

I WAS so very busy when the last mail left that I forgot to write until it was too late. This is the unhealthy time of the year, and there was a great deal of sickness in the station, which kept me engaged day and night. Our own baby too caught cold and fever, and gave me a great deal of trouble. She soon however got over her sickness, and is now as healthy and fat as I could wish. She has a very good constitution, and is much admired by every one here. We are always very glad to hear that the little boy is doing so well. My wife, however, is not very well pleased to hear that he has red hair, and will scarcely believe it. I tell her that "golden," the word used, means red. For my part, I like a slight tinge of red. In this country it is a clear proof that there is no Indian blood. We still give our baby ass's milk, and now we have begun to mix it with arrowroot, grown at Monghyr. She seems to thrive on this, as well as if she were suckled, but I fear it may not suit so well when teething commences. Still I hope, as the baby is strong and healthy, that she may cut her teeth easily. The wet-nurses, Dhyrs, are so low and dirty, and so troublesome, that I did not like having one for our little baby. We have not yet fixed on a name. I wish to call her Francesca or Helen, but Annette prefers Lucie. It is still quite uncertain when I shall leave Monghyr, but I wish, for the baby's sake, to remain here till the end of October. You must not suppose that I wish to go to Calcutta merely for the sake of making a fortune, although I should like to return to England with plenty of money. My chief object is to become more generally useful, as a more important member of society. I think I am more likely to succeed in this at Calcutta than in any other place.

TO HIS MOTHER.

MONGHYR, *October 3d*, 1864.

I AM still at Monghyr, but am expecting daily to hear something about going to Calcutta. I am in no hurry to leave, for it is still hot there, and our baby is doing well here. She is in first-rate condition, and her cheeks are getting red. Every one admires her, and we, of course, think she deserves to be so admired. Annette is so constantly occupied with her little daughter that she finds time for nothing else. We have had a houseful for the last month. Mrs. G., the wife of an old friend of mine, and Colonel S.'s wife and child, have been staying with us for a month. The latter brought his baby down from Dinapore, because it was supposed to be dying, and a change of air was recommended as a last hope. Their baby is now stout and healthy, and the parents are delighted. Our home has become a sort of hospital for our sick friends, because Monghyr is one of the healthiest places on the plains of India, and certainly the prettiest. Remember me kindly to Isabella. I do not know how to thank her for her kindness to our little boy. I hope you will send another photograph soon.

TO L.

MONGHYR, *October 20th*, 1864.

I HAVE just received your letter, in which you speak of my prospects in Calcutta, and also give an interesting account of our little boy. The appointment at Calcutta is not yet vacated, but Dr. Beatson (the late Governor-General's doctor), who holds it, is at the top of the list of Assistant Surgeons, and as soon as his promotion is in the *Gazette* he will have to leave. I have great hopes of succeeding in Calcutta, and I am determined to work hard and do my best, but there is a great deal of uncertainty. I must be patient, wait, and spend more than my pay, for the appointment is not well paid, and expenses at Calcutta are great. It is fortunate that we shall have a good house, in the healthiest part of Calcutta, for I quite agree with you that health should be economised. The climate of India suits my constitution very well. I have now completely recovered from the ague which I caught in China, and people say that I look as healthy as if I had just left England. Our little baby is doing remarkably well. From what I hear of Calcutta, I daresay she will be as well there for the first few years of her life as in any part of the world. A great deal of the sickness of children in this country is due to neglect. The ayahs are careless and untrustworthy. You are right in supposing that by going to Calcutta I shall have a better chance of paying Europe a visit soon. Annette is charmed with your description of the little boy, and with the kind manner in which you speak of him.

TO HIS SISTER.

MONGHYR, *October* 20*th*, 1864.

WE have got through the heat of another year in this country, and are now enjoying the best climate in the world. We rejoice at the approach of winter as you do in England at the approach of summer. Certainly the scenery about Monghyr, of its kind, is as beautiful as possible. Without leaving our house we see the most charming views: on the one side the Ganges and mountains, and on the other our garden, full of flowers and curious flower-bearing trees, luxuriant acacias, and funny-looking cactuses, and euphorbias—brilliant flowers contrasting with the freshest green. We enjoy too our evening drives, along winding picturesque lanes with natural hedges, formed of all kinds of bushes and trees, which are often covered with enormous parasitical plants and creepers. The variety is so great that at every turn we see something new, and the luxuriance of the vegetation is such as you who have never been in the tropics can scarcely imagine. Any description can give you but a faint idea of the reality. Annette looking over my shoulder says I ought to mention as a drawback the abundant animal life of the country,—the mosquitoes, the grasshoppers, the flies, fleas, and flying bugs and ants, which swarm, and do anything but improve the flavour of our soup, coffee, etc.

We are not going to leave Monghyr so soon as we expected, and we consider ourselves very fortunate in that we were not at Calcutta in the great storm, of which no doubt you have read in the papers. If we had been there I suppose we should have suffered. E., a friend of mine, wrote to me from Calcutta that the greater part of his furniture was destroyed, to the value of 7000 rupees. Every one at Calcutta has lost more or less. The poor natives down the river are starving, and thousands will die, although people are subscribing handsomely, and doing all they can to aid them.

Our little girl is thriving, and becomes prettier and more engaging every day. She keeps Annette constantly employed, and even takes up a considerable portion of my time. We had her christened about a fortnight ago, and I took the liberty of making you the godmother; we call her Beatrix, not after any one, but simply because I think the name pretty, and applicable to her, as she seems to be of a very happy disposition. I hope it may be a name of good omen.

K

TO HIS MOTHER.

MONGHYR, *November* 21*st*, 1864.

LATELY I have had a great deal to do. I have been expecting daily to leave Monghyr, and been kept in such a state of uncertainty that I have felt little disposition for writing letters. The appointment was promised to me by the Governor-General six months ago, but since then the Commander-in-Chief has promised it to some one else, and it appears there is some uncertainty as to whom the gift of the appointment belongs. The matter must shortly be decided, for in three weeks' time the place will be vacant. If I do not get to Calcutta, I shall console myself by thinking that perhaps it is better for the health of our little girl that we should remain at Monghyr. She is perfectly healthy, and never cries now. Every one admires her, and is astonished that she should have so much colour and be in such good condition. I think that the reason of this is that her mother is constantly looking after her. She is never left alone with servants. I have reproached myself for not writing to Isabella oftener to thank her for all the kind care she is taking of our little boy, but I always hope she will feel sure that I fully appreciate and am grateful for her kindness. Allie frequently writes and tells me of Isabella's assiduous love and care, and both Annette and I rejoice to think that our boy is so well looked after.

CHAPTER VI.

LETTERS FROM CALCUTTA.

"I was sick, and ye visited me: I was in prison, and ye came unto me... Inasmuch as ye have done it unto one of the least of these my brethren, ye have done it unto me."—St. Matthew xxv. 36, 40.

TO HIS SISTER.

GENERAL HOSPITAL,
CALCUTTA, *December* 20*th*, 1864.

... I think we shall like Calcutta very well. We have a good house in the healthiest quarter, and that is a great advantage. The pay is not particularly good, but I have a prospect of obtaining another appointment shortly. The new Medical Warrant which has just come out to India, I fancy, will give me Rs.800 a month, and I have a house besides. Nearly every one is dissatisfied with the new Warrant; it is slightly advantageous to the younger assistant-surgeons, but after-prospects are bad. However, people in England who do not know what a quantity of money is necessary in India will think it good. Common clerks in offices are better paid here than army doctors. I am glad that I have got to Calcutta, for it is the only place now in India where a doctor has a chance of doing tolerably well....

TO L.

GENERAL HOSPITAL,
CALCUTTA, *February* 15*th*, 1865.

I HAVE had so much to do since I came to Calcutta that I have not had time to write to you and Allie so much as I would have liked. In addition to my work at the General Hospital, I have been officiating as Superintendent of the Alipore Jail, and as the management of a jail is quite new to me, my time has been completely taken up in learning the details of the work. I am very glad that we came to Calcutta, for we both of us find life more interesting than in our up-country station.

One great advantage to me is meeting with other doctors, and the doctors here are pleasant companions, and excellent in many respects.

... You mentioned in one of your letters that we should establish a branch of the Medical Association at Calcutta. I find that this was done some time ago, and I have become a member. We meet once a month to read and discuss papers. Calcutta is very full just now, and there are reviews, balls, and parties, or something of that sort, every day. We are going to a ball to-night, and to Government House to-morrow evening. The Duke of Brabant is staying there, and my old schoolfellow Eustace Smith with him.

I have just received a long letter from Allie. We feel deeply grateful to you both for the interest you take in our little boy. Beatrix is a great delight to us; from observing her we can imagine what pleasure we should have in our little boy. She does not talk yet, but she knows every one about the house, and screams with delight when she sees her mother or me. When anything amuses her she bursts into fits of laughter, so natural and infectious that those who see her cannot avoid joining her in her laugh. It seems to me remarkable that a baby so young should laugh so heartily, but I never observed any other baby so closely as this one. I hope I have not bored you by talking so much of her.

TO HIS MOTHER.

CALCUTTA, *April 4th*, 1865.

THE date I see on a little tablet on my writing-table reminds me that to-day is your birthday, and I cannot help thinking of the anniversaries of this day long ago, when we used always to bring you little presents, learn hymns, or do something to give you pleasure in honour of the day. Afterwards, when we were separated, but not so far as we are now, I used to write letters (knowing what you valued most) so that you might receive them on your birthday. Now I am too far away to be able to calculate on your receiving a letter on any particular day, so I write a letter on the day itself to show you that I have not forgotten the old custom, and that I think as much of my mother as ever. We received letters from Isabella and you a few days ago. It always delights us to hear such good accounts of our little boy. When I hear that you are so fond of him, I feel glad that he was left in England, for I hope that by his cheerful temper he amuses and interests you, and is perhaps a pleasanter companion than his father would be. We still like Calcutta, although this is the hot season; but there is this advantage over up-country stations, that the nights are cool, for we feel the sea-breezes. Although I am writing in a cool house, the thermometer on my table is at 95°. As soon as the sun sets, however, it will be quite cool. I have much more to do now than I have ever had since I came to India. In addition to my work at the General Hospital, I am Superintendent of the largest prison in India, and Deputy-Inspector of Prisons in Bengal. The work that I have to do suits me very well. I have to prevent as well as cure disease; to see that evil-doers are not badly treated, but punished, taught, made to work, and improved. I see that they are made to work until all the wickedness is worked out of them for the time, and I know that this result is attained by the quietness that prevails in the prison at night. After a good day's work, the prisoners, like other people, sleep soundly.

TO HIS SISTER.

CALCUTTA, *May 20th*, 1865.

I NEVER had so much to do in my life as lately, and this is the reason that I have not written to you for some time. The state of great uncertainty about my appointment also had some effect in preventing me from writing, for I did not like to tell you about it until all was settled. I only heard yesterday for certain that I am to continue to act as Superintendent of the Alipore Jail and Deputy-Inspector of Prisons in Bengal. Before I was only officiating; now I am regularly appointed. For the present I am also to keep the General Hospital appointment, but shortly I shall be Superintendent of Lunatic Asylums instead. . . .

I read the articles on America in the Review with interest, but I do not altogether agree with the author. Having lived so much among savages I think has made me inclined towards slavery, and wishful for the extension of the institution in savage countries. Obedience ought to be the first lesson taught to races, as to children. The English allowed too much liberty, and were too gentle with the New-Zealanders, and here it is found absolutely necessary to govern the rude tribes very despotically. Too much freedom was allowed to the hired coolies in Assam, consequently the tea-planters were, many of them, ruined, and the progress of civilisation and cultivation was very nearly stopped in that country. Savages, like children, will not work unless they are forced to do so. Englishmen are the best masters they can have. At present the Bengal Government is making laws to force the coolies to work after they have engaged to do so, but at the same time it is intended to appoint inspecting protectors of coolies to see that no cruelty or injustice is exercised. The American Government should have done something of this sort.

P.S.—I am glad to hear such good accounts of our little boy. I have great hopes he will not disappoint us.

TO HIS SISTER.

July 19*th*, 1865.

WE have just received letters from you and L. chiefly relating to our little boy. We neither of us care particularly about his being handsome, so are not disappointed to hear that strangers are not struck by his beauty, but we are delighted to hear that he already begins to show signs that some day he will be intelligent, and possess manly qualities. Beatrix is very pretty and intelligent for her age. She is nearly thirteen months old, has cut eight teeth, can stand alone, but cannot walk. She understands a good deal that is said to her, and imitates whatever strikes her fancy. As yet she can only say "papa," "mamma," and "ayah." I mention all this in order that you may compare her intelligence with that of her brother at her age. She is rarely ill, and is always in good condition. I have had a little more time to myself than I have had the last three months, and this is rather fortunate, for the weather is getting too hot for work. In olden times cutcherries and public offices in Calcutta used to be shut up when the weather was very hot, but now the work is too important to be stopped, however hot the weather may be. The Judges complain of Sir Barnes Peacock, who himself will do any amount of work, and expects others to work as he does. The house that we are shortly going to occupy is one of the nicest in Calcutta, "the city of palaces," so we expect to be very comfortable. The garden and grounds are very extensive, and will suit well for the children.

TO HIS MOTHER.

GENERAL HOSPITAL, *August* 7*th*, 1865.

A LITTLE girl was born on the evening of Sunday, July 23d, whom we intend to call Margaret. She is just thirteen months younger than Beatrix. The work that I have to do is of an interesting character, and I consider myself very fortunate in having such useful work to do. The pay and prospects too are good, and these are not to be overlooked, with such a rapidly increasing family as mine is.

TO HIS SISTER.

ALIPORE, *September* 21*st*, 1865.

WE are both delighted with the portrait of our little boy, which Isabella was so kind as to send us. The likeness to Beatrix is so striking that we need scarcely send you a portrait of her; the brother and sister, although neither resembles their parents, are very like each other. Beatrix is a charming little girl, but occasionally very violent. This fault is very difficult to correct here. She is most despotic in her manner towards her bearer and ayah, in fact to all the servants about the house.

I am glad to hear that Sir C. Trevelyan's son has been elected member for Tynemouth. Although he has not as yet written anything of any value, he has a great deal of talent, and as he comes of a good family he will probably do Tynemouth credit some day. I travelled in the same steamboat with Sir C. Trevelyan, and have often seen Lady T. in Calcutta. She is excellent in every way.

Tell L. that I have followed his advice, and have been occupying myself with sanitary matters. A short pamphlet that I wrote about a month ago has brought me more credit than I deserve, and letters from all parts of India.

TO HIS MOTHER.

ALIPORE, *October* 3*d*, 1865.

I HAVE really had a great deal of anxiety and trouble of late, and I think this has made me overlook the post-days. I have also had a great deal of work. I always have about seventy sick sailors to treat in the General Hospital. This, as you may imagine, takes up a good deal of time; and besides this, I am Superintendent of the Alipore jail, where I have to manage about 2000 prisoners, as well as to look after the medical treatment of those who are sick. By degrees I hope to get the jail well organised, and then I shall have less to do. In May and June I was acting as Inspector-General of Jails, and this of course gave me additional work. I am very glad to have so much to do, for the work interests me.

TO HIS SISTER.

CALCUTTA, *December* 29*th*, 1865.

YOUR letters arrive as regularly as the mails. We are always delighted to receive and read them. They keep us acquainted with all that goes on at home, and strengthen our sympathetic connection with you. It is very painful to me to hear that our dear mother is losing her strength and cheerfulness. I like to think of her as I saw her seven years ago, and still hope that when I do see her again I shall not find her much changed. We are glad to hear such good accounts of our little boy.... It has been so warm that few English flowers have flourished this year. Christmas, I suppose you know, is the time that the corn and English flowers grow in this country. People here try to make their Christmas as like English Christmas as possible.

TO HIS MOTHER.

ALIPORE, *January* 19*th*, 1866.

I WAS glad to hear from Allie that you do not suffer from neuralgia nor the cold so much as you did last year. How I wish you could spend your winter with us! You would enjoy this climate at this time of the year. Every day is alike; there is no wind nor rain, and the temperature is that of a mild English summer.

TO THE SAME.

ALIPORE, *April* 4*th*, 1866.

THE anniversary of your birthday falls on a delightfully cool day. Of late the weather has been terribly hot, but to-day a most refreshing change has taken place, and I am enjoying the cool sea-breezes while thinking of you. We were delighted to hear such a good account of your health from Allie. Our youngest baby, Margaret, has a most charming temper; she has a smile for everybody, and rarely cries. She is remarkably fair, and has a great deal of colour for an Indian child. I think and hope that she will be like her grandmother.

TO HIS SISTER ISABELLA.

ALIPORE, *May* 20*th*, 1866.

YOU ask me whether you should lend money to our nephew G. to enable him to take a share in a saw-mill in New Zealand. I have little doubt that a saw-mill, properly managed, would pay well, and that G. would perform satisfactorily his part of the management; but we know nothing of the partner, and have no security that he is to be trusted. The only advice I can give is to consider the loan as a gift, and to act accordingly. It gave me great pleasure to hear of your generosity towards ———. I am charmed to have another proof of your kindheartedness and devotion to us. I feel that I owe you thanks for this as well as for all your other kindnesses. You will always reflect on what you have done with pleasure.

TO HIS MOTHER.

July 7th, 1866.

WE heard from Allie by the last mail about our little boy. It is a great satisfaction to us that he is so well cared for, and that he is liked so much by all of you.

TO L.

ALIPORE, *August* 1*st*, 1866.

I WAS very glad to receive your long kind letter a few days ago, and Annette was delighted with your description of the little boy. I agree with you that it is not of any serious consequence his being a "spoilt child" for the first three or four years of his life. It will necessitate a little rough treatment at school from the other boys, before a cure can be effected, but then he will, I hope, be all right, and not suffer too severely. I should prefer his not being spoilt; but what can be done? It is Isabella's nature to be too kind, and nothing anybody can say will induce her to treat the child differently. One thing is certain, that she is exceedingly good, and I should be the last to find fault. I am sure that the little boy will be better brought up than his sisters whom we are with continually. Indian children as a rule are detestable, yet they always recover with proper tuition in England. The servants are wonderfully patient and attentive, yet they always yield and submit to the most tyrannical treatment, which of course spoils the children. I hope, but can scarcely expect, that our children may be exceptions to the rule. Up to the present time our children like us better than their servants, and this makes me think that we may possibly be able to keep them in order, and counteract the evil influence of the servants.[1] You and Allie both ask if I have lost money by the Agra Bank. I am happy to say that I have escaped, but many that I know have been terrible losers. Allie seems to have a great aversion to all speculations. You know she sent me the £50 left her by Mr. Pow to invest. I did invest this in a company for spinning and weaving cotton in India, which I think was a good object. The company is very likely to do well; but as she objects to speculation, I will buy her investment, and pay for it by transferring the cottages near Derwent Bank to her.

[1] He was then but three years old. My dear Isabella had the principal charge of James my brother, as well as of his son James; and both were the better for her gentle loving care.

You will be glad to hear that the **Lieut.-Governor** of Bengal has given me the officiating appointment of Inspector-General of Jails until Dr. Mouat returns to India. This will probably lead to my being Dr. Mouat's successor, if in the meantime I do not get a better appointment. The better appointment would be one admitting private practice in Calcutta, but I think I prefer moderate Government pay to a large private practice. There is a good deal of jealousy, on account of my short service, but I can afford to disregard this now that I have the appointment. You see doctors are as jealous of each other here as at home.

You cannot be more desirous to see me again than I am to see you. The chief pleasure that receiving a better paid appointment gives me is the thought that it will enable me to visit England and see you all again. I often think of Derwent Bank, and all the trees we planted, and the "improvements." What an alteration the eight years must have made! My wife thinks you will be much struck with the change in me,—complexion quite changed, and instead of a slim boy, a stout strong man. I think it is as well to prepare you for a change, but you must not suppose that I have yet got the complexion of a guinea. The liver does not extend below the ribs yet. I am happy to say Annette is quite well and strong, and the two babies enjoy excellent health now. Beatrice is pale, but the baby is as healthy-looking as any English child at home. Annette joins in love to you and Allie.

TO HIS SISTER.

ALIPORE, *August 2d*, 1866.

You will be glad to hear that J. P. Grant, the new Governor of Jamaica, was much disliked by a certain party here for his leaning towards the natives, and I suppose you will hope that the conduct of the emancipated negro will not upset his calm impartiality. I am afraid he will find Jamaica more difficult to govern than Bengal. He led a most extraordinary life here. People could scarcely ever see him, for he rarely got up before three o'clock, rarely talked, but used to lie about on the sofa in pyjamas in most extraordinary postures. At night he wrote his orders, and transacted business, always by writing, never by interviews or conversation. He succeeded well, for he was clever with his pen, and thoroughly conversant with all questions connected with the government of Bengal. This plan will not do in Jamaica, where everything will be new to him.

If kindness, talent, and humanity are all that is required of a Governor of Jamaica, he will succeed. I am afraid, however, that the natives require severity, but in this you will not agree with me. Remember me most kindly to Mr. Wm. Smith, if he is still in your neighbourhood.

TO THE SAME.

ALIPORE, *September 20th*, 1866.

I HAVE just returned from Dinapore, Deegale, and Patna, where I have been inspecting jails. I enjoyed my visit to Patna very much. I was hospitably entertained by the Commissioner. My first regiment, the old 70th B. N. I., was at Dinapore, and of course it was a pleasure to see my old comrades, also to revisit old haunts. Patna is a very pretty place at this time of the year; the compounds (parks or fields surrounding the houses) are beautifully green; they all looked neat and park-like; the trees are very fine, and accidentally well placed. The train in which I returned to Calcutta was crowded with pilgrims, all old men and women. I should say there were a thousand of them. They were on their way to Gya, but probably numbers would die before reaching the end of their journey. The poor purdah-women seemed much bamboozled with the train and the crowd. Whenever they got separated from their guide, they squatted down on the ground, muffled up in their clothes, determined (like a little dog that we once had) to stick to the place where they were lost. Some of the high-caste pilgrims were objecting strongly to the *fraternité* of the railway carriage. They were appealing to the guard to turn a Chumar (low-caste man) out of their carriage, and when their appeals were useless they tried to bribe the Chumar to leave them. The natives who are accustomed to travel by train have given up the idea that they are defiled by contact with low castes.

TO HIS MOTHER.

ALIPORE, *Dec. 7th*, 1866.

I HAVE been away from Calcutta for three weeks on my tour of inspection of jails. I have been at Darjeeling, a station high up among the Himalayas, where our soldiers are sent to recruit their health. The station is 7000 feet high, and is as cold as England. As you climb up the mountain side, in an hour you pass from the vegetation of the tropics to that of the temperate zone. The forests through which I had to pass are magnificent, composed of Indian fig-trees, magnolias, chestnuts, oak, etc., all tangled together with curious creepers, and covered with mosses and endless varieties of orchids. There were canes about 500 feet long arranged on the trees like the rigging on the masts of a ship, and rendering the forest perfectly impenetrable. The scenery about Darjeeling is the grandest I ever saw, so grand as to be almost terrible. The highest mountains in the world, Mount Everest and Kinchin-junga, are about ten times as high as Skiddaw. They are distinctly seen from Darjeeling, and appear high up in the sky, brilliantly white, and look so near that you fancy you could throw a stone on them, although they are forty-five miles distant. When I was at Darjeeling the weather was perfectly clear and fine, without the least wind. I enjoyed myself very much, taking long rides on the mountain ponies, and I had magnificent views of the snowy range of mountains for upwards of one hundred miles. It was a great treat to get among the mountains again, but I do not think I should like to live at Darjeeling. It is too gloomy and terrible; no lakes or smiling valleys, as in Cumberland, to relieve the severity of the mountains; not even a visible river, for all the rivers are hidden from view by their steep banks overgrown with wood. The most cheerful object is the cold snowy range. The extensive view of ranges upon ranges of mountains, every one so distinctly seen, without any habitations, rivers, or evidence of life, makes one feel very lonely among these mountains, and the complete silence—for not the slightest sound is to be heard—enhances the feeling. It is most remarkable that there are scarcely any birds or animals to enliven the Darjeeling forests. There were even very few noisy insects when I was there, but plenty of most beautiful butterflies. I returned to Calcutta well, but the next day I was laid up with fever, caught probably by passing through the jungles.

TO HIS SISTER.

January 1867.

I HAVE such a lot to do now, travelling about, and writing inspection reports of the Bengal jails, that I find it difficult to avoid missing the post sometimes. I think, however, that Annette writes whenever I am unable to do so. I have just returned from Orissa, of which no doubt you have heard, for the famine has directed public attention to the district. I went there with the Commissioners who have been appointed by Government to inquire into the causes of the famine, and the best way of preventing famine in future. The Lieut.-Governor, Sir Cecil Beadon, has been much blamed, but I do not think he could have done much more than was done. The only way in which the famine could have been prevented would have been to have constructed canals and railroads years ago to convey rice into the country. Rice is too heavy and bulky to convey in carts, and the coast of Orissa being dangerous and without harbours, sending rice by sea was a very hazardous proceeding. Thousands of bags were lost last year in attempting this. I am very glad that I have to make these tours of inspection, because by so doing I learn my work thoroughly, and become acquainted with the Bengal civilians, my correspondents; but being away from home is a great nuisance, and travelling about in this country is a very difficult, fatiguing business. I have only two months more of this work, and then I shall revert to my old employment.

. . . It is very kind of you to wish to take care of our children. There is no one in the world I would trust them to more willingly than to you, but I should be afraid of giving you too troublesome a charge. Isabella and William and John also have offered to receive them, and I do not know how to thank them sufficiently for their kindness, for really the charge of children is no joke. I should have more faith in your method of exercising discipline than in that of any other member of the family, except my wife, who is a little more severe than you would be. She has completely succeeded in conquering Trix during my absence.

TO HIS MOTHER.

ALIPORE, *April 4th*, 1867.

I WISH you many happy returns of your birthday, and wish very much that I could do it in person. I have made the calculation that you taught us all, and conclude that you are seventy-six to-day.[1]

1867, add ten, subtract one, and that leaves seventy-six. I always think of you as you were eight years ago, and fancy that the eight years have not changed you so much as it has changed me. However, I think I am only altered in appearance, not in disposition, and I know that my love for my mother is not in the least diminished. I long to see you again; every year of absence increases my impatience to return. I enclose a little birthday present for you, which I think you will be as

---

[1] My dear mother's method of reckoning her age was an old joke against her. She added ten and subtracted one from the year of the century.

pleased to receive as if it were more valuable. The portraits are all good, except that of the little Margaret. Her chief beauty now is her colour, and that is not given in the photograph. Mine is very like, but in reality I am not so severe-looking as the photograph would lead you to suppose. We are delighted to receive such good accounts of our little boy, and hope that he will not disappoint your expectations.

TO HIS SISTER.

ALIPORE, *May 29th*, 1867.

It has been so terribly hot of late—alternately a furnace and a vapour-bath—that I have not had the energy to write to you. I have felt satisfied, after doing my necessary work, to repose quietly with a book under the punkah, or to watch with surprise the energetic play of our two babies, who appear quite unaffected by the extreme heat. The thermometer is only at $100°$ in the house, but $100°$ in Calcutta, where the air is moist, is as insupportable as $110°$ in the drier parts of India. Men and horses are dying of heat and apoplexy. Out of doors the heat is almost unendurable, but fortunately I very seldom am obliged to go out in the heat of the day.

We were very glad to receive letters from you and L., and to hear that our boy has gone to spend some time at Derwent Bank, where he will meet with as much kindness and more salutary discipline than at Etal Villa. We are both fully alive to the danger he runs of being spoilt by too much kindness.

I have felt the heat more this year than ever I felt it before; this probably is because I have been a little too long in India, and require a change. Every year one stays in India one tolerates the heat less. You must not be surprised if you see me returning to invigorate myself in England in a year or two.[1]

Annette tells me that our little boy's name is inscribed at the Mairie in Paris, as William Paul James. I told her that I wished him to be named William, and she of her own accord made the incongruous addition. You say you like the name Edward. So do I, but it has been an unlucky name in our family. Please select another name, and if I have an opportunity, I will carry out your wishes. Mother made a mistake in making me one of her executors. What can I do so far away? Why should you not be executor? or L.? I suppose our stupid laws will not allow of the former.

---

[1] Alas! he did not come until it was too late to save his valuable life.

TO THE SAME.

ALIPORE, *August 7th*, 1867.

I WROTE to you about a week ago, but mislaid the letter, and had not the courage to commence another then, for I was suffering from fever, and there is nothing so depressing or provocative of laziness as the species of fever one catches at Calcutta. Annette also has been ill, suffering from a malarious affection. I very much fear that the climate will have a bad effect on one or other of us, so that we shall require a change to Europe perhaps next year. The trip home and the sight of you all again would be delightful. I do not think that I should regret much being obliged to leave Calcutta, but I am doing so well here, and would run so much chance of spoiling my prospects by abandoning my work, that I shall not leave unless I am forced to do so. The children are in first-rate health, but Beatrice is more than three years old, and I should not like her to stay here beyond five. I think you would like our little girls; they are both pretty and well-behaved. My wife is expecting another baby. What shall I do with such a family? I think I must have a house built for them near Derwent Bank, hire a "gouvernante," and ask you to superintend.

TO HIS MOTHER.

ALIPORE, *August* 31*st*, 1867.

I WAS so delighted to hear from Allie, the other day, that you have been to Derwent Bank, and were enjoying excellent health and spirits. I suspect, from her description of you, that I shall find you when I return to England much the same as when I left eight years ago. We are all tolerably well now, but for the last month we have had a sick household. The two little girls have had fever, and my wife also has had fever for more than a month. Last Monday she was confined, and since then has been much better. Another little girl—but we are not sorry, for I like girls better than boys.

TO HIS SISTER.

ALIPORE, *October* 18*th*, 1867.

I AM afraid it is a long time since I wrote to you. Your kind letters however come as regularly every mail, and although I feel ashamed of not replying, I do not fear that my laziness will deprive me of the pleasure of receiving letters from you. Yet it is not altogether indolence which has prevented me from writing. I have been very hard worked of late. My colleague at the General Hospital has been ill, and I have had all his work to do. I have also been doing the work of Inspector-General of Jails, for Dr. Mouat has been a tour with Mr. Grey, the Lieutenant-Governor of Bengal. Now I have more leisure; my wife and the children are well; the weather is becoming cool again, and we are all feeling the beneficial effects of the change of weather. The little baby is very small, but is doing well, and I daresay ultimately will be all right. The other little girls are charming, and are remarkably healthy-looking for Indian children. They are very well-behaved, although inclined, when not checked, to be tyrannical and uproarious. I think you are right about people in India becoming indifferent regarding the loss of life, but I suspect there is the same tendency all over the world, and that the carnage in America and Germany was not regarded with much more horror in England than the Orissa famine in Calcutta. We all subscribed tolerably liberally, but I do not think we felt so much sympathy for the poor starving creatures; this is to be accounted for by the apathy of the natives themselves, their willingness to die, and indisposition to make efforts at self-preservation. It seemed sometimes as if they were glad to die, and gave the famine the same welcome as Juggernath's car. I must say, however, that whatever may have been the feelings of the inhabitants of Calcutta, the English officials of Orissa exerted themselves to the utmost. Most of them behaved nobly, and many that I know have ruined their health by working beyond their power. Sir Cecil Beadon too, on whom has fallen the greatest blame, is not a man to disregard his responsibility, or to be wanting in feeling for the poor sufferers. He was much abused during the mutiny for advocating clemency, and for prevailing on Lord Canning to pardon freely. Now, people admit that he was then right, and I have little doubt that when all the circumstances of the Orissa famine are thoroughly understood, it will be discovered that Sir Cecil Beadon did as much as could have been expected from him, and not only more than those who blamed him, but more than almost any one else could have done in his place. I have not formed this opinion carelessly or hastily, for I was much interested in the matter, and have read carefully most of the papers connected with the famine. I have also conversed with many of the officials in Orissa. I travelled with the Famine Commissioners, and passed through the districts where the famine was most felt. I have no doubt, as you say, that we take very different views of many questions, but I am not more violent than formerly,—if anything, less so. When we meet I have no doubt we shall talk quietly and argue calmly.

Perhaps I shall persuade you to think as I do on many subjects. Of one thing I am certain, that we shall do anything but quarrel—*tout à fait le contraire.*

TO HIS MOTHER.

ALIPORE, *November 7th,* 1867.

WE were glad to hear from Isabella and Allie by the last mail that you have been well throughout the year, and that you enjoyed your visit to Derwent Bank. We wish that you could spend a week at our house occasionally. You would so much enjoy the charming weather we have at present, but we are unfortunately too far away, and even if the railway were completed you would find the journey too long. We were in a tremendous hurricane the other day, an account of which you will no doubt have seen in the papers. Few people at Calcutta slept that night, and nearly every one took shelter on the ground floor of their houses. Many solid walls, and all the huts of the natives, were blown down. Our house, fortunately, is very solid, and sustained little damage. Its verandahs however were swept away, much to the terror of my wife, for the crash was tremendous. Next morning we saw the heavy beams of the verandahs sticking in the ground at a distance from the house, and looking like arrows hurled by a giant. Our children were taken down-stairs, and they slept with a few interruptions through the hurricane. Although windows and doors were carried away, and the wind blew fresh through the house, and the rain came through it in torrents, we found that in the morning only about £20 worth of damage was done to our furniture, for we had time to stow it away carefully. Hurricanes of this sort are very unusual in Calcutta. They occur on an average once in ten years. I am glad to have been in one, and do not wish to see another.

We are delighted with the last portrait of our little boy. He certainly promises to turn out well. We do not know how to thank Isabella and you for your kind care of him.

TO THE SAME.

April 4th, 1868.

YOU see I never forget the 4th of April. I always think of you, more especially on that day, and wish that I were near enough to wish you many happy returns in person. It is nine years now since I left England, and in another year I shall be entitled to leave, whether sick or well. The children will be then too old to remain any longer in India, and it is most probable that I shall return to Europe with the whole family, and that on your next birthday I shall be with you. I shall be so pleased to introduce our little girls to you. They are all three pretty, very good, and have charming dispositions. The two eldest are very fond of each other. The other day they were playing together on the verandah. A large owl made its appearance, and Beatrice ran pale and trembling with fear into the house; then it occurred to her that she had forgotten her little sister, and, notwithstanding her terror, she faced what she thought was the danger a second time, and brought her sister into the house, all this time trembling with fear. I tell you this, as I think it shows what a good loving little child she is, and that she has the courage to overcome fear.

I hear of you from Allie and William, who are both very good in writing, and it always delights me to learn that you enjoy such good health. Isabella also frequently sends us a letter, and tells us about you and our little boy. How kind she is! Annette sends her love to you. She has a most affectionate recollection of your kindness to her.

TO HIS SISTER.

CALCUTTA, *April* 10, 1868.

I HAVE just read your letter to Annette. I am sorry that she should have written to tell you about my pay being diminished, while the matter is still uncertain. I said nothing about it, partly because it caused me very little trouble, and partly because it was difficult to explain. The "cutting," as we call it here, is done by the Accountant-General, or some clerk in his office, and neither Sir J. Lawrence nor the Lieutenant-Governor, Mr. Grey, have had a word to say on the matter as yet. I know very well that they are both very well disposed towards me, and would willingly give me as much pay as I am entitled to. The difficulty at present arises from a misunderstanding of a Government resolution either on my part or on the part of the Accountant-General. This will be shortly cleared up, and I trust probably my views will be adopted by Government.

In any case I have little to complain of, for my salary, even if curtailed, will be greater than any other Government servant, civil, military, or medical, of my service and standing.

My good fortune has given rise to a considerable amount of jealousy, which so far misled some that they sent a petition against me to the Secretary of State in England.

This, as you may imagine, did me good rather than harm. These proceedings of my enemies do not annoy me in the least.

TO HIS BROTHER.

April 19*th.*

THE weather is now terribly hot, and I feel often quite done up with my necessary work, and little disposed to make any extra exertion. I am now sitting under a punkah with scarcely any clothes, and yet am dripping with perspiration. All last night I was in the same state, and awoke this morning feeling as if I had been boiled, and as tired as when I went to bed. I never felt the heat so much before, and I suppose every year I shall feel it more and more. This is the rule in India; new-comers suffer from the heat much less than old Indians. We have been very anxious about our daughter Beatrice; she has had an attack of malarious continued fever; for five days she took absolutely nothing but water; then we became alarmed, and forced her to drink a little soup and milk, but for eight days she took next to nothing. We left Alipore and went with her to the General Hospital for a week, thinking that the change of air might do her good, and now we have returned to Alipore, and she is rapidly recovering, but too weak to stand.

TO L.

ALIPORE, *July* 17*th*, 1868.

I AM so glad you were pleased with the Lieutenant-Governor's praise of me. The satisfaction you expressed I think pleased me as much as his publicly recorded opinion, which will probably be of value to me hereafter. Annette was delighted with your account of our little boy. We hope he may turn out as well as you expect, but often fear, from the accounts that reach us, that aunt Isabella is spoiling him. Allie, I know, can manage him well, and the thought that she will watch him carefully *nous tranquillise*. We both feel very grateful to you for inviting him so often to Derwent Bank. Our three little girls are very lively and happy. Of course we think them good and pretty, and are very much attached to them, but we shall have to separate soon, as it will not do to keep them much longer in this country. I often think of Derwent Bank. You would see the effect of what I learnt there if you were to come to Alipore. The land surrounding my house is more extensive than the Derwent Bank estate, and it is a great pleasure to me to plant trees on it, and decorate it, making *circumbendibus* paths with careful attention to the line of beauty, in the true old Derwent-Bank style. I have not very much time however to spend in this way, for besides looking after a hospital and jail, I have engines and complicated machinery for spinning jute to look after, to superintend a large printing establishment; I am also Justice of the Peace for Calcutta, and take a great deal of trouble about the public health.

TO HIS SISTER.

ALIPORE, *Sept.* 26*th*, 1868.

I CONTINUE to receive your kind letters regularly, but I scarcely deserve them, for I am terribly indolent in not writing to you. I am nevertheless very grateful. The kindness you and L. have shown to our little boy is very highly appreciated by me and Annette. We know how much good he derives from his visits to you, for everybody in writing from Shields says he returns there quite a good child. I hope he may fulfil our expectations and turn out well. Energy and vivacity form a good basis to work upon.

. . . We have had a wonderfully cool summer. All the rain that has fallen in India this year appears to have been concentrated in Bengal. In consequence Central India and the north-west are burnt up, and it is feared—in fact it is almost certain—that there will be a famine there, for which, I suppose, some poor Lieutenant-Governor will be called to account. I was walking through the burial-ground here the other day, and saw two tombstones, not very far from each other, one bearing the name H. W. M. Thackeray, and the other Philip Firmin. Thackeray you know was born at Calcutta, and I should think these must have been connections of his.

P.S.—I have read Piazzi Smyth's book on the Pyramids with great interest. He is too enthusiastic to be trusted, and I do not believe in his idea of inspiration. The correspondence in the measurement with the earth's axis must be an accidental coincidence.

TO THE SAME.

ALIPORE, *Jan.* 19*th*, 1869.

YOUR letter telling me about the elections arrived when the Calcutta community was also in a state of excitement about the arrival of the new Viceroy. The day that Lord Mayo arrived, the troops were all arranged for his reception, and all the Government servants were assembled on the grand staircase of Government House. Of course we were all eager to see him. He is very different from Sir John Lawrence, and I think will be more popular. Lord Mayo is affable, fond of talking, and easy in his manners. He is a robust, healthy-looking man, with a great square head, reminding me of the portraits of O'Connell. The Countess appears amiable.

I was afraid at one time that Sir John was going to leave India without receiving any public demonstration of respect. But the day before Lord Mayo arrived, he was entertained at the Town Hall by the military and civilian officers of Calcutta. At the dinner there were about 250 present, and Sir W. Mansfield presided. Sir John made a very good speech, but he is out of health, and his voice was not strong enough to fill the room. One of the aides-de-camp was telling me that he becomes quite affected, and breaks down in conversation when he talks about leaving India. It is not surprising that he has a great affection for the country in which he has spent thirty-nine years of his life. Last night I met him at Government House. It is sad to see how worn and old-looking he has suddenly become. This makes me fear that he will not survive his viceroyalty longer than Lord Dalhousie and Lord Canning survived theirs. We are all well, and enjoying the calm cool weather. This year we have had no really cold weather, for there has been no rain since October, and it is always unbearably hot out of doors. In the house, however, with the door and windows open, it is pleasant enough, and also out of doors in the mornings and evenings. Our garden is charming, full of roses, and all sorts of English flowers, besides a number of magnificent Indian flowers. The Bignonia Venusta and the Bougainvillia are in full flower. I cannot describe their magnificence to you, but I believe that small specimens are to be seen at Kew. If you could see them, you might form some idea of their beauty when growing luxuriantly as they do here.

TO L.

ALIPORE, *Feb.* 21*st*, 1869.

I RECEIVED your kind letter about our little boy. It gives me great pleasure to hear that you like him, and I hope he will be as much as possible with you. I often think how pleasant it will be to meet you and him in Cumberland, and to climb some of our old mountains together again. I can get leave now for a few months, but I do not think that would be satisfactory, so prefer waiting a little longer and then taking leave for two years. Our children are in robust health this year, so we think we will keep them for another hot season in India. Sometimes I feel very tired of my work, and long to take a rest. From morning to night I am every day hard at work, and in the hot weather it is very exhausting. My work is not disagreeable, but I have a lot of responsibility, and have to keep my subordinates in order, and this is not always an easy task. I suppose that I govern the largest jail in the world. The average number of prisoners is 2500. Lord Mayo came to see the jail almost immediately after his arrival in India. He has had great experience of jails in Ireland, and he told me that the subject was one to which he had paid great attention, and in which he took great interest. We had a long conversation, about an hour and a half, and when he left the jail he wrote in the visitor's book that he "was astonished and greatly pleased with what he had seen."

Lord Mayo has a most charming manner, and is very much liked. He entertains in much grander style than Sir J. Lawrence. We have at present invitations for a concert, a dinner, and two children's parties at Government House.

TO HIS SISTER.

ALIPORE, *April 6th*, 1869.

THE children are good, affectionate, lively, and obedient. I do not think you will find them troublesome, but they will give you sufficient occupation to be pleasant. I need scarcely tell you that it will be very satisfactory to me to know that you have charge of them, for I know that they will be as well cared for as if they were with their parents. They are in excellent health now, but we cannot keep them in India, and it is possible that we may find it necessary to send them away or take them to Europe before the end of the year. Our hot season has fairly commenced now; the sun is very powerful, and the air is so hot and dry that blotting-paper is not necessary. The thermometer in the house is at 94°. Nevertheless, on account of the dryness of the air, the weather is pleasant and wholesome. It is true that the natives suffer from cholera, but this is due probably in a great measure to the filthy water which they drink, and to the dirty houses and neighbourhood in which they live.

TO THE SAME.

ALIPORE, *April 26th*, 1869.

THERE are so few medical officers in India that Government has been obliged to refuse furlough to many, and I see no prospect of my obtaining furlough for a very long time. Sick-leave is the only leave that is granted, and this only in case of extreme sickness. My only hope of seeing you soon is by taking privilege-leave for three months. Privilege-leave is leave for one month in every year, which is allowed to every one, and this can accumulate for three years. I am entitled to three months' leave, and I have applied for it to commence in July, so that if my application is granted you may expect to see me in August. This will not interfere with my furlough, so that a few years hence I shall pay you another visit, and remain in Europe for two years. I shall be disappointed if my application for privilege-leave is not granted, for I am very anxious to see mother this year. There are great difficulties in the way, for it devolves on me to find some one who will do my work during my absence, and it is not easy to arrange this matter. Since making my application I have been very impatient to know the result. I am eager to be off, to be home, and to see you all again. The trip I suppose will cost us very nearly £1000. This seems a large sum of money to spend for one month in England, but we shall enjoy our visit to you all immensely, and on our return we will economise. We are both so glad to hear that our little boy is going to stay with you until June.

TO THE SAME.

ALIPORE, *May* 11*th*, 1869.

MY application for privilege-leave for three months has been refused on the ground that there is no one to do my work, so I must be patient, and wait until some more doctors arrive from England. I was enjoying in anticipation the pleasure of passing a week with you at Derwent Bank, and am disappointed that it cannot be managed. Captain Murray was here last evening, and we had a talk together of Keswick, and the old and new inhabitants. His account of our boy is very satisfactory.

TO THE SAME.

ALIPORE, *August* 6*th*, 1869.

YOUR kind letters arrive regularly, and are always eagerly opened and read by us. It is very good of you to write so frequently, and not even to complain that your letters are not answered. Since my disappointment in not obtaining leave, I have felt more than usually indolent about writing, and the kind letters which I have lately received from home, expressing delight at the prospect of seeing me soon, have only added to my embarrassment, for I feel that I ought not to have excited expectations before I was sure that my leave would be granted. We have all kept remarkably well through the hot weather so far, and although the weather is horribly steamy now, I suffer from nothing but a sensation of fatigue and laziness. I have to stand about the hospital and jail for about four hours every morning, and after I have gone through this, feel very much disinclined for office-work, which I am obliged to do during the rest of the day. The weather in Calcutta during August and September is certainly very oppressive, and all those that can, escape from it. Unfortunately I am one of those that must remain at their post.

TO HIS SISTER.

August 27*th*, 1869.

MR. B. gives a good account of ——, and I hope he will continue to improve. The estate on which he is employed is not in a very thriving condition this year. Mr. B. has spent £2000 more than he has gained, and prospects are bad. There is scarcely any grain in the surrounding country, and unless the crop of rice this season is a remarkably good one, there will be a famine in the north-west. Mr. B. takes a very gloomy view of affairs, and anticipates a very horrible famine. However, those who have most experience are often wrong, and it is to be hoped that a timely fall of rain may save the crops. In any case there must be great distress, for at Gurrockpore the price of rice is now more than three times as great as it usually is. Bengal and Orissa are well off this year, and rice is being exported to the north-west, but the carriage is very costly.

TO THE SAME.

ALIPORE, *December* 7*th*, 1869.

YOU ask, in a letter which I have just received, whether I intend sending our youngest little girl along with the others, or keeping her here to console us. After much deliberation and hesitation, I have determined on sending her off. I think it better for her that she should be in Europe, for she is more than two years old,—and better for me too, for the longer the children are with me the more I become attached to them, and the more painful is the thought of parting with them. I absolutely am afraid to think of parting with Trix. I fancy I am different from many fathers, for I scarcely can comprehend the parental feeling for young babies, and I have a totally different feeling for those I know well, and those I know but imperfectly or not at all. I can understand Isabella's dissatisfaction in my apparent want of interest in my little boy. She is mistaken however in supposing that I take no interest in him. I am on the contrary very pleased to hear good accounts of him, and sorry when I hear the reverse. I am prepared also to exert myself, and do whatever I am able to help in making him a useful member of society. When I see and know him I shall probably take a deeper and more loving interest in him. In the meantime it gives me the greatest pleasure to hear how kind you and L. are to him; and to feel that he cannot possibly be better cared for and more kindly treated than he is. You will, I think, be delighted with our little girls, for they appear to me to have charming manners, and are very loving and intelligent. I shall be very anxious to hear what you think of them. I hope to collect my family together, and be with them for two years, when I take my furlough, to which I shall shortly be entitled, and of which I shall avail myself when I have an opportunity.

TO THE SAME.

ALIPORE, *January 8th*, 1870.

I HAVE received your letter in which you suggest that our youngest daughter should be left at Etal Villa. I perceive that you are rather afraid of so many children being too much for you, and I am not astonished, although I think your apprehensions will disappear when you see the children. I do not think they will trouble you, if you are able to get a good governess to look after them. It will be necessary probably to increase your house-accommodation by building a room to the south. You will then be able to cut them off from the rest of the house, and L. will not be disturbed by their noise, if they ever should become noisy. At present they are in capital order, very obedient and affectionate, as you will see in a few months. I should like, if possible, that they should be with you, for I know they will be happy at Derwent Bank. I do not like troubling mother with them, for I fancy she is not strong enough to bear with their vivacity, or to keep them in order, and I prefer England to France. I shall not hear from you again in reply to this letter, before the children leave me, so you and Annette must decide together what has to be done. She will take the children to see you, and I hope will leave them with you. If not, I shall not be annoyed, for I know perfectly well how kind and good you are, especially to me, and that if you do not keep the children, you have a very good reason for not doing so. Please give my love to L. and thank him for his very kind letter to me.

TO HIS SISTER.

ALIPORE, *February 7th*, 1870.

I HAVE just received your letter describing your journey through the snow to Shields, and telling me how glad you will be to see Annette and the three little girls. It is very kind of you to consent to take charge of all of them; it will be a great consolation to me to think that they are with you, and certainly well looked after. At the same time I hope you will not hesitate, if you find them too troublesome, to let us know, so that we may make other arrangements. I am firmly persuaded that you will like them very much, for they are all pretty, lively, intelligent, and loving, but three is a large number, and it is possible to have too much of a good thing. I myself feel now that I cannot have too much of them, but of course I am prejudiced in their favour. I can scarcely tell you how painful the thought of being separated from them is to me. The pain is not in the least lessened by the consideration that I have brought all this on myself, and that in leaving my home I inflicted as much pain on those who loved me as I am now suffering. Annette is not at all happy at the thought of being away for several months. She is disposed to return immediately, but I am anxious that she should not return before September. I know that she will not consent to stay away after she has taken the children to England. She will be so unhappy, that she will at once hurry back to India, and so lose the advantage of being away for a hot season. For this reason I wish her to stay two or three months in Paris before going to England. There she will be tolerably happy with the children and her own relations. We were on board the "Mongolia" yesterday, and saw the cabin which she will occupy. As a cabin it is a good one, but it looked terribly dismal, and Annette's heart sank when she saw it. The whole appearance of the lower deck was far from engaging, and the "board-of-ship" smell gave her *mal au cœur*. I daresay if we all had been going off together the ship would have appeared more cheerful. Can you remember Cowan, who lived at Dr. Lorimer's with me in 1851? He is staying with us just now because he is very ill, and requires looking after. I am very anxious about him, for I fear he has abscess of the liver commencing. This is a very fatal disease.

TO HIS **SISTER** ISABELLA.

ALIPORE, *Feb. 24th*.

I HAVE just received a very kind letter from you telling me about our little boy's birthday, and giving such a good account

of his character and intelligence. I certainly am very anxious to
make his acquaintance, and wish I could manage to get off with
Annette and the children. I am almost reconciled to the idea
of being separated from my children, by the thought that they
will be loved as much, and certainly looked after as well, if not
better, than if they were with me. It is, however, very hard
to part with them, and the rapid approach of the time for separation makes me very sad. I think you will be pleased with
our little girls. They are considered pretty, but at their age it
is difficult to say what they will be. At present we can trace no
resemblance either to their father or mother. Perhaps, however,
you, who knew me so well at their ages, may be able to see a
likeness. They will not be able to talk to you in English when
you first see them, but they will soon learn enough to be able
to say all they require, for the vocabulary of a child is small.
My love to mother and my son, and many thanks for all your
kindness to the latter.

TO HIS SISTER ALICE.

ALIPORE, *March* 10*th*, 1870.

I HAVE just received your letter dated Feb. 4th. It is quite
true that at the fancy ball I wore a dress similar to that which
Henry VIII. is supposed to have worn. I was scarcely, however,
stout enough to personate the king whom you dislike so much.
It was not admiration of his character that induced me to wear
the costume, although I believe he was no worse than his con-
temporaries. My only reason for adopting the costume was
that it was the only one I could easily obtain at the last
moment when I decided to go to the ball. I should infinitely
have preferred not making a guy of myself, and only did so
because I wished Annette and a lady who was staying with us
to see the ball, which in truth we found very amusing and
perfect of its kind. Most of the costumes were very pretty,
and Lord Mayo looked particularly well as Lord Cornwallis. Our
present Governor-General appears to have a talent for arranging
pageants. He got up the investiture of the Duke with the Star
of India in grand style. I must say, however, that I think the
day for these displays has gone by, and when one comes to
think about them their absurdity is more striking than their
grandeur. An accident which occurred during the proceedings
had a very comical effect. There was not sufficient room to
wave the banner over the Prince's head, and in consequence his
hair was brushed three times over his eyes.

We all liked the Prince; he is a first-rate, manly fellow, is
well educated, and does his work thoroughly. When he came

to the jail he was very affable, and appeared to take much interest in what I told him of the management of the jail and of the prisoners. I gave him a photograph as a souvenir of the place.

Annette and the children left on the 1st of March. You will probably hear of their arrival in Paris before you receive this letter. The parting, as you may imagine, was very sad, and recalled vividly to my mind our parting in London eleven years ago. As the steamer went off I heard the pretty voice of Trix calling to me across the water to come with her, and felt inexpressibly sorrowful. Now I am beginning to get reconciled to my solitary life, but the house appears terribly lonely. I am anxiously waiting for a letter from Madras. As we have had very fair weather here, I hope they have had a good voyage. Annette will have so much trouble and anxiety with the children that she will not have time for melancholy. As I told her, "La tristesse est pour celui qui reste."

Constant occupation and moderate exercise, which I am obliged to take, keep me in good health.

My love to L. and kisses for my son, of whom I am glad to hear such good accounts.

TO HIS SISTER.

ALIPORE, *April 9th*, 1870.

I HAVE received your letter telling me of the sort of religious education you propose giving our children. I am quite of your opinion that their minds should not be troubled with dogmas. If they were with me, I should only teach them what I firmly believed myself, and should carefully guard against their being terrified by stories of hell and the devil.

As yet I have only heard from Aden, but I am anxiously looking out for a letter from Suez. I am glad that you think of teaching our little boy to swim, and think it would be well if his sisters were taught to do so also. Costumes might be made for them, and they might all be taught together. I dine out a great deal just now. Last week I dined *en famille* with the Lieutenant-Governor, and again with Sir Barnes Peacock, the Chief-Justice. These dinner-parties are oppressive in hot weather. It is a horrible Calcutta custom to prolong the dinner with a succession of wines and dishes for two hours. The Governor-General has gone to Simlah. He was very popular until the Budget was read the other day, and now people are beginning to speak against him, and they are absolutely furious against Sir Richard Temple, the Finance Minister. It is on account of the $3\frac{1}{2}$ per cent. income-tax, as this falls chiefly on Europeans. The tax cannot be screwed out of the natives, for they never tell the truth about their incomes. The tax is equally unpopular with the natives, for they do not like paying money. Many will be unjustly over-taxed, but the majority will escape. The former will be actively discontented, and the latter will pretend to be so.

TO THE SAME.

ALIPORE, *May* 11*th*, 1870.

By the time this letter reaches you I daresay you may have seen, or at all events you will shortly see, our little girls. How I wish I could be present also! You can scarcely imagine how I miss them, for I am immensely fond of them. They used to come into my office at all times of the day. Their play and talk never disturbed me. In fact I think I got on better with my work when they were present than when I was alone. Now I feel as if I had lost them for ever. When I see them again they will be totally changed, and will not know me. It is a great consolation to me to think that they will probably be with you, and I long to hear what you think of them. You must tell me truly. I would much rather myself suffer a disappointment than that you should have your peace of mind disturbed by a troublesome charge. I think you will like the children, but it is possible that like other fathers I may not see the defects of my children, and that they may not appear as nice to you as to me. If this should unhappily be the case, you must not hesitate to tell Annette. By the last mail, although it brought English news up to the 15th April, I only received news from Annette up to the 8th. I fancy she has failed to make herself acquainted with the dates on which the post for India is despatched. You think she ought to have stayed in the south of France for a month. I wish she had done so, for that would have delayed her return to India. I very much fear that she may come out before the hot weather is over, and so do away with the good which she would otherwise derive from the change to Europe. I hope you will try to persuade her to remain until the middle of September. I am miserable alone, but I endure this willingly for the sake of the good which I hope her stay in Europe will do her. It is terribly hot in Calcutta, and we shall probably have a very hot summer. The crows and sparrows are all panting with their beaks open, and no one leaves the house who can avoid it. I have a great deal to do, and would much prefer taking it easy.

In this hot weather drinking **iced water and smoking** are the most tempting occupations.

TO HIS SISTER.

ALIPORE, *June* 18*th*, 1870.

I HAVE received your kind letter, in which you tell me that you intend going to London to meet Annette. It is very kind of you to do so, and I am sure she will be delighted to see you. Annette has certainly had a very troublesome time of it since she left me. Misfortunes and annoyances seem to have been heaped upon her. At first I used to look forward with impatience for the arrival of the mail, now with dread, and when I receive the letters I am afraid to open them, for fear that they may announce that the children have got small-pox, or that some other dreadful calamity has fallen upon them. I shall not feel happy until I hear that the children are comfortably settled at Derwent Bank. There they will be well clear of all infectious diseases, and I shall not fear any harm coming to them from revolutions. It is very depressing to receive such bad news of the children; at this distance one feels so helpless. It is useless even to give advice, for it is sure to arrive too late to be of any use. I wish I could, as you suggest, get away in autumn, and bring Annette back with me. I fear I must not think of this, but it is impossible to say what may happen.

TO L.

ALIPORE, *July* 22*d*, 1870.

I RECEIVED your kind letter, and the photograph of our little boy and the donkey by the last mail. The boy appears wonderfully big and strong for his age. I have great difficulty in forming a very definite idea of him. Photographs are excellent as aids to recollection, but few of them are sufficiently complete to enable one to form a picture in the mind of the person represented, unless one has previously seen the individual.

I am very glad that you like the little boy, and that you think well of him. I think you will like them all. I am afraid sometimes that you may find them too noisy, but then I remember that you have a big house, and that you can keep them at a distance when you find them troublesome. I am eagerly looking out for an account of their arrival at Derwent Bank, and am anxious to hear how you like them, and what you think of them. Beatrice is very good, thoughtful of others and kind. She is my favourite, but chiefly because, being older, I have known her longer, and time has strengthened my attachment to her. I am by no means cheerful when I think about them, and suspect that I made a mistake in coming to India. There is a prospect now, and this is cheering, that I shall be able to retire before I am old.

TO HIS SISTER.

ALIPORE, *Aug.* 18*th*, 1870.

I HAVE received the letter announcing the arrival of my family at Shields. My wife says that you are all very kind to her, and that she is delighted with the manner in which you have received her. I felt certain that she would meet with a kind reception, but it is pleasing to me to hear of it. I am glad you like the little girls. The other day I received their portraits. As you may imagine, I often look at them, and think how sad it is to be separated from them. I felt terribly losing Trix, but the worst is over now, and I am pleased to think that they are in a climate where they can be out all day long, and be happy and healthy. I am surprised to hear that they struck you as being so delicate; we used to consider them remarkably robust and strong, but then we compared them with Calcutta children, whereas you see them alongside of the ruddy children of East Northumberland. The sea-air I fancy will soon give them a colour, and this will improve them immensely.

The telegrams of the war are intensely interesting. I hope those Prussians will not overrun France. Is it not horrible to think of their getting into Paris?

TO L.

ALIPORE, *Aug.* 26*th*, 1870.

YOUR letter written when Allie had gone to meet my family at Shields was very welcome. I have not the least doubt that the children will be as happy, as well cared for, and as well educated with you and Allie, as they could be anywhere. I am consequently delighted at your having undertaken the charge, but fully understand that you have done so with the proviso that they do not interfere with your comfort and repose. If ever this occurs I expect you will let us know. I am glad that you have agreed to build a story to the south wing, for this will enable you better to keep the children at a distance when troublesome.

As you may imagine, the news of the war in Europe is intensely interesting to me. I am afraid France is in a very bad way. The Prussians seem to be carrying everything before them. I sympathise with the Frenchmen, and am sad when I think of their humiliation. It appears to me that the two nations are equally in the wrong; they have both been preparing for and longing for the war. The penalty to both is terrible to think of.

TO HIS SISTER.

ALIPORE, *Nov.* 11*th*, 1870.

YOUR letters of the 13th of October have just arrived, and we are delighted to hear such a good account of the little girls. I am so glad to see from your letter that Beatrice is "orderly, and delights in helping" you. I think she is charming, and believe that you will become exceedingly attached to her, and she to you. Her thinking of us after so long a separation shows that she is a very affectionate little child. Laura also, but in a different way, is equally nice, more independent and careless about sympathy, and less sensitive. The account of little Mary is charming. It affected Annette so much that she could not restrain her tears. You say that the French are infatuated not to accept the terms Prussia offers. It appears to me that the Prussians are equally infatuated not to accept the French offers, and are moreover both cruel and criminal. The French are as it were, in a corner; they have to choose between civil war and war with the enemy. The latter seems to me preferable. The English, I feel sure, would not, in similar circumstances, insist on the humiliation of a conquered enemy, and it is evident to me that the Prussians are still strongly tinged with barbarism.

TO THE SAME.

ALIPORE, *Nov.* 1870.

IT makes me sick to read in the German papers the attacks on the French people, who are described as debauched, and so wicked as to be only fit for extermination, and I wonder at Englishmen repeating their fallacious reasons for pursuing their horrid vengeance. Glad that you agree with me in thinking that the Prussians should be prevented from destroying Paris.

TO L.

ALIPORE, *Nov.* 9*th*, 1870.

I HAVE just received your long kind letter dated October 9th. I can scarcely describe the pleasure I felt in reading your description of the little children. Do not for an instant suppose that I have any doubt of the judicious hygienic treatment they would receive at Derwent Bank. When my wife was at Shields she wrote begging me to write to you on the subject of cold baths, and I simply complied with her request, but I think I also said I had perfect faith in your treatment, and willingly left all in your hands. If I did not say so, I meant it, and felt it. I am delighted to hear that you find the children so engaging. Your letter convinces me that you take a great interest in them, and that you will become attached to them. I sometimes fear that the anxiety of looking after them will be too much for Allie, and these fears are confirmed by your statement that she is losing flesh. It makes me very unhappy to think that she is exerting herself beyond her strength, and I hope you will prevent her from doing so. I do not think now there is any cause for anxiety. The children have all good constitutions, and as regards external circumstances could not be better off than at Derwent Bank. Allie should not exert herself; she should have all the assistance she requires, and merely superintend. Please tell Allie that I have received her kind letter, but as Annette is writing to her to-day, I will defer replying until next mail. Allie asks if anything can be done for my wife's parents in Paris, but it is clear that nothing can be done for them. They would not leave, even if they could. They are very old, and would rather die than leave the place where they have lived all their lives. I still hope that the French will be victorious, and that little harm will be done to Paris. The King and Bismarck made a mistake and committed a crime in refusing to make peace after Sedan, and I think they will be punished.

TO HIS MOTHER.

ALIPORE, *Nov. 20th*, 1870.

I THINK it right that I should tell you before any one else of my good fortune in having been appointed Inspector-General of Jails. It is not only right that I should impart this news to you first, but it is also my natural inclination to do so, for I feel that no one will be more pleased to hear of my success, and there is no one whom I am more delighted to please. I am always grateful for all you have done for me, and the long years we have been separated have not diminished my strong filial affection for you. My inclination has always been to return to England and see you, but I think that, for the sake of my wife and children, I was right in not yielding to it. Now I have an assured position, and shall be able to pay you frequent visits during the remainder of my service in India. The work I have to do now is of a responsible nature, but not so hard as hitherto. You will have some idea of this when I tell you that there are about sixty prisons under my direction. Shortly I shall have to undertake a tour through Bengal and Assam; and as we have no children here now, my wife will accompany me. To me travelling will be especially pleasant as a change, after having led a somewhat monotonous and hard-worked life at Calcutta for so many years.

We receive good accounts of our children, and consider ourselves very fortunate in having them in such good hands. I sometimes fear that they will be too much for Allie, and that she will be wearing herself out with anxiety. Fortunately Margaret has gone to help her.

TO L.

ALIPORE, *Nov.* 22*d*, 1870.

... I have have just time to write you a few lines to tell you of my good fortune in having been appointed Inspector-General of Jails. The appointment generally gives satisfaction, but of course I must expect a certain amount of jealousy, as I am junior to many of the officers who will act under me.[1]

---

[1] "No one acquainted with the progress of the Bengal Jail Department during the past five years will learn with surprise that Dr. Fawcus has been appointed to succeed Dr. Mouat as Inspector-General of Jails; nor will any one so informed doubt that the Lieutenant-Governor has exercised a sound judgment in the selection. Apart from the extraordinary development which the Alipore Jail has undergone in Dr. Fawcus's hands, and the perfect knowledge of detail, as well as the governing faculty implied in such success as he has achieved, he has been for several years Deputy-Inspector-General of Jails, and has officiated in the principal office. This position in itself includes a natural claim to the higher post, the recognition of which gives a stimulating hope to every officer of the Jail Department.

"It is only quite lately that a Jail Department could be said to exist in the sense of a body of officers devoting themselves to the service of the jails, and relinquishing, with that object, all other prospects; and as there can be no reasonable doubt of the material advantages which have followed this organisation, so is it desirable that permanent efficiency be secured, by enabling incumbents to feel that their labour is not devoid of fruit to themselves—that they have, as other branches of the service have, a future before them. On the first creation of special departments it is often inevitable that men should be selected for their government on grounds of general ability and probable fitness, who are without special experience of the work before them. Even later it is occasionally found expedient to postpone the nascent claims of incumbents to outside merit of exceptional kind. The Jail Department is fortunate in having produced in its infancy an officer of rare and well-attested fitness to administer its affairs, and so, by the precedent, establishing a succession of preferment within its ranks; fortunate also in the opportunity having occurred under the Government of Sir William Grey, with whom no opinion or consideration prevails that has not the public good for its aim and foundation."—*From the Calcutta Englishman.*

TO HIS SISTER.

ALIPORE, *Nov.* 23*d*, 1870.

. . . Your charming letter dated 19th October has just arrived, and I feel forced to write and thank you for it. I see that you fully appreciate Beatrix's good qualities, and that you will soon love her almost as much as I do. I am glad Margaret is with you. Our uproarious little family require a great deal of looking after, and would be too much for you alone. As you do not think it necessary to build the other wing to Derwent Bank, I have another improvement to suggest,—a large bath-room with a stone floor, and a stove to keep it warm and free from draughts of cold air.

CHAPTER VII.

THE LAST LETTERS FROM INDIA.

"The fame is quench'd that I foresaw;
The head hath missed an earthly wreath."

TO L.

ALIPORE, *Jan.* 11*th*, 1871.

... For the last month I have been in a very unhappy condition with my spleen. On Sunday last I tried a change of air. Annette and I went off to Serampore, the old Danish settlement, and headquarters of the Baptist missionaries, and editors of *The Friend*, the old enemies of the East India Company.

We found very comfortable quarters in an hotel on the banks of the Hooghli. The change was very pleasing, and did me a little good. The views from our verandah up and down the river were very fine, especially towards sunrise and sunset. The wind was refreshing, and the sight of boats of all descriptions, passing rapidly up and down the river with the tide, very cheerful. In my weak state it was a pleasure to sit in the verandah watching these. We explored the town on foot, and were interested in seeing the curious old Danish buildings. This, however, rather exhausted me. We also went out several times in a boat, crossed over to Barrackpore, where there is a small zoological garden, and a lot of tigers. We left Alipore on Saturday and returned on Monday. My appetite, which had almost gone, has returned to a certain extent, and I have regained a little of my colour. But this change is not enough, and I intend now to go by steamer to Juggernath, which is on the sea-coast, a charming place, where there is always a tremendous surf, which renders bathing safe, as the sharks avoid it.

There are a lot of curious old temples at Juggernath, and the scenery to the south is very fine, mountains, lakes, and sea being all there. I am looking forward to this trip eagerly, as I feel sure that it will restore me to health, and fill my veins with red blood instead of yellow, which, to judge by my complexion, appears to be the colour of the little I have at present. I congratulate myself on not having fallen sick before getting my present appointment. Now I can treat myself to a change of air, which I could not do formerly. You may imagine that our home is not very cheerful at present. We miss our children, and Annette cries when she thinks of Paris. . . .

Give my love to Allie, and kisses to the children. Thank Margaret for her attention to them.

TO HIS SISTER.

GOBALPORE, *Feb.* 3*d*, 1871.

I HAVE been here a week doing little else but breathing the sea-air, and watching the big waves break on the shore. For the last two months I have had too much to do, as I kept charge of the jail, in addition to my own appointment. At last I found I was quite incapable of doing the work, so I went to the Lieutenant-Governor, who saw at once how ill I was, and relieved me of the charge of the jail. The next day Annette and I started in a coasting steamer, and arrived here in three days. I cannot say that I am much better for the change as yet, although nearly all the symptoms from which I suffered in Calcutta are less severe, and I have got a little colour, which I had completely lost. My chief complaint now is want of appetite, but this is a very serious one, for it prevents me from getting strong. I seem to get weaker daily, and I am losing weight very fast. As, however, I am better in most respects, I hope my appetite will return, and then I shall soon be all right. We are living in a very comfortable house, which has been placed at my disposal, with all that we require in the way of eating and drinking, by the friend of a friend of a friend of mine in Calcutta. I mention this to show how hospitable the gentleman is, for I am a perfect stranger to him. The house is well situated on high land, well exposed to the sea-air. The verandah in front overlooking the sea is charming, and it is there that we pass the greater part of the day. I have read two novels since I came here, the *Antiquary* and *Redgauntlet*. I found them in this house, and as I am incapable of work, I thought I should like to see if the former would interest me as much as it did when I was at Gale Cottage with you. I daresay you will guess that I found it terribly dry and long-winded; I think I could only have got through it in a place like this, where I have only my wife to talk to, no books and nothing to do. There are only two good houses at Gobalpore, this and the hotel, which was built many years ago by a ship captain. He lived in this house with his daughter for many years, and made money by trade. His daughter survived him, and lived a solitary life here for forty years. She had £100,000, but did not care to go to Europe. At the age of ninety she died. The exports of this place are rum, sugar, and gingelly seed. I daresay you do not know what the latter is, so I shall enclose a little in this letter that you may see it. Usually large quantities are exported from here and from other ports on the Madras coast to Marseilles to make oil, but on account of the war the exports are much diminished this year. A wretched little place like Gobalpore, you see, is even affected by this horrible war. We are far away from newspapers and telegrams, so I know little about the war.

TO HIS SISTER.

BERRICOL, *Feb.* 13*th.*

IF it were not for the sea Gobalpore would be a very dreary place. For some considerable distance inland there is little verdure, and the land is a collection of high sandhills, which frequently change their position in storms. About fifteen miles inland there are wooded mountains about 5000 feet high, but these are generally too hazy to improve the landscape. After being a week at Gobalpore, and finding little improvement in my health, and increasing weakness (I was losing 1 lb. per diem), I felt somewhat disheartened and tired of the place, so I sent for bearers, and we started in the direction of Juggernath. We had twenty-four bearers for our two palkees—a torch-bearer, and a bearer to carry our luggage. We set set off at a tremendous pace for palkee-bearers, and kept this up for several miles the bearers screaming, yelling, and laughing. The jolting was alarming. I seemed sometimes to be midway between the floor and roof of the palkee. This jolting seems to have done me good, for on arriving at the end of our first stage, at six o'clock in the morning, I felt that I walked with a firmer step than I had had for a month. The place we arrived at is called Rumba. It is situated at the head of a large salt-water lake, called the Chilka Lake. It is a most charming place; the shores are wooded to the water, but as the water is salt there are no rushes, and the edge of the lake is well defined. Near the lake there are numbers of small wooded hills, like Fawe Park, and in the distance high mountains, covered with trees and jungle. At Rumba there is a magnificent house in a somewhat ruinous condition. There we put up for the day, but were not very comfortable, as there was no furniture in the house. The house contains twenty-four rooms; there is stabling for fifty horses, and lots of outhouses and buildings after the old Indian fashion, which is now out of date. It was built by a Commissioner, an Indian civilian, who appears to have been an out-and-out rascal. He spent a great deal of money on it, getting marble floors, chandeliers, and expensive furniture from Calcutta at great original cost, as well as cost of carriage. The money he spent, however, was not his own. He collected the revenue of the district, but of this none found its way into the Government treasury. He was repeatedly asked why he sent in no collected revenue, and his reply was that he spent it on improving the roads of his district. At last it was discovered that he was sending large sums to England; an inquiry was held, and he was dismissed. He afterwards lived in London in grand style. There are no such Indian civilians now-a-days, but a long time ago there were many like this man. The position in which the house is built shows that he had taste, and appreciated fine scenery. The views from the house in all directions are very fine. Four enormous wild monkeys have taken possession of the ruined kitchens. Annette was afraid they might attack us, and I felt that we were in their power, for I was too weak to offer anything but the feeblest resistance. We intended to go to Juggernath across the lake, but as I found the boat small, uncomfortable, and without any cover, and that we should be two or three days on the water, I did not think it advisable to risk the chance of catching a severe fever, which would certainly kill me in my present condition. Neither would I think of exposing Annette to such hardship. We therefore commenced our journey round the lake in our palkees. It is too hot to travel by day, although it is exceedingly pleasant and cool in the shade. Last night we travelled eighteen miles skirting the lake, along a very good road. The lake was to our right, and to our left mountains covered with forest and jungle. This jungle began at the road-side, and is said to be full of bears, tigers, and leopards. By the shores of the lake, and on its islands, there are lots of spotted deer, and deer of other sorts, and numbers of pea-fowl, and on the lake millions of wild ducks and flamingoes. I find I am getting too tired to write, and am making a mess of my letter, so I will finish it another day.

Cuttack, Feb.—We arrived here last night, and I feel exceedingly glad to be in a civilised place, where I can get the sort of diet I require. Our intention was to go to Juggernath first, but we found it more convenient to come here, when we arrived at a place distant thirty miles.

Feby. 10th.—The next post for England leaves to-day, almost immediately, so I must finish my letter. Since coming to Cuttack my health has improved immensely. This morning I absolutely had an appetite for breakfast, and ate more than I have eaten at any one meal for two months. Now I think I shall be soon quite well. Weakness and slight fever are all that I suffer from now. You must bear in mind the state I am in, and excuse the confusion and bad writing of this letter. To-night we start for Pooree (Juggernath), and expect to find letters there, and I hope there will be one from Keswick. I often think about the family at Derwent Bank, and feel very happy that the children are in your hands. Annette joins with me in love.

TO HIS MOTHER.

MIDNAPORE, *Feby.* 21*st*, 1871.

You have no doubt seen the letter I sent to Allie by the last mail, so it will be useless for me to give you the same account. I shall tell you therefore how we have fared since we left Cuttack. One night in the palkees took us to Juggernath, or Pooree, as it is usually called. By the way we saw numbers of pilgrims from all parts of India, who were going there to be cheated and ruined by the priests who inhabit the temple. The poor people, when all their money is spent, are induced to give bonds, which are carefully and certainly exacted afterwards. Often they have not sufficient money to return, and in consequence die in numbers by the way. There is no remedy for this, of course, but education, and I think it probable, although I do not know it for a fact, that the numbers of pilgrims are yearly diminishing. Pooree is by the sea-side, very sandy, and the surf the same as everywhere on the east coast of India. The great Juggernath temple is exactly like a sugar-loaf squared and grooved. We saw it when we were five or six miles from Pooree, and it appeared, in the early morning, quite near. Europeans are not allowed to see the interior, but we could see quite enough to satisfy us by looking in at the door. It is surrounded by a wall, and in the enclosure the car is kept. There was nothing beautiful to be seen. Hindoo architects seem to delight in the hideous and the horrible. Their grotesque is not even comic. The figures seem to be carved with the intention of terrifying the ignorant worshippers and bringing them into such a frame of mind as to be at the mercy of the priests. We only stayed a night at Pooree, as I was anxious on account of my health to return to a dry climate. On returning we stayed two days at Cuttack, and then started for a place called Balasore, which is two nights from Cuttack. By the way we saw canals which have been constructed with the intention of rendering another famine impossible. It is said that even in their incomplete state they have this year saved many square miles of crops. We rested a night at Balasore, and then pursued our journey to this place, which is two nights from Balasore. We always travelled by night, as the days are too hot. During the day we rested in little houses called dak bungalows, consisting of two rooms and two bath-rooms. There is also a resident cook, who provides chickens, eggs, milk, curry, and rice. These Annette and I used to eat with an appetite, for although the voyage is fatiguing we are both deriving benefit from it. Now we are at Midnapore, living in a grand house with the judge whom I knew in Calcutta, and the comfort and repose which I now enjoy, I think, will do me much good. On arriving here we received a telegram saying that Annette's friends in Paris are all safe. You may imagine with what joy this telegram was received by us. We had had no news for five months. Annette joins with me in love to you and Isabella.

TO L.

MIDNAPORE, *Feb.* 21*st*, 1871.

As Annette is writing to you, I also will write a short note to enclose with hers. Your letters give Annette the intensest delight, but she cannot read them without tears. I also am so weak now that I am as much affected by your letters as she is, and I can scarcely think of the children without actually weeping. At one time I scarcely expected to recover, and I am sure I have had a very narrow escape. I had absolutely no appetite, and was losing at the rate of one pound per diem. I was also so weak that I could scarcely walk. A sudden change to a dry climate brought back my appetite by degrees, and I was thus saved. I was on the point of returning to Calcutta by steamer, and this I feel now almost certainly would have killed me. I felt that it mattered little whether I went by sea or by land, so I stuck to my original intention. Your teaching, I think, had something to do with leading me to this decision. In our Cumberland journeys you remember we did not turn back, unless the obstacle was almost insuperable. From you I have learnt the habit of completing the programme, and I think my life in this instance has thus been saved.

TO HIS MOTHER.

CALCUTTA, *March* 1*st*, 1871.

I WRITE you a very short note, but I daresay you will be better pleased to receive it than any I have written since I left England **twelve** years ago. **Although** I am doing well, the doctors here **say that it will be** unsafe for me to remain during the **hot weather** in India. It is therefore decided that I **must** leave for **Europe as soon** as possible, and I have taken my passage by the **first** steamer that leaves **Calcutta, which is on** the 8th of **this month.** I expect to be delayed *en route*, **for it will not** be safe **to** go straight **to** England, before habituating myself to the cold. You may feel certain, **however,** that we shall have the great pleasure of meeting in April.

TO HIS SISTER.

CALCUTTA, *March 7th*, 1871.

THIS letter, as it will go by Bombay, will probably reach you a week before I arrive at Marseilles. We sail to-morrow, and although I wished to remain here working for two years, on the whole I am not sorry to be compelled to pay you all a visit. One great cause of joy to me is the pleasure which I know the thought of seeing me soon will give mother. I cannot say that I am decidedly better, but I think I am no worse. I have fever every day between ten and two, and every night perspire tremendously. These two causes prevent me gaining strength. Write to *Poste Restante*, Marseilles, and I shall write to you from that place **as soon as I arrive.** I hope I shall be in a fit state to enjoy a summer in England.

P.S.—Written during an **ague-fit, so** please excuse mistakes.

CHAPTER VIII.

LAST LETTERS.

> "I will come back to you when all my wanderings are over."—*Old Letter.*
>
> "And all is well, though Faith and Form
> Be sundered in the night of fear."—*In Memoriam.*

TO HIS MOTHER.

MARSEILLES, *April 6th,* 1871.

ON the 4th, your birthday, we drank the health of her whom we think the best woman in the world. We wished you many happy returns of the day, and hope that in future we may spend many of the anniversaries with you. We arrived here to-day, and I went at once to the post-office to look for letters, but there was not one, neither from Keswick nor Shields. This was a disappointment, but I hope to hear soon. I have improved immensely in health and general appearance since leaving India, but I still suffer from fever from 8 to 12 A.M., and I am in consequence somewhat afraid to go too quickly into a cold climate. I feel undecided as to what I shall do, but probably we shall stay here for a few days, and then go on to Geneva. My plans are however very uncertain. I have made several, but cannot decide on any. We are impatient to proceed homewards, and wish that this wretched fever would disappear and allow us to do so.

TO L.

MARSEILLES, *April 8th,* 1871.

No doubt you have heard of our arrival from mother, to whom I wrote yesterday. We arrived just in time to avoid the small revolution, and we feel comfortable and secure here. We have two cheerful rooms in a very nice hotel. The diet suits me, and is even a great treat after that of the steamer. We have had calm weather all the way from Calcutta to Marseilles, and it was neither hot in the Red Sea nor cold in the Mediterreanean. In passing through the Canal I felt a decided improvement in my health. I ceased to suffer from depression, my colour improved, and I gained flesh; but I still suffered from ague every day; in fact the attacks are as violent as they have ever been, and I also suffer from a lot of little ailments, dependent on the condition of my spleen. I am consequently afraid to move northwards too rapidly, for I feel the cold very much, and a chill is sufficient to bring on a fit of ague. Before leaving Calcutta I told the Lieutenant-Governor that I hoped to be back again in eight months; and I think I shall be able to keep my promise, but as regards this, I shall be able to judge better in a month. I should like to be able to spend as much of our time as possible at Keswick. I know you will wish us to live with you, but we are determined not to derange in any way your household arrangements.

With love from Annette and myself, to you and Allie, etc.

P.S.—Annette remarks that I have said nothing about the children. Please tell them that papa and mamma will be with them soon.

TO HIS SISTER.

MARSEILLES, *April 9th*, 1871.

I WROTE to L. two days ago, but I feel doubtful if my letters arrive at their destination. It is extremely probable that letters from England do not reach this place, for I have no doubt some of you have written to me. I find now that Marseilles does not agree with me, for the attacks of ague are not less severe, and last night I had an extra one. We have fixed to start for Geneva *via* Lyons to-morrow, and I intend looking for some dry place in the neighbourhood. We shall not however go any great distance from Geneva. Please therefore address to *P.-R.*, Geneva. You may be sure that I do not like hanging about in these regions, and that I am very anxious to see you all, and the dear children, but I am afraid of the cold at present, and I am so weak that I can scarcely walk. Nevertheless I am not unhappy. Annette looks after me; I have a good appetite, and I vegetate in a quiet way. Our old friend A. C. must have felt somewhat as I do, when he said, "I feel like a fungus." We wish to spend as much of our six months as possible near you; and should like you to hire two good rooms for us. We know that you will be opposed to this at first, but consideration will show you that there is not room at Derwent Bank. As it is, you are very much pressed for room. Annette joins me in love to you both. She is very busy all day long, and has little time to write.

TO L.

GENEVA, *April 21st*, 1871.

I HAVE now received several letters from you and Allie, which have followed me about from place to place. When I found no letters for me at Marseilles, I never for one moment suspected that none had been sent to me, but at once came to the conclusion that the disturbed state of France had caused this miscarriage. We were delighted to receive several very kind letters from you and Allie, and to hear such good accounts of the children. We long to see them, and I am very impatient to be in England. The weather here is abominable, it rains almost constantly, and the north wind, *la bise*, is almost unendurable. At Montreux the weather was warm, but for the last three days that we were there it rained constantly; we could not go out, and from our windows we saw nothing but rain and clouds. This state of weather hastened our departure, and now our intention is to proceed to London, *via* Germany (Basle, etc.) My health is much improved, but I am very weak and indolent. Reading even is a labour to me, and I sometimes sit for an hour at a time doing absolutely nothing. Annette frequently reads to me, and this I like. The hotel we are living in is charmingly situated. From our window we have a fair view of the lake. The Rhone absolutely washes the foundations of the hotel. I enjoy the sight of the clear and rapid stream, and am fond of watching the swans and ducks swimming about in it. With love to Allie, and kisses for the children, etc.

TO HIS SISTER.

LONDON, *May 3d*, 1871.

WE shall soon see you now, for I am anxious to get on to Shields, and am only waiting on account of some business at the India Office. Our journey across the north of France was a very pleasant one. The country is most beautiful, and traces of the war are scarcely to be noticed, unless looked for. There were too many Prussian soldiers about to please Annette, but I daresay their presence rendered our journey secure. We travelled by day always, and generally not more than six hours per day, but sometimes the trains were delayed for a few hours. The hotels generally were well filled, but we always obtained rooms easily. The day travelling, and seeing the towns which we stayed at, generally occupied our whole time. I have made most rapid progress towards recovery, and consider myself almost well. I feel perfectly so, but my body is much emaciated, and I am still unsteady upon my legs, on account of weakness. The hollows in my face are rapidly filling up, and sometimes I have a fair amount of colour. Our lodgings are very comfortable, but the dimness of the sky and the smokiness of the air appear to me very dismal, and I shall not be sorry to be in a clear atmosphere again.

With love to L., and kisses to the children, whom I long to embrace, etc.

TO HIS SISTER ISABELLA.

LONDON, *May 3d*, 1871.

WE have been travelling at such a rate, and have had so much to see and do, that I have not had time to reply to your kind letter until now. You see we have followed your advice, and lost no time on the way. I also intend trying your prescription with respect to diet, for I have an excellent appetite. We arrived here yesterday afternoon, having enjoyed our journey from Boulogne, which was like a pleasure trip, exceedingly. It was a great treat to me to see English fields, trees, and cattle again. I shall write and tell you when to expect us, as soon as I know myself. I feel quite well now, but I am thin and weak.

TO HIS SISTER ALICE.

KENSINGTON, *June 1st*, 1871.

IT is evident to me now that warmth is what I require to put me all right. I regret leaving London when it is so pleasant, and where there is so much to see, but I fancy it is too cold for me yet. On returning to England I hope to spend some time in London, and that you will meet us there and stay with us. I reported and showed myself to Sir Ranald Martin to-day. This I am bound by the rules of the service to do. He told me that he thought I should have to stay over the winter. I require his permission before returning to India.

TO THE SAME.

BOULOGNE-SUR-MER, *June 4th*.

WE arrived here last evening after a very pleasant journey both by land and sea. The last day of our stay in London was very disagreeable. There was a cold north-east wind, which gave me ague almost the moment I felt it, and I was consequently obliged to pass the greater portion of the day in the house. We intend leaving Boulogne to-morrow, and shall probably stay for a day or two at Amiens, but as this is uncertain, do not write to me until I give you an address. I do not like losing letters. I feel that I have done quite right in leaving England, and think that it would have been better if I had come to France at once, instead of going to Buxton, which is really an awfully cold place.—With kisses for our little ones, and love to L., etc.

TO HIS SISTER.

HÔTEL DE L'EMPEREUR JOSEPH,
RUE DU TOURNON, PARIS, *June 9th*, 1871.

I KNOW you will feel anxious about me now that I am in Paris, therefore I hasten to assure you that there is not the slightest danger. The stench, if it ever existed to any extent, has completely disappeared. Newspaper agents cannot be trusted; the temptation to write sensationally is too strong. I am delighted with Paris; it is much more beautiful than when you and I saw it together fourteen years ago. It is true that I have not yet seen the Champs Elysées and the portions of the city which are said to be in the worst state; but in coming here from the railway station we crossed Paris from one side to the other, going through the heart of the city. We saw several houses of which the interiors were completely burnt; the good stone walls seem to have resisted the fire very well. The Hôtel de Ville is a sad sight, but its blackened walls still stand. Marks of rifle-bullets are visible on many of the houses, and glaziers are to be seen everywhere plying their trade. Most of the windows in this house were broken by the explosion which took place in the Palais de Luxembourg. We are in the healthiest part of Paris, well raised. All the streets in the neighbourhood are kept beautifully clean. The *balayeurs* commence their work at half-past three A.M. The weather is mild, but there is a little too much rain to be agreeable. I cannot say that I am much better, but I think I shall be so after a few days' repose.

We are always talking about our dear little children, and feel so happy at knowing they are so well with you, and this reconciles us in a great measure to the separation.—With love to you both, and kisses to the children, etc.

TO L.

. PARIS, *June 22d*, 1871.

I HAVE not written to you regarding my health, because hitherto I have had nothing definite to say on the subject. Since I came to Paris, the improvement has been slow but decided. The night-perspirations became less frequent, and at last disappeared altogether. I never now have an attack of ague more than once a day, and the attacks are much less severe. The pulse is never more than 108, and is sometimes as low as 88. My complexion is much clearer, and I feel stronger and more cheerful. Two days ago I walked the whole length of the Rue Vivienne, and twice round the Palais-Royal, and yesterday we went to St. Maur, a village about twelve miles from Paris, where Annette's parents are living. We went by rail, but had also about a mile to walk. I was obliged to give up the vapour-baths after the third; they were too unpleasant. Every bath I took was more difficult to support than the preceding, and the unpleasant effects lasted longer. My appetite is excellent still; I eat lots of fruit and vegetables, which are exceedingly good here, and I drink a bottle of Médoc every day.

Yesterday in going to St. Maur, which is beyond Vincennes, we passed through the quartier St. Antoine, and the Place de la Bastille. Many of the houses showed evidence of hard fighting, but few were completely destroyed. The Pillar was perforated in many places by cannon-balls, but it has sustained no serious damage. The Hôtel de Ville is the greatest loss to Paris. Even in ruins it is a fine building. The outside wall has sustained wonderfully little injury, considering the state of the interior. Annette joins in love.

P.S.—I am glad to hear that you are preparing to build.

TO HIS SISTER.

PARIS, *June 28th*, 1871.

FOR the last few days I have not been very well. The weather has been somewhat cold, and I caught inflammation of the windpipe, which increased my fever and gave rise to a very unpleasant cough. I am better now, but somewhat weakened by the attack. I must expect occasional relapses, and be satisfied with a gradual improvement. My complexion is now whiter and clearer than it has been since I left England years ago. This I regard as a good sign. As I am doing well at Paris, I do not feel inclined to make any change. Farther south the climate is no doubt too hot, and I am afraid to return to England. Annette and I would both like to be at Shields when you and the children are there, but I am afraid of the climate, and am getting sick of the bustle of railway stations, seeing boxes packed and looked after, etc. "Leave well alone" is my motto at present. I am getting on tolerably well at Paris, and like the city. Quietude agrees with me. Please excuse this long stupid letter that I write to you about myself. Your very kind letters of inquiry and advice, which show the interest you take in my health, induce me to write more freely about myself than I otherwise would do. The garçon here tells me that the Duc d'Aumale is in our hotel *en haut*. We were thinking that the hotel was scarcely clean enough in some respects for us. It appears that one of the Royal Family of France is less particular.

The doctor here has treated lots of cases similar to mine coming from Algeria, and I perceive that he understands them. He told me that the cold douche on the spleen was the treatment for my case. The effect of the first douche was certainly startling, and nearly knocked me down. That day the fever was delayed three hours, and I had a very slight cold stage. On the second day I had only a slight feeling of cold about the spleen, where the douche had been directed. On the third day I had no cold at all, and the fever was much diminished in intensity. I feel now as if I were going to recover.

TO HIS SISTER.

PARIS, *July 5th.*

SEVERAL of my friends from London have been here lately. They all say that the climate of Paris is infinitely better than that of England, and strongly advise me to remain here until I get quite strong. When that will be it is difficult to say. In the meantime I hope you will pay us a visit, and the sooner you do so the better pleased we shall be. We go to Auteuil to-morrow, where we have taken "un appartement." I am sure you will enjoy the trip. Auteuil is close to the Bois de Boulogne, and pleasantly situated. Annette hopes that you will not be long in deciding to come. If you come only for a week, you will enjoy the change, and it will do you good, but we hope you will stay longer. I am very anxious for you to come, for unless you do, I do not know when I shall see you. For your own sake too I think you should come, for I think you require a holiday. With love to mother and Isabella, etc.

P.S.—I return the plan of the new room. All I have to say is that I think there ought to be two windows, as at the other side of the house. The windows may be made to open like doors.

TO THE SAME.

AUTEUIL, *July 25th,* 1871.

I HAVE just had a solitary walk along the Rue Michel Ange, to warm me after my bath. The wind was strong and in gusts, and I thought of you and the Channel. I hope however that there may be less wind at Boulogne. Do not forget to write soon. I am anxious to know the effect of your trip to Paris.

TO L.

ETAL VILLA, *August* 13*th*, 1871.

I CANNOT tell you much about myself. Progress is slow and uncertain. I certainly feel clearer about the head, and have more blood than formerly, but I have lost seven pounds in weight during the last two months. As regards horseback exercise, I am afraid it will be long before I am able to mount. Carriage exercise is even too much for me, and I feel great fatigue after sitting for an hour without support to my back. I am glad to see Allie looking so well. The children gave her the heartiest welcome, which pleased me very much to see.

TO HIS SISTER ISABELLA.[1]

CALCUTTA, *Dec.* 16*th*, 1864.

I WAS sorry to hear such a bad account of our nephew George's health. I do not think that you can reasonably reproach yourself for having encouraged him to go to New Zealand. The climate of New Zealand is excellent for persons with his hereditary tendency. It is the war that he engaged in that has been the exciting cause of his present disease, and when you sent him to New Zealand you were far from wishing him to have anything to do with that. If he had continued to work at the farm, to cut down trees, etc., he would probably now be much stronger than when he left England. I will write to him at once and advise him to go to Australia, where the climate is warmer than in New Zealand. The sea-voyage and change of air may possibly do him good. Queensland, I think, would be the best place for him to go to. I have often intended writing to you about our little boy, to thank you for all your kindness to him, of which Allie continually keeps me informed. In all her letters she tells me of your devotion to the little boy. Annette and I are both exceedingly grateful. Your kindness to the boy is beyond thanks, but I hope he may recompense you in a measure by turning out a fine boy, and by loving you.

---

[1] This letter was omitted in its proper place.

ACCOUNT OF THE LAST WEEKS, BY HIS SISTER ALICE.

AFTER landing at Marseilles my brother hurried from place to place with the restlessness of an invalid, never during the next two months staying anywhere more than five or six days. Like a hunted creature, he seemed to fly for his life. Now reading these letters, records of the wasting fevers, it seems as if the end was plain from the beginning; but then we imagined, as he did, that he would recover. Many things were against him. He came to England in May, when the weather was extremely cold. He said to me in August that he thought he had made a series of mistakes since he left India. This was true. But these untoward chances, over which we grieved, were the means appointed to bring the destined end.

After spending a few days in my mother's house, he came with her and his wife to us at Keswick, and at the end of one week he said he must leave the north, and seek a warmer climate. It was heartbreaking to see him leave Derwent Bank and the home-comforts he so much needed, where his mother and children were, where he had been so long looked for, again to become a wanderer in his weak, shattered state of health. He said he would soon come back, but this was not to be; it was his last visit to the loved home of his youth. How sad, how sweet is the memory of that short week! He was delighted to see his children so robust and healthy, felt their firm limbs, and was astonished at the improvement a year had made in their condition, said how well our climate had agreed with them, and was full of gratitude for the care we had taken of them. He was pleased with the beautiful scenery and the aspect of the old place, noted little alterations, remarked that our trees looked smaller than he had expected to find them. He was solicitous to give no trouble, made light of his ailments, would say cheerfully, "Now I have had my fever, and had my dinner, let us go into the garden." He would stroll about the grounds with me talking in his old pleasant way of the past and of a future which was not for him. He was but the shadow of his former self—so changed that I should scarcely have known him. Twelve years of work in the exhausting climate of India had indeed wrought a change in the beautiful youth whom I had seen leave England full of hope and buoyant life. He was amiable and loving as ever, but instead of the radiant glad look there was an expression of deep sadness on his features, of the eyes especially. He resembled some of the pictures of Christ. I recollect him speaking of our Great Teacher as having given the highest and purest lessons to mankind. Truly my brother was one who loved his fellow-men. He followed the golden rule to "do to others as ye would that they should do unto you." He was ever ready to sacrifice himself at the call of duty. He has been often known to leave the society of his friends to look after some poor Hindu patient, and would spend nights in the hospital or jail watching anxious cases.

Alipore jail was self-supporting whilst under his superintendence. Sir William Grey, then Lieutenant-Governor, at my brother's solicitation, granted funds for the purchase of machinery, the use of which in a short time repaid the first outlay. Objections were made on the ground that "punishment" was not made of primary consideration; but my brother considered the reformation of criminals the more important object. He sought to make the prisoners better and more useful members of society. I recollect him telling me of two men, both condemned to imprisonment for life. One was an old Sikh chief, who had been taken prisoner during the Sikh war, fighting for independence. He was a fine fellow, pining in captivity. James represented his case, and obtained his pardon. The old chief was most grateful, and became a good subject to the British Government. The other, condemned for murder, was a Dacoit, whose business was to kill. James said that whilst imprisoned he had become an excellent workman, and was exemplary for good behaviour, but that if he were let loose, he would return to his trade of murder,—that therefore the best thing for this individual and for society was to keep him in perpetual durance. A few months after my brother's retirement there was an *émeute* in Alipore jail. All had been quiet and orderly during the five years and a half he was governor. Colleagues, subordinates, and prisoners were alike attached to him.

My brother was for two or three years engaged with Dr. Douglas Cunningham[1] in scientific researches into the pathology

---

[1] The following is a letter from Dr. Douglas Cunningham to a sister of Dr. Fawcus:—

"4 ALIPORE LANE, CALCUTTA, *July* 10*th*, 1877.

"... I always have an uneasy feeling that I indirectly contributed to cause the illness of your brother by the additional fatigue which his unexampled kindness in attending me during an illness of some weeks in the rains of 1870 must have caused him. I knew at the time that he used to come twice a day to see me, and to stay for long hours from his work, doing everything that could be done for my comfort, and even for some weeks bringing his work over during the day, at great inconvenience to himself, in order that I might not feel myself left alone; but I did not know until long after, when one of my servants told me, that he used to walk over from Alipore late in the night to see how I was getting on. I do not know a more beautiful instance of utterly self-forgetful kindness than his attendance on me at that time was, harassed as he was by office-work, and specially trouble connected with the Wahabi trials. He was the noblest specimen of humanity of cholera. His reports show the result of long labour and great numbers of post-mortem examinations made under circumstances more favourable for arriving at just conclusions (respecting embolism, for example) than any which could have occurred in this country. Such labours as these must have cost great effort in the exhausting climate of India.

I went to Paris in July. We lodged at Auteuil, near the hydropathic establishment, in order that my brother might take baths and douches. About his health he remarked, "I do not think that my complaint of itself will prove fatal, but in my weak state I should easily succumb to any fresh malady; for instance if I were to get pneumonia, I should die!"

How often I remember our pleasant little journeys from Auteuil to Paris, sometimes by rail, sometimes in omnibuses by the banks of the Seine; our walks in the Place de la Concorde, with its broken statues and fountains, the ruins of the Tuileries, and the Hôtel de Ville, their outer walls alone standing against the blue sky; the looks and words of my gentle brother as we wandered amongst these scenes. He said that Paris in its beauty and desolation reminded him of Byron's description of modern Greece, so changed from its former glory.

He was able to walk two or three miles in a morning, and would say playfully that he feared he was tiring me out. And yet in a postscript to one of my letters, he thus describes his condition to L. :—

"*July* 19*th*.—For the last three days no definite distinct fever, but pulse in morning 96, rising to 105 in the middle of the day and evening, after slight exertion to 120. The spleen has diminished two fingers'-breadth, and in volume also. I am still very weak, and generally suffer from an overpowering sensation of fatigue."

When I parted from him on the stairs of that house at Auteuil, he clasped me affectionately to his heart, saying, "Whatever happens, we have had this week together." The memory of that solemn farewell will remain whilst I am left to "wander on a darkened earth."

A fortnight afterwards (August 12th) we met again at my mother's house. He was in worse health than when he left England in spring. He wrote to my husband that he had lost

I ever encountered, or hope to encounter again. His large-minded liberality was wonderfully combined with such transparent uprightness and hatred of all forms of sham, and the extreme gentleness and (to use a term which has been so often misapplied as to pass into disrepute) sweetness of his character were such as to make one thankful, as they certainly ought to make one better, for having encountered them. It is a great privilege to have had an opportunity of seeing what a noble thing human nature can be in a world where the mean side of it so often predominates. . . ."

7 lbs. in weight during the two months he had been in Paris. His complexion was grey and yellow. He used to come down to breakfast with the family about eight o'clock, and during the forenoon would lie on a couch in the drawing-room and listen to my reading. The Letters of the Rev. F. Robertson of Brighton, The Straits of Magellan, by a brother of his friend Dr. Douglas Cunningham, Miss Mitford's Biography, were among the books of which I read portions to him. He was weak, said that he felt wretchedly ill in the morning. He often seemed very desponding and low, and sometimes I heard that he had shed tears whilst dressing. On one of these occasions, when Isabella was with him, he said to her, "It is only weakness." Often whilst I was reading to him he would fall asleep, his hands usually clasped on his breast, his features, ever placid and sweet, wearing a look of great weariness and sadness; sometimes the eyelids would be slightly open, and I saw the shadow of the coming Angel upon his face. Oh beloved one! we feared, but we hoped then! Yet he welcomed all his friends with smiles. He was pleased to see our old servant Ann, who had waited upon him in his boyhood. He wished mother to invite her to stay in the house, which was done. He liked to see our good neighbour Mrs. Pow. When told an instance of her forgiveness of injuries, he said, "How good of her! how truly Christian!"

During the first week or two, after he came to Shields, he used to go daily to the Turkish bath; afterwards he took drives to the seaside, and bathed in the sea. The sight of the rocks and shores, the familiar places of his youth, pleased him.

On September 2d I was obliged to leave him to take his three little girls to Derwent Bank; they troubled him in his weak state. He looked sadly at them as he bade them good-bye. The parting from them in India had tried him exceedingly. When at Derwent Bank in May he had said to me, "I have given them to you, Allie; I do not want to love them again. I have suffered so much in parting from them."

I returned to my mother's house on the 13th September, on the occasion of my brother Robert's death. James did not seem worse, and told me to let L. know that from various signs he thought he should recover. When he first saw me, alluding to our poor brother's departure, he said, "You must not be doleful; we are all cheerful here. I was dreaming last night that I was writing a letter to you, and that I added in a postscript, It is a duty to be gay." When he had heard from my eldest brother some painful details of Robert's illness, James desired me to beg John not to let my mother know how Robert had suffered.

After a few days I again left him and returned to his

children. He then complained of a sore gum. This increased, and prevented him eating solid food. (It was a small fish-bone which had caused inflammation in the gum.) He grew weaker, yet took daily drives to the sea-side, bathing occasionally. My brother William used to accompany him. His wife, my mother and sister, were there. Isabella anticipated all his wants, and tried to tempt his failing appetite. Other members of the family were ready to help; all feeling his precarious state. (How I longed to be near him!) I received his last letter on September 29th, in which he said that his gum was recovering, and that he "hoped now to regain lost ground."

It was suggested that he should try the hydropathic establishment at Melrose. He himself wished to do so.

My husband saw him set off for Melrose, October 2d. His little boy, eight years old, was placed beside him in the carriage at my mother's door, and twice he stooped to kiss him tenderly. When the boy took off his hat as the train moved, James smiled approvingly,—a sweet last farewell to his child.

He enjoyed the journey; his spirits and health seemed at first to revive; he was amused with fresh scenes, and pleased with the beauty of the banks of the Tweed. On Wednesday, October 4th, he walked through the long suite of rooms at Abbotsford. On the next day he drove in an open carriage to Dryburgh Abbey. Whilst his wife and William walked about the grounds, James sat on a seat on the grass. The afternoon was chilly, and when he returned to the house his hands and feet were icy cold. He had caught a fatal cold! He had pulled a piece of ivy from the ruins of the old Abbey, and desired William to send it to me. I received this last gift with tears,—that ivy from a sepulchre seemed to my heart a prophetic token. He had fever the two following days, followed by diarrhœa. On Sunday he desired to return home to my mother's house, and charged William to be careful that there should be no hindrance. On Monday morning they were early at the station, the hoar-frost on the ground, and he sat on the open platform, waiting for the train, suffering from pneumonia!

The journey of five hours, with changes, was long and trying, but he bore up resolutely, got out of the carriage at mother's door, and walked into the house, kissing my mother as he entered. He was carried up-stairs in a chair to his bedroom. He declined to have any doctor sent for. He then dictated his last letter, a few lines to me. He was heard coughing all night, but no one was in the room but his wife. At seven in the morning he sent for my brother William, and requested that a telegram should be sent to my husband. He signed with great difficulty a codicil to his will, made in 1862, in order to appoint my brother William his executor. He prescribed for himself,—linseed poultices to his side, the room to be kept at an even temperature, champagne and milk to be given every half-hour. He thanked those who ministered to him, was patient and sweet as ever. Once, when he saw mother standing near him, he said he feared she was unhappy. She did not realise that her darling was dying, and answered, "No, I am thinking of the Psalm, 'Bless the Lord, O my soul, and forget not all his benefits.'" James smiled lovingly, and pointed to his feet, that she might see that he wore the shoes she had knitted for him. These went with him to the grave. To Isabella he said, "You are a good woman, Bella."

At eleven at night I arrived. More than once he had asked, "Has Allie come?" (Oh that I could have been there sooner!) When I went into the room he was breathing with great difficulty, taking no notice of what was passing around him. He was roused to take some champagne, and then he saw me standing by his bedside; his whole face lightened up with a sweet smile of welcome, and he held out both his thin pale hands eagerly towards me. He immediately desired that all others should leave the room, "except Allie." I leant my ear to his mouth, for he could only speak in the faintest whisper then. He said, "Have you anything to ask me? Do not be anxious, they (the children) will all be brought up Protestants." I said, "I shall do all I can for them." "Yes." "Wherever you are we shall still love each other." "Yes." It was but for a few moments. Even then I did not think that these were his last words to me. He never spoke again, except to ask my husband, "Will it be long? Is there any hope?" He smiled sweetly when my brother William and my husband raised him up. He was roused at intervals, and drank a little champagne, holding the glass in his own trembling fingers; heroic, sweet, patient, and yielding to the last. A little after two in the morning his breathing became gentle, and grew fainter and fainter until it ceased. He passed away without a sigh or struggle, and our beloved one lay still and silent—beautiful yet, but with that strange unearthly beauty of death. His wife was on one side of the bed, my brother William on the other, holding his left hand, my husband and I at the foot of the bed, when he died. Isabella came, full of woe, Wilhelmina and Janie. What a night of sorrow! We did not call poor dear mother. William said, "I do not like to leave this warm hand." I took it from his; it was yet soft and warm, that loving, gracious hand, so dear to me. I held it until it was cold. The waning moon was shining ruddy and bright through the east window as we passed through the corridor leading to the room where he lay, still and alone. All his wanderings were over

In the morning I went to my mother. "How is my darling?" she asked. She looked at my sad despairing face, and cried, "Is he gone? I always thought he would recover!" Afterwards she became calm and said, "By their fruits ye shall know them." Remembering his gentle, unselfish, useful life, she thought that surely his heart was right in the sight of God.

On the third day (Friday) we buried our loved one by the side of his father and grandfather, and the little brother and sister who had been laid there long ago. Our funeral was very quiet. There was no hearse, no carriage. His body was carried to the grave by six workmen. Part of the service was performed at the house, as there was no church at the cemetery. My mother was present, and seemed comforted by the service. She watched, with my sister and me, the little procession as it wound through the garden and gate, and on the road that led to the cemetery,—the road he knew so well. The bier was covered with flowers. It was a still day, the sun a little clouded.

How empty seemed the house when he was gone for ever! How sad, how dreary, to go on our way without him! I have loved him from his cradle to his grave, and I shall love him until my own life is ended. Shall I not meet him then? Shall I not know him again?
A. L.

APPENDIX I.

LETTER FROM MY BROTHER WILLIAM TO DR. CARLYLE.

Oct. 11*th*, 1871.

YOUR kind letter reached me this morning, and from no one would I sooner have received a friendly greeting on this to me sad day; for James died this morning in mother's house, as he had lived, bravely and gently.

Alice I see has told you about him leaving India seven months ago. . . . I think that consideration for the feelings of others, and his anxiety to see his friends, led him to come to England when he should have gone to a more suitable climate for one suffering from malaria; but that is all past now. He was asked to continue at his work, when he should have given up, and, as often happens, the willing horse was pressed; but this too is past, and should be forgotten. . . .

In outward appearance and in inward worth he was the finest man I have known, and he lies struck down by the climate of India at the age of thirty-eight, a soldier of civilisation of the noblest type, just as he was becoming most useful and honoured. He was singularly beloved, from being a child to his last days, by all who knew him. I can see in memory the 120 boys at Mill School, crowding round James as a new boy, then only nine years of age, and declaring that he was painted, as they had never before seen such purity of red and white. And at Melrose the other day, though all that was gone, though thin and wasted, there was a hush of admiration as he passed along with his own sweet expression on his noble features, and with that graceful courtesy which wins all hearts, as of Sir Lancelot of old, or of a greater than he whom the daughters of Jerusalem followed.

APPENDIX II.

From a leading article in "THE ENGLISHMAN," *Calcutta,*
Oct. 16th, 1871.

A PRIVATE telegram has been received from England announcing the death of Dr. James Fawcus, Inspector-General of Jails in Bengal. Distinguished as a student before he came to India, opportunity alone was needed to bring into prominence the rare faculties and qualities of mind Dr. Fawcus possessed, and the rapidity of his advancement to one of the highest offices within the reach of a medical officer is we believe without a parallel in the service. Opportunity would have been long wanting if it had depended on any self-seeking aspirations of his own, but fortunately he was early brought to the notice of Government by Dr. Parkes of Netley. His connection with the Jail Department began in 1865, in his appointment to the charge of the great jail at Alipore. So perfect was the confidence he inspired in a Government given to the most critical scrutiny, that though he had not then ceased to be an assistant surgeon, he was marked as the successor of Dr. Mouat on his retirement. He had held the office for a few weeks only when the illness began which has ended in his death, and the persistency with which, against the most urgent advice, he refused to leave his work in time, is now among the memories which, while enhancing the admiration of his friends, adds much to the bitterness with which they mourn his loss. He was not in his lifetime a man of many words, and praises in a journal must be few, if they would be in harmony with this. Calm and dispassionate in judgment, earnest and strong to think and act, he gained the high regard of every man with whom he had relation either of work or friendship. They loved him best who knew him best, and though brought into daily contact with a large number and variety of men, he never had an enemy.

www.ingramcontent.com/pod-product-compliance
Lightning Source LLC
Chambersburg PA
CBHW021728220426
43662CB00008B/748